POLITICAL SOLIDARITY

POLITICAL SOLIDARITY

SALLY J. SCHOLZ

THE PENNSYLVANIA STATE UNIVERSITY PRESS   UNIVERSITY PARK, PENNSYLVANIA

LIBRARY OF CONGRESS CATALOGING-IN-PUBLICATION DATA

Scholz, Sally J.
Political solidarity / Sally J. Scholz.
p.   cm.
Includes bibliographical references and index.
Summary: "Examines the relations and obligations of committed individuals working to create social change. Addresses issues involving forms of solidarity, the role of violence in activism, the moral and epistemological privilege of the oppressed, the relation between solidarity and social justice, and the prospects for global solidarity"—Provided by publisher.
ISBN 13: 978-0-271-03401-0 (pbk : alk. paper)
1. Solidarity—Political aspects.
I. Title.

HM717.S36 2008
306.201—dc22
2008007995

Copyright © 2008 The Pennsylvania State University
All rights reserved
Printed in the United States of America
Published by The Pennsylvania State University Press,
University Park, PA 16802-1003

The Pennsylvania State University Press is a member of the Association of American University Presses.

It is the policy of The Pennsylvania State University Press to use acid-free paper. Publications on uncoated stock satisfy the minimum requirements of American National Standard for Information Sciences—Permanence of Paper for Printed Library Material, ANSI Z39.48–1992.

CONTENTS

ACKNOWLEDGMENTS VII

INTRODUCTION 1

ONE
Solidarities 17

TWO
Toward a Theory of Political Solidarity 51

THREE
The Moral Relations and Obligations of Political Solidarity 71

FOUR
The Solidary Collective 113

FIVE
The Paradox of the Participation of the Privileged 151

SIX
The Social Justice Ends of Political Solidarity 189

SEVEN
On Human Solidarity and the Challenge of Global Solidarity 231

REFERENCES 265

INDEX 275

FOR MY FAMILY

Acknowledgments

This book has jumped from front to back burner and back again for many years. Throughout the entire process, countless people provided inspiration, offered support and encouragement, argued with ideas, and read or heard portions of the text. It is with sincere gratitude that I thank them all—those named below as well as all those other friends, philosophers, activists, and strangers who gave me food for thought and reason for continuing.

For their interesting and thoughtful comments on various parts of this project, I would like to thank the members of the North American Society for Social Philosophy, the Society for Philosophy in the Contemporary World, the Society for Feminist Ethics and Social Theory, the American Philosophical Association, and philosophy departments at Bryn Mawr College, the University of Portland, Temple University, and Villanova University.

Villanova University provided useful summer support, a generous sabbatical, and ample space to allow me to complete the manuscript. Special thanks especially to my Dean, Kail Ellis, O.S.A., and to the Vice President for Academic Affairs, John Johannes. Numerous students have had a hand in this book, whether they know it or not. I benefited from discussions in and out of the classroom, I was inspired by the student activists I saw, and I was pushed on by those students who believed that this project was something they would like to read one day. I would especially like to thank the students in my Social and Political Philosophy; Ethics; Philosophy of Women; Race, Class, and Gender; and Social Contract Theory courses. Many graduate and undergraduate students gave generously of their time in discussing parts of this book—often unbeknownst to them. I thank them all. They have helped me think through ideas and kept me from taking myself too seriously. Thank you.

I am grateful for my many colleagues at Villanova. Although there are too many to name them all, I want to especially thank Joe Betz and Tom Busch for their encouragement and example. Brett Wilmot suggested the formative/substantive distinction and although I may not have carried it out as well as he articulated it, his comments were extremely helpful to me. Joe Betz and Michael Prosch sent me articles and commentary on solidarity in theory, practice, and literature. Michael pointed me in the direction of the Brecht poem "Solidarity Song" and was incredibly generous with his time in discussing issues with me. Friends in the Peace and Justice Center were among the most influential in bringing this book to fruition. They continue to challenge me with their committed lives as they live out the relations of political solidarity. Carol Anthony, Sharon Discher, Rick Eckstein, Sue Toton, Bill Werpehowski, and Joyce Zavarich, thank you for all the comments, encouragement, fun times, and fair-trade chocolate! Colleagues at other universities have also been generous with their time in discussing ideas or reading drafts. Most especially, I want to thank William McBride, whose support has been invaluable and whose life and philosophical work demonstrates the hope for a global solidarity. This book is also dedicated to him.

The anonymous reviewers offered invaluable advice for revising the manuscript and I thank them for their time, attention, and kindness in reading so carefully the draft of this book. Sanford Thatcher at the Pennsylvania State University Press believed in this project from the beginning and I thank him most sincerely for his professionalism, encouragement, and consideration.

The teachers and staff at Ken-Crest Child Development Center in Rosemont, Pennsylvania, offered loving care of my children while I worked on this and other projects. They not only gave me peace of mind but also taught me how to be a positive parent (though I don't always succeed) and inspired me with the spirit of collective social responsibility for all children. In a similar way, our friends on Barcladen Circle showed us what neighborliness means. They watched children while I cooked dinner and kept me sane during difficult times.

Finally, my family has been a never-ending source of fun for the off hours and support for those work days. Tessa Scholz Kilby's gentle, caring spirit balanced with strong opinions gives me hope for the next generation of activists. Luke Scholz Kilby's passionate enthusiasm for just about everything, tempered by his sense of justice, challenges me to look for new avenues to express the fun of social responsibility. Finally, Christopher P. Kilby's belief in this project, insistence on my ability to complete it (including teaching me how to say "no" to less-important demands), and patience with the mess that I call a desk—our kitchen counter—has been unwavering, invaluable, and absolutely essential.

Introduction

Why Solidarity?

When I was in college, I took a one-credit course in sociology called the "Urban Plunge." The course took about a dozen students and two professors from a lush, suburban campus that sat on a bluff overlooking the Willamette River to downtown Portland, Oregon. For three days, we stayed on the smelly, hard floor of an upstairs room of a church. Downstairs, in the basement of the church, was a homeless shelter for men. Each day our intrepid crew marched out into the rainy Portland weather to experience life on the street—or, in the rhetoric of the course, "to be in solidarity with the homeless." We served and ate at soup kitchens, cleaned mice feces and roaches out of food pantries, met with advocates and social workers, listened as two former prostitutes told us of their life, and generally wandered through streets unshowered and proud of our liberal efforts to change things for the better and "truly experience" what it meant to be homeless. Although I look back on that experience with a mixture of humor at my naiveté and cynicism about whether our efforts really had any impact at all, the course got me thinking a lot about *solidarity*. The word itself was inspiring—as if in spending three days in that church meant I suddenly became transformed to be one with workers struggling for the right to unionize, the poor and oppressed in Latin America fighting oppressive regimes, prisoners at the mercy of impersonal criminal justice systems, and countless other struggles. I had a vague understanding that solidarity was some combination of compassion and social justice but beyond that, I just was not sure.

What does "solidarity" mean? Some scholars have suggested or implied that solidarity means a shared consciousness, experience, history, or identity.

Yet how then could someone who not only had no experience of oppression, like me and my colleagues in the Urban Plunge, possibly share the same consciousness with those who live the oppression relentlessly? Others suggest that solidarity is a feeling, but feelings alone do not always motivate us to act, nor do we even understand all the feelings that we may experience. Still others say that solidarity is the bond uniting individuals whatever their life circumstances may be. Most appeals to solidarity appear to be deliberate differentiations from unity, camaraderie, sociality, sympathy, or community. So what makes solidarity distinctly different and yet also allows it to be meaningfully used in such different ways? What did we mean when we claimed solidarity with the homeless and what did workers in Poland mean when they chose it for the name of their movement in 1980?

Philosophical literature on race and the history of the women's movement offer two pertinent examples that illustrate both the appearance of common understanding and the different possible uses of the concept of solidarity. A recent debate within the literature on race pertains to the moral obligations of racial solidarity. W. E. B. Du Bois used the term "racial solidarity" to draw out the familial analogy for race, and Alain Leroy Locke used "race solidarity" to indicate consciousness of and pride in cultural difference or artistic achievements within racial groups (see Scholz 2003a). But Locke also used it to indicate the ties that bind whites in a race-supremacist society: "The vicarious satisfactions of the poor whites, with a small share in the benefits of restricted labor competition, have been used to create a specious solidarity of interests based on the perpetuation of the discriminations of color caste" (Locke 1946, 235). Locke also mentions the bond that forms among colonized peoples in reaction to the dominance of the colonizer (Locke 1946, 531). Contemporary critical race theory further unpacks this term and challenges its social and moral content. What emerges is a complex, and at times vague, appeal to racial solidarity as an ontological concept, moral imperative, and social descriptor. Some argue that racial solidarity is meaningless because there are no races (Appiah 1996). Others argue that racial solidarity ought to be analogous to the ideal family and thus justifies giving partial treatment to members of the same race so long as no harm is done to others (Stubblefield 2001). Still others want to retain the notion of racial solidarity not for its truth or falsity as an ontological concept and not in order to justify moral partiality but as a recognition of the social construction of race (Mills 1997) or the political empowerment such a concept entails (Shelby 2005). Clearly, different conceptions of solidarity are at work in at least some if not all of these invocations of the term. More often than not, the understanding of solidarity is blurred as scholars use it to discuss external identity, shared experience, shared consciousness, and political resistance separately *and* simultaneously.

The second example is drawn from feminist activism and theory. Since the 1960s, the possibility of solidarity among women has been in the background of almost every feminist political theory. Activists of the 1960s and 1970s asserted strong connections among all women with their use of the term "sisterhood." But sisterhood belied the range of divisions between women and the diversity of oppressive experiences often interconnected with racial and class oppression. This critique, put forth (among others) by bell hooks in her well-known essay "Sisterhood: Political Solidarity Between Women," challenged conceptions of solidarity grounded on similar experiences of oppression or shared experience. She argued that male-supremacist ideology encourages women to bond only with men. Sisterhood was meant to show that women could bond on the basis of our shared oppression. But, as hooks explains, "The idea of 'common oppression' was a false and corrupt platform disguising and mystifying the true nature of women's varied and complex social reality. Women are divided by sexist attitudes, racism, class privilege, and a host of other prejudices" (1984, 44). Solidarity as a political movement, she argued, is built on resistance struggle and emphasizes shared strengths and resources. Perhaps even more radical, the shift in the understanding of solidarity challenged feminists and others who fight for liberation to see connections between their efforts and the efforts of other resisters. As hooks sees it, "Women must learn to accept responsibility for fighting oppressions that may not directly affect us as individuals. Feminist movement, like other radical movements in our society, suffers when individual concerns and priorities are the only reason for participation. When we show our concern for the collective, we strengthen our solidarity" (1984, 62).

Solidarity as a political movement superseded sisterhood or solidarity as shared experience when women recognized the need to unite based on shared strengths, common goals, or even identification with struggles. Sara Ruddick describes this transformation and adds that "solidarity extends indefinitely with different emphases depending on the feminist" (1989, 240). Solidarity among and between women became the ideal to strive for even while vast class and race divisions forced women to acknowledge their own role in upholding systems of oppression. Ruddick characterizes the ideal of solidarity as capable of uniting women in struggle across national and state boundaries because it favors "a closer look at what women actually suffer and how they act" (1989, 240). Feminist solidarity, she continues, seeks to "identify with women's culturally specific struggles to work, care, and enjoy, to think and speak freely, and to resist abuse" (1989, 240–41). These passages, like the material cited above for racial solidarity, reveal different, shifting, and even contradictory conceptions of solidarity often differentiated by a fine line between the unity for a purpose and the unity based on shared experience. Identifying with women's culturally specific struggles is different than uniting women in struggles. Two different notions of solidarity are at work.

One way to think about the apparent perplexity of the concept of solidarity is to scrutinize the social ontology of the group relation described by the term. The social bonds, strength of sentiment, identity, and overlap of interests among people in solidarity differs in many of the examples used above. Alternatively, because "solidarity" clearly carries some moral or political import, perhaps examining various solidarity relations for that content would clarify things. Racial solidarity or the solidarity among women might imply an obligation to patronize minority- or woman-owned businesses, to support cultural events and artistic endeavors that demonstrate race or gender solidarity. But that is different still from the political meaning of solidarity's socialist roots. Although not as explicit as the social ontology or the moral and political aspects, solidarity also seems to have an epistemological side. It has been described as sharing consciousness and as empathetic understanding. But many of the different forms of solidarity overlap in their social ontologies, moral and political norms, or epistemologies. These categories may aid in distinguishing forms of solidarity for ease of theoretical discussion, but there is not always an easy alignment of actually existing solidarities solely along these theoretical lines.

How, then, can forms of solidarity be delineated? Is there reason for keeping them connected? Should vastly different phenomena be similarly labeled solidarity? Is solidarity best understood as a description of the relations of human persons or community, a moral virtue, a political activity, or a state of mind?

Political Solidarity, a monograph in moral, social, political, and feminist philosophy, defends a system of classification for levels and types of solidarities and develops a theory of one of those types. I argue that there are three levels of solidarities. The first and most general level describes the content or expectations of every form of solidarity, thereby identifying the traits that distinguish solidarity from camaraderie, community, association, and other social groupings. This marks solidarity as a morally rich concept for political theorists in that it describes some form of unity (however tenuously the members might be united) that mediates between the individual and the community and entails positive moral duties. Each of these components informs the richness of the concept *solidarity* while also contributing to the challenge of articulating a theory of solidarity.

From this general level, a second level adds specificity and nuance to the different moral relations of solidarity. Three types of solidarity emerge that may be distinguished by their social ontologies, moral relations, and corresponding obligations. Consider, for instance, the solidarity of a tightly knit society. There is something different between this solidarity and the solidarity that unites individual workers in their collective efforts to win free unions or just wages. Similarly, the solidarity that victims of domestic abuse share with each other is not equivalent to the solidarity of a social activist movement aimed at changing a culture of abuse. In both cases, the initial sense of solidarity marks the bonds of a community united by some shared characteristic or similarity (social solidarity) while the second sort of solidarity indicates political activism aimed at social change (political solidarity). A third sense of solidarity is found in the obligations of civil society to protect citizens against vulnerabilities through the provision of healthcare, welfare, and consumer and environmental protection (civic solidarity). These three types meet the general features of solidarity and even have some other important traits in common. Their social and moral structures, however, make them distinct forms of solidarity and worthy of separate study.

The third level of solidarity might be thought of as "parasitical solidarity." "Solidarities" at this level are not rightly solidarity at all insofar as they fail to meet at least one of the criteria for solidarity generally. Parasitical solidarity draws on some of the elements of a form of solidarity but rarely has the strong positive duties that constitute social, political, or civic solidarity. Parasitical solidarity is a rhetorical tool rather than a moral relation. By identifying and delineating the other forms of solidarity, we stand a better chance of rescuing this important moral and political concept from slipping into cant.

We have witnessed or even been part of those more or less spontaneous groups that manage, somehow or other, to work together to bring about significant social change in spite of not having any formal mechanisms for decision-making, social criticism, collective action, or even ascription of responsibilities. In this book, I articulate a theory of political solidarity that focuses on the active duties of individuals and groups "in solidarity." I argue that political solidarity carries important distinctions from other forms of solidarity, social and civic in particular. Political solidarity is a moral relation that marks a social movement wherein individuals have committed to positive duties in response to a perceived injustice. This understanding of solidarity allows us to dissect its various parts while maintaining its concreteness or embeddedness in a practical political situation. En route to this theory of political solidarity, I lay out a social ontology of political solidarity, set a framework for categorizing the moral relationships within it, and address some potentially troubling epistemological questions regarding authentic participation in solidarity.

A Brief Look at the History of the Concept of Solidarity

Any history of the concept of solidarity would be incomplete, and my aim here is not to give a definitive account of its development. Instead, I would like to offer a few relevant historical touchstones that demonstrate some of the background for the current use and understanding of the term. Many of the accounts I present here only in passing will be developed much more completely in the course of the book.

The word "solidarity," originates in French and was adopted by biologists and sociologists to indicate bonds of commonality. Karl Metz (1999) offers a fairly extensive history of the term and also notes that it is rooted in "common liability." Auguste Comte, the father of sociology, used the term to indicate the cohesiveness of a community or society, clearly playing on the biological origins. He saw sociology as a science like the life sciences. Using them as a guide, Comte conceived of humanity as an organism. Solidarity was a measure of the stasis and variation within social institutions, elements that are instrumental to the reproduction of society (see Wernick 2001, 54). Emile Durkheim refined Comte's conception of solidarity by distinguishing two types: mechanical and organic. I go into greater detail about the sociological use of "solidarity" in Chapter 1 but for now we can note that the sociological roots of the term describe the cohesiveness or commonality of a group or population. Max Scheler's extensive study of sympathy added a phenomenological turn to the concept of solidarity. While these developments occurred in sociology and philosophy, the Catholic Church entered the debate with what has come to be known as Catholic Social Teaching.

Catholic Social Teaching is distinguished by a set of papal encyclicals and other documents that address the Church's role in society. It is said to originate with the encyclical *Rerum Novarum* in 1891 by Pope Leo XIII. This first social justice encyclical addressed the plight of the worker in the wake of the industrial revolution. Among the most important subsequent documents are Pius XI's *Quadragesimo Anno* (1931), which stresses the principle of subsidiarity and addresses the oppression of the poor, and *Mater et Magistra* by John XXIII (1961), which, together with *Gaudium et Spes* (Pastoral Constitution on the Church in the Modern World, 1965), examines the relation between rich and poor nations, suggesting that the Church has a responsibility to help people living in the world. In 1967, Pope Paul VI published *Populorum Progressio* on development, and twenty years later, Pope John Paul II paid tribute to that document with his *Sollicitudo Rei Socialis*. Solidarity appears throughout Catholic Social Teaching, beginning in the mid-twentieth century, as one of the primary principles. It applies both to individuals and nations as an obligation to aid those in need, with special emphasis on full human development—educational, religious, and social as well as economic development.

Expounding on Catholic Social Teaching and influencing it in the process, Heinrich Pesch articulated a theory of solidarism sitting soundly between the individualism of capitalism and the collectivism of socialism. Pesch argued that human beings were both individuals and social beings; social theory must take account of these two indivisible aspects of the human person (Mueller 1952, 488; Pesch 2003). Individuals maintain their own projects but are able to achieve success only within a society. For Pesch, this meant that moral obligations were cooperative. Solidarism indicated not collective responsibility wherein the individual was merely part of a whole but interdependent responsibility and joint obligations. The assumption here is that solidarity is an ontological fact; individuals are members of society and society exists for individuals. Mueller argues that "solidarity, because it *is* part of the very nature of society, is also a model for social action, something which society in the making *ought* to realize" (1952, 489). You can see here a clear recognition of the dual purpose of solidarity. Solidarity descriptively connotes the cohesion of the civil society for the benefit of individuals (i.e., for the common good). Prescriptively, it contains moral obligations to one another and may be seen as a call for social action/social change for the ends of social justice.

In a related vein, solidarity is among the rallying cries for liberation theology. Liberation theology, a particular branch of theology originating in the Latin American Catholic Church in the late 1960s, seeks to reinterpret the gospel in light of the plight of the poor. It takes seriously the gospel message to be one with the poor, and solidarity is the guiding principle in calling for a "preferential option for the poor." Theologian Clodovis Boff outlines three models of participation for privileged theologians in solidarity with the poor and oppressed: the specific contributions model, the alternating moments model, and the incarnation model. These models of solidarity with the poor reflect liberation theology's challenge of a "preferential option for the poor." According to the specific contributions model, the theologian contributes to solidarity activity via his or her theology. The theologian uses the tools of theory to participate in social criticism while also choosing themes that support the cause of the poor (Min 1989, 55). Liberation theology strives to blend theory and practice into a praxis that challenges dominant ideologies simultaneously with its confrontation of unjust political regimes. It is important, however, that the theoretician not become isolated in theory—the theologian must actively engage in liberation activities. The alternating moments model directly addresses this tension between participation in theory and participation in activism by alternating scholarly work and social justice work/activism on a regular basis. According to the third model, the incarnation model, "The synthesis of theology and politics takes the form of social insertion in an organic, even physical way, sharing in the life conditions of the poor" (Min 1989, 55). The identification between the scholar and the poor is effected via an abdication of privileged social status, class, and location. The risk with this last model of solidarity with the poor is that theory, in this case theology, is sacrificed for activism.

Perhaps the most noteworthy development of the concept of solidarity was its use as the name of the Polish workers' movement from September 1980 to October 1982. Many credit the influence of Catholic Social Teaching generally, and the inspiration of Pope John Paul II specifically, for offering some direction in the movement (see, for example, Libiszowska-Żółtkowska 1991, 103). Solidarność (Solidarity) may have been decades in the works, but it was the massive movement across Poland and eventually around the world that cemented the notion of solidarity in our consciousness. Solidarność originally fought for the right to establish independent trade unions that would depend on and serve the workers rather the Communist Party (Goodwyn 1991). It grew to a widely known movement of approximately four million workers. Seen more broadly, Solidarność was a protest against violations of human rights and citizen rights of workers. The movement targeted not only the exploitation of workers but also the unjust economic conditions, increasing poverty, and state control of information. Workers argued for free trade unions, the right to strike, and freedom of expression based on the moral values of human dignity and the freedom of conscience, truth, and justice. Although the goal of free trade unions served as the explicit end of the movement, it quickly encompassed a critique of the entire Communist Party regime. Many credit the Polish Solidarity movement with breaking the grip of Communist hold on Eastern Europe. The movement "articulate[d] common complaints against a dictatorial regime" (Walzer 1988, 15).

Frequently, solidarity is referred to as a European value. The fourth chapter of the Charter of Fundamental Rights of the European Union is titled "Solidarity." It lays out the rights of workers in Articles 27–32, familial life in Article 33, the right to social security and social assistance in Article 34, and the right to healthcare, "services of general economic interest," environmental protection, and consumer protection in Articles 35–38.

Finally, the song "Solidarity Forever," with lyrics by Ralph Chaplin, captures one of the most well-known applications of solidarity: unions. The song lists the many contributions of workers and the chorus echoes "solidarity forever / for the union makes us strong." In the early part of the twentieth century, when workers' unions exercised their strongest influence in both the lives of members and national politics, solidarity captured the spirit of loyalty to one's union as well as the struggle for rights that served as the justification of unions. While these two functions of solidarity—loyalty to a union and struggle for rights—are united in the solidarity struggles of unions in the early part of the century, there are compelling moral and social philosophical reasons to think about them as distinct. The next section furthers the process of distinguishing forms of solidarity by looking at some contemporary solidarity theorists. Chapter 1 offers a more sustained discussion and defense of the distinctions.

The Current Status of the Concept

In addition to the historical, sociological, and theological uses of the term, solidarity has been used to stand in for sympathy, to mark the ties of friendship within civil society (Kahane 1999), to indicate the level of peer pressure in the purchase of consumer goods (Sunstein and Ullmann-Margalit 2001), to rally social protest, and to mark any sort of unity. With all these varieties of solidarities in use, it is evident that there will be some slippage from one form to another.

There is a surprising gap in the moral literature with regard to solidarity. A few thinkers have tried to discuss solidarity systematically, based on Marx's concept of history (most notably Lenhardt 1975). While it is often assumed in accounts of individual and group motivation for action, it is rarely discussed and analyzed. Kurt Bayertz offers one of the most extensive discussions of solidarity as a moral concept to date. Bayertz challenges political and moral philosophers to examine the concept of solidarity in the same manner as the concept of justice (1999a, 3–4). What is called for, in other words, is a vigorous dialogue about solidarity.

Bayertz delineates four uses of the term "solidarity" in what he describes as an attempt to "lay the ground work for a future solidarity theory" (1999a, 5). The first, according to Bayertz, is solidarity as the binding force for all of humanity. In this usage, "solidarity" replaces "fraternity" in the patriarchal lingo of old. A number of scholars have attempted to articulate a universal solidarity, and I discuss some of these theories in Chapter 7. I also challenge the conception of human solidarity as a distinct category; I instead argue that there are forms of human solidarity that are best understood as extended versions of the three basic forms of solidarity discussed in Chapter 1.

The second usage of solidarity centers on society. Solidarity might be used, for instance, to describe the cohesion of a smaller community such as a city or civic public. Members of solidarity would thus be obliged to one another because of their membership in the community. Bayertz links this to Durkheim's mechanic and organic solidarity. Following Durkheim, I refer to this form of solidarity as "social solidarity" and contrast it with political and civic solidarity in Chapter 1.

The third use of solidarity describes a group that comes together based on common interests. But common interest alone is somewhat misleading; their opposition to injustice or oppression unites the group. As Bayertz explains, "Here, 'solidarity' denotes the emotional cohesion between the members of these social movements and the mutual support they give each other in their battle for common goals" (1999a, 16). I call this characterization of solidarity "political solidarity," and it forms the heart of the arguments in this book.

Finally, the fourth use of the term solidarity is the welfare state's work in redistributing wealth. I group this form of solidarity with two relevantly similar others and refer to them as "civic solidarity" in Chapter 1.

Klaus Peter Rippe similarly classifies solidarity but into only two groups. The first, "project-related solidarity," resembles Bayertz's third category and my category of political solidarity. There are some differences between project-related solidarity, political solidarity, and Bayertz's third category, but those will become clearer as my articulation of political solidarity unfolds. The second classification of solidarity, according to Rippe, is that "found in the family, in the neighborhood, in the village, in clubs and in guilds" that includes a "disposition to help and assist" (1998, 356). In other words, Rippe divides solidarity into political solidarity and social solidarity. One might be able to discern a form of civic solidarity in his notion of a "network of joint rights and obligations" (Rippe 1998, 371), but, at least in this article, it is undeveloped.

Bayertz speculates that one reason solidarity has not gained the attention of philosophers until very recently is because solidarity entails "positive obligations to act" and these are "difficult to incorporate within mainstream ethical and political thought" (1999a, 4). Moreover, the duties that do arise are, by and large, particular to the activity in solidarity. Bayertz suggests we consider "solidarity" as a "political watchword" rather than an "ethical concept." It is political because the social groups interact in such a way as to uphold or challenge social and political practices.

Another reason may relate to the attempt at doing philosophy apolitically. Philosophers have long held on to an ideal of objectivity. Political biases only cloud our analyses in the search for truth. But social philosophers, feminists, critical theorists, race theorists, and others have challenged that understanding of philosophy's task, in part pointing out that even seemingly "objective" claims carry with them certain prejudices or biases. In some ways, these developments open the door for a more sustained study of solidarity. Solidarity is context dependent; understanding its moral and political import means acknowledging its social and historical circumstances.

In addition to the reluctance to study "solidarity" per se, there has been an even greater reluctance to study the resistant or revolutionary version in political solidarity. While sociologists have done extensive work on social solidarity, and political scientists have worked, albeit often under a different organizing concept, on civic solidarity, philosophers have largely avoided offering sustained theoretical defenses of political solidarity. Theologians are slightly better with regard to political solidarity in the area of liberation theology, but philosophy clearly has some unique contributions to make to the study of solidarity generally and political solidarity specifically.

Summary of the Book

After developing a system of categorization for forms of solidarity and highlighting the problems that accrue when solidarities are conflated, I articulate a theory of political solidarity that focuses on the moral relationships and positive duties of individuals and groups united in solidarity for social change. I argue that political solidarity has a different impetus, social structure, and moral content than civic or social solidarity. Political solidarity also has implications for such topics as sustainability and globalization that necessitate a foray into the meanings and possibilities for human solidarity. For instance, our individual consumer choices have political repercussions that extend far beyond national borders. So too the international community bears some responsibilities in the face of gross violations of human rights. I take up the topic of human and global solidarity in the last chapter. Throughout the book, I use compelling examples from social movements to illustrate key aspects of the argument. My aim is not to defend these movements as justifiable forms of solidarity or even to explore the solidaristic potentialities of social injustice, but rather to defend and in some sense rescue solidarity as a moral and political concept.

In the first chapter, I develop a taxonomy for solidarity and begin to articulate the differences between social solidarity, civic solidarity, and political solidarity. While there are certainly important commonalities between these three forms of solidarity, the significant differences reveal markedly contrasting moral obligations. A look at the literature on solidarity also reveals a tendency toward slippage among the three that obscures some of the fundamental questions of solidarity. After a section on each of the three forms of solidarity, by highlighting the commonalities I offer some insight into how the three bridge one another. Finally, I present "parasitical solidarity," that is, the rhetorical use of solidarity that aims to tap into the associated feelings without the moral obligations.

After this survey of the terrain of solidarity, I begin to articulate a theory of political solidarity. Political solidarity is a relation that forms a unity of individuals each responding to a particular situation of injustice, oppression, or social vulnerabilities. Each individual makes a commitment to a cause. This commitment shapes relationships with other members in solidarity and, depending on the nature of the political cause and the extent of the commitment, has the power to transform the individual's life and lifestyle as well. The second chapter examines the nature and strength of commitment to solidaristic activities and defends solidarity as a form of collective responsibility. Subsequent chapters elaborate on the theory.

In the third chapter I further discuss the initial individual commitment to participate in political solidarity looking primarily at an existentialist model of commitment. Section 2 examines moral sentiments as components of solidarity. I then suggest that there are three primary moral relations with corresponding obligations and responsibilities within political solidarity. The first is among the members of the solidary group. This relation mandates consciousness-raising, cooperation, and mutuality. I explore some of the possibilities and limitations of these drawing from the literature on collective responsibility.

The second moral relation of political solidarity is the relation to the cause, goal, or ends, most broadly understood as liberation. Because the individual action has the politically transformative power to change social relations, this relation mediates other relations. The primary duty here is social criticism. The goal or end of the solidarity movement is inspired by social criticism, but that social criticism must remain active throughout the course of the movement in order to accommodate changing needs and interests. Moreover, social criticism is also turned back on the solidary group and solidaristic activity itself to encourage consistency and, as much as possible, avoid the antinomies of action for social change.

The third moral relation is the relation between the solidary group and the larger society. This relation encompasses many different relations: those in solidarity assume an obligation to each other, to those who suffer an injustice but do not join in solidarity, to those who are privileged by oppression or injustice but do not directly perpetrate it, and to those who do directly support unjust systems or regimes. The primary duty here is activism but there are, I argue, multiple and varied means within activism. In the last section of the chapter, I argue that political solidarity is nonviolent because of its oppositional relationship to oppression or injustice that is itself violent. Political solidarity is a confrontation or challenge to the status quo and as such has the potential to be quite combative. I argue, on the contrary, that the values that inform political solidarity must not assume the values opposed in the oppressive system.

In the fourth chapter, "The Solidary Collective," I study more closely the solidary collective or group. In keeping with the literature on solidarity, I use the adjective "solidary" to refer to the specific group or collective that is said to be "in solidarity." I do, however, confine my use to describing the group or, in rare instances, the group activity. Solidarity is unique not only because it maintains a balance between individual interests and group interests, but also because it marks a group that at times looks more like a seriality or loose collective than a tightly knit group. In the fourth chapter, I show how political solidarity can include the participation of a wide variety of peoples, with sometimes radically different ideologies or motives, who nonetheless commit to a similar cause. Each individual commits to solidarity and at times the commitment may be weak or strong. The strength of individual commitment, the exigency of the cause, the urgency of the struggle, and the inspiration of others united in solidarity help to define the group. In political solidarity, as opposed to social and civic solidarity, the goal or cause is instrumental in the measure of group cohesion rather than the bonds between members. This is not to say that members in political solidarity do not share a bond—they do but it is primarily a bond to the cause that subsequently brings individuals together for collective action. The chapter also includes a discussion of democracy and solidarity. The solidary group acts in concert but often the activity of political solidarity is not organized or is organized by a subgroup. Decision-making within political solidarity then becomes something of a challenge for theorists.

Throughout the book I emphasize a need to distinguish the solidary group and the oppressed group for political solidarity. When social and political solidarity are conflated, the solidary group is circumscribed by experiential knowledge of the injustice. I argue that theory needs to distinguish social solidarity and political solidarity, thereby separating the oppressed group and the solidary group, though there may be significant overlap between the groups in practice. Chapter 4 provides the argument for and defense of this distinction.

One of the distinguishing features of political solidarity is that it is not equivalent to the social group of oppressed peoples. At times, oppressed and privileged alike join together to create the solidary group. But this raises some epistemological questions associated with privilege and solidarity. Political solidarity indicates solidarity formed in response to injustice or oppression. As such, the group that forms necessarily excludes others. Individuals from among the privileged social ranks who renounce their privilege have and do participate in political solidarity. Most of the literature on solidarity grants the oppressed a privileged knowledge, and some also assert a moral superiority as well. In Chapter 5, "The Paradox of the Participation of the Privileged," I look at three different models of epistemological privilege for solidarity drawn from feminist theory and critical studies. Each features important challenges to traditional epistemology in an effort to avoid excluding voices from political participation, but none of these models adequately address the possibilities for participation in solidarity of those who were formerly oppressors or formerly privileged by the oppression. I examine both the desirability and feasibility of the participation of the privileged in solidarity and suggest some epistemological strategies that might be entailed in the solidary commitment in order to avoid repeating social structures of domination within the solidary group.

As I argue in Chapter 2, individuals unite in political solidarity to achieve a goal or end. The goal can be quite concrete or quite fluid; it might be accomplished within a matter of days or span decades. Chapter 6, "The Social Justice Ends of Political Solidarity," explores the ends of political solidarity as a movement to end oppression, injustice, or social vulnerabilities. I explore what counts as a justifiable goal and how praxis is sustained once the original goal is no longer the driving force of the movement. The energy of the collective derives in part from the collective praxis toward a goal. Once the goal has been accomplished, a new exigency has replaced it, or the goal itself has undergone significant transformation, the solidary group either dissolves or remakes itself according to a new end. This chapter explores some of the philosophical issues of a cause that inspires individual and collective commitment.

The final chapter analyzes one of the most controversial topics within the literature on solidarity: human solidarity. After presenting a number of prominent approaches to human solidarity, I argue that human solidarity, depending on its agenda, is best understood as a subcategory of social solidarity: that is, it is the social solidarity of all humans united by a shared attribute or characteristic, or civic solidarity, as a unity of all humans in an international community committed to protecting its members and providing aid to the world's most vulnerable. Global solidarity, in contrast, is a subcategory of political solidarity. When peoples of the world share a common enemy, universal political solidarity or global solidarity might arise. There are some candidates that might form the oppositional group but, given the universality of global solidarity, the prospects are quite limited. In this chapter, I use the question of genocide, especially focusing on the way rape has been used in genocidal campaigns, to frame the questions of human solidarity and the challenges of global solidarity.

Solidarity is a rich and complex concept. In many ways, this book is a continuation of my early reflections on solidarity. Back in college, when I was working and learning about the problem of homelessness, I convinced myself that I could not be in solidarity with the homeless because I could always leave. I had family who would protect me from that fate and more than a few doors opening to provide opportunities that would further secure my social status. But many years later, I look back and think that my assessment of what counts as solidarity was too limited. Certainly I did not share in the experience of homelessness for any length of time, but I had made a commitment to live a different way—a commitment I have sometimes failed to keep. I also tried in some small manner to take a political stance. Solidarity has many forms and is manifest in many different ways. By recognizing what solidarity can mean in any given context, we open up the possibilities for personal and political transformation. Solidarity demonstrates the potential for social change and the hope for a better world. In this day of ever-expanding relations among peoples all over the world, solidarity—whether social, civic, or political—offers a new way to think about those relations and enact our moral commitments.

ONE

Solidarities

The term "solidarity" is used variously to mark the cohesion of a group, the obligations of civic membership, the bond that unites the human family, shared experience, expressions of sympathy, or struggles for liberation. As a moral concept, solidarity has been interpreted as a virtue, a duty, a feeling, a relation, and a conscious choice. Solidarity is used to describe a particular type of community and it is used to describe the bonds of any community. Solidarity is a feeling that moves people to action and it is an action that invokes strong feelings. Although there are times when different forms of solidarity overlap, the distinctions between them are revealing and important. What do these forms and functions of solidarity have in common? How do they differ? Has solidarity come to stand in as a description of any sort of unity or is there something more meaningful, more content driven, about the term?

In this chapter, I propose a classification system of solidarities that begins by offering three characteristics of every form of solidarity. These characteristics are necessarily very broad and general but they help to illustrate what it is we all understand or mean when we hear or use the term. This brief discussion of the "genus" or "meta-concept" of solidarity reveals what all forms and presentations of solidarity have in common. But there are also significant differences between the "species" or forms of solidarity. Using the same unmodified term for all of the various forms of solidarity hampers our ability to see the rich variety of social relations contained within the concept. The next three sections delineate some of the crucial descriptive and normative differences between the three basic forms of solidarity: social, civic, and political.

I then discuss two models for how these three forms of solidarity relate to one another: the continuum model and the discrete model. Examples of both models are evident in social practice; understanding the differences between them, however, allows for a more nuanced account of the origins and ends of the various forms of solidarity. With this background, we can take a step closer to articulating a theory of political solidarity.

Finally, "solidarity" is often used inappropriately—in a way that ignores or even contradicts the moral content of the concept. This I call "parasitical solidarity," and I suggest that there are rhetorical reasons for its use. Given that an important part of my aim in this book is a recovery and defense of solidarity for moral and political philosophy, I argue for some caution and critical awareness of the parasitical uses of the term. Nevertheless, I call these inappropriate uses of the term "parasitical solidarity" rather than "pseudo-solidarity" because they do attempt to feed off of at least some aspect of social, civic, or political solidarity.

I turn now to examine those characteristics found in every form of solidarity in order to help illuminate those features that make solidarity different from other moral relations. Although present in all, the manifestation of each of these three primary characteristics differs in each of the various species or forms of solidarity. Subsequent sections of this chapter illustrate those differences. The first characteristic is that solidarity mediates between the community and the individual. That is, solidarity is neither individualism nor communalism but blends elements of both. Individuals are valued for their uniqueness but solidarity is also a community or collective (whether it be the formal state, society generally, or some subgroup or voluntary association). We could also say that the community of solidarity might be identified through contrast or opposition with a larger or different social grouping. The group or community described by solidarity is somehow more than an aggregate of its parts. The solidarity collective is constituted by individuals but simultaneously enriches the lives and identities of those individuals through their communal engagement. This is not to say that the community exists independently of the individuals or that the community takes on the status of a super-entity (Ladd 1998, 19–22). Rather, in solidarity the individual sees him- or herself as part of a unique grouping (though he or she may not always consciously be aware of this grouping) and the community itself exists because of who the individuals are. When we speak of solidarities, we speak neither solely of the individual and his or her interests, nor solely of an abstract or idealistic notion of a community or the state. Instead, solidarity describes both through a focus on the relation between the individual and the community or group.

Solidarity need not be contrary to autonomy, but it is contrary to individualism. The latter emphasizes independence but solidarity, while not losing the individual in the community, emphasizes the bonds with others or interdependence. So too solidarity is not a form of communitarianism, though it shares certain similarities insofar as community takes a pride of place. The good of the community is tied up with the good of the individual and vice versa in solidarity (whereas communitarianism places the good of the community over and at times against the good of the individual). The solidarity community also demands particularity; that is, the details of context and unique combination of members contribute to how solidarity is conceived, which leads to the second characteristic.

The second characteristic of the broad category of all solidarities is that solidarity is a form of unity. All the various uses of the term assume that there is an identifiable group, though not all will be as formal as an association or as long-standing as a tribe or society. Something binds people together. The nature of the unity also varies tremendously as does the motivation for the unity. One cannot be in solidarity with oneself; nor can just any community be in solidarity. There is something distinctive about the unity of solidarity but, as we shall shortly see, that distinctiveness is best expressed within the various forms that solidarity takes—even that level of specificity, however, will be incomplete.

The third primary characteristic, and perhaps the most distinguishing, is that solidarity entails positive moral obligations. Political philosophy has historically been preoccupied with articulating rights and privileges of citizens or describing negative duties. Kurt Bayertz speculates that political philosophers have been reluctant to develop theories of solidarity precisely because solidarity entails positive duties (1999a, 4). While it would be quite impossible to articulate the content or particularity of the positive duties of all the various instances of solidarity, it is possible to provide a general structure, outline, or procedure that will indicate how the positive duties vary across forms of solidarity and how they resemble each other. Solidarity is a moral relation, but the different forms or species of solidarity can be differentiated according to their varying moral priorities and constituent relations.

While every form of solidarity shares the general characteristics of being a form of unity that mediates between individual and community and entails positive duties, different forms of solidarity differ a great deal in how they motivate and manifest these characteristics. As we saw in the Introduction, Bayertz identifies four uses of solidarity. I roughly follow his distinctions and, although I disagree with his characterizations of human solidarity and some of the details within the four types, I find his four uses quite useful in thinking about what might be called the various species of solidarity. Some forms or uses of the term focus on the bonds between members of a group or society. Some forms emphasize the obligations a society owes its members and vice versa. Still other forms make an explicit connection to social justice. What distinguishes these is not so much the particular type of unity but rather the logic of the moral obligations and the solidary bonds. For some forms of solidarity, the bonds cause or bring about moral obligations; for others, a moral commitment causes social bonds to form. Of course, parasitical solidarity stands outside this characterization more or less entirely by falling short on some aspect of the social or moral structure of solidarity but nevertheless sponges off the implied relation it invokes.

Human and global solidarity will be touched on only briefly in my discussions of social, civic, and political solidarity, in part because human solidarity is so controversial and in part because I argue that it is merely a subcategory of one of the other three depending on how one understands human solidarity. Far from trivializing the ideal of human solidarity or the necessity of global solidarity, placing human solidarity as a subcategory of social and civic solidarity allows for the specific nuances of the moral relations to come to light for the specific uses of the term. A fuller account of human solidarity as forms of social and civic solidarities, as well as an account of global solidarity—a form of political solidarity—is developed in the final chapter.

For social and civic solidarity, I will explore some of the prima facie moral elements that will be useful in clarifying the differences between them and political solidarity. Social solidarity has roots in the thought and writings of Jean-Jacques Rousseau and Emile Durkheim but more recent discussions are also presented. Civic solidarity is perhaps best developed in the European Union Charter, but it is a long-time European value and appears in contemporary discussions of development and universalized healthcare as well. Political solidarity has its roots in revolutionary praxis. After discussing these three basic forms and their normative dimensions discretely, I bring them back together for a look at their connections and a defense of the schematic of keeping them theoretically separated, even if practically they often overlap or intersect.

The next chapter lays out a theory of political solidarity. Broadly speaking, political solidarity is a unity of individuals who have made a commitment to struggle for liberation. The rest of this book develops and defends the theory of political solidarity by looking more intently at the moral relationships, obligations, and contexts first articulated here.

Social Solidarity

In the case of social solidarity, solidarity is a measure of the interdependence among individuals within a group; primarily descriptive and secondarily normative, social solidarity pertains to group cohesiveness. But this simple statement belies a much more complicated structure that entails some degree of shared consciousness, shared experience, or some other uniting feature among group members. Social solidarity is a community relation that also entails some binding obligations. These obligations, however, are quite different from the obligations of political solidarity articulated more completely in Chapter 2 and subsequent chapters of this book. The cohesion of the group or the sense of community by and large dictate the types of obligations found in social solidarity. Established customs, social mores, laws, or codes express the expected obligations individual members have to one another in the group. An important difference between the obligations of social solidarity and the obligations of political solidarity is that the latter are chosen and oriented toward a particular goal in response to an unjust situation. Within social solidarity, by contrast, the obligations accrue with group membership and thus may be externally imposed. In addition, the moral ties pertain to day-to-day responsibilities to others in the community and are not explicitly aimed at alleviating injustice or oppression.

Consider some different types of groups: a family structure wherein an individual's interests are intertwined with the interests of others in the family, a group with a high degree of group consciousness or shared consciousness, a group of individuals affiliated merely by a shared goal of gaining a seat on a bus, or a group attending the same sporting event. Each of these exemplifies social solidarity insofar as there is a group, however loosely defined, about which we may analyze the group cohesion. The family, wherein there is a great deal of interdependence among members, may be described as having a high degree of social solidarity. Bus passengers, on the other hand, demonstrate a relatively low degree. Groups that fall in the middle, according to the general sociological model, display less interdependence among their members than the family but more than the random seriality of the bus passengers. The groups with shared consciousness or group consciousness—like a club, association, or perhaps a political party—have a relatively high degree of social solidarity insofar as they demonstrate some shared and overlapping interests. Attendees at a sporting event likely have a low degree unless they are season ticket holders who develop longer-term relations with one another (much like regular churchgoers who develop a "pew community").

Cultural solidarity is a subcategory of social solidarity and occurs when the social cohesion rests on shared traditions, languages, and practices that are normally understood as constituting culture. In the Introduction, I used the example of "racial solidarity." At least one of the uses of that term connoted social solidarity as in cultural solidarity. Alain Locke and W. E. B. Du Bois both use the concept of solidarity to mark the racial grouping connected by shared forms of artistic expressions, linguistic patterns, and other cultural norms. Even Locke's use of "racial solidarity" for the pernicious bond among whites demonstrates a sort of cultural solidarity—white supremacist culture—even if the culture it marks is not only not admirable but even unjust.

Perhaps the most famous account of social solidarity comes from sociologist Emile Durkheim. Solidarity, according to Durkheim, describes the bond that ties a society together. He distinguishes two kinds of solidarity: mechanical and organic. Mechanical solidarity, found in lesser-developed societies, is grounded on a notion of group cohesion resulting from resemblances or similitude. Individuals within the group share attributes, location, and experience such that there is a low level of individuality within the group and a high level of shared consciousness. In fact, the individual conscience is so engrossed in the collective conscience that the latter appears to be independent of the former though that appearance is mistaken. Durkheim argues that there is always a realm of psychic life that is unique to the individual (1973, 84). So long as it is united, society acts as a whole, that is, mechanically (Durkheim 1973, 78). Individuals share an attraction to one another that corresponds with a desire for the other's good as well, but, in its most extreme form, individuality is almost—though not completely—nonexistent. Altruism develops because of the similarity of conscience or the strength of attraction based on similarity of sentiments (Durkheim 1973, 84, 110; Doran 1996, 4). In other words, one desires the good of another as one desires the good for oneself.

Organic solidarity, on the other hand, is based on the function or role of individual members that leads to an intricate interdependent community with a highly developed division of labor. Organic solidarity arises from mechanical solidarity as society develops. Altruism in the case of organic solidarity arises because of the division of labor. The division of labor allows greater individuation to occur; each person becomes like an organ with "its proper sphere of action where it moves independently without imposing itself upon others" (Durkheim 1973, 79). Changes in society change the individual rather than the other way around, but individuality and community are compatible in organic solidarity (see also Bayertz 1999a, 15). Shared interest, according to Durkheim, does not have the power to hold individuals together enduringly (as in solidarity). Only when individual consciences intermingle and reciprocity appears does organic solidarity form. The division of labor allows for individuality to emerge but also illustrates the dependence of each person on society and restrains individual activity through the moral and legal rules that develop. The division of labor, in short, "becomes the chief source of social solidarity, . . . [and] at the same time, the foundation of the moral order" (Durkheim 1973, 139). Within the division of labor the individual realizes his or her dependence on society thereby forming the foundations for morality (cf. Doran 1996, 19).

Durkheim, it has been argued, was heavily influenced by Jean-Jacques Rousseau (Cladis 2003). In the *Discourse on the Origin and Foundation of Inequality Among Mankind,* Rousseau examines the state of nature, the evolution of inequality, and the development of civil law with the increase of a division of labor. The purpose of the *Second Discourse* "is to point out, in the progress of things, that moment, when, right taking place of violence, nature became subject to law; to unfold that chain of amazing events, in consequence of which the strong submitted to serve the weak, and the people to purchase imaginary ease, at the expense of real happiness" (Rousseau 1967 [1755], 176).

In the state of nature, according to Rousseau, the individual is perfectly free, independent, solitary, and naturally good. The individual's desires, confined merely to preservation, are easily fulfilled through his or her own power. There also would be no progress, however, if the state of nature continued; insecurity would keep people from working the earth, for example. Hence, we begin to rely on others and develop a division of labor, thereby creating social and moral life. Natural differences become more entrenched as their effects are differently valued by society. The toolmaker and the farmer may work equally hard but their products are valued quite differently. Civil law replaces natural law and cements this inequality; the greater the inequalities found in a society, the more laws will be required to maintain it. Rousseau's *Social Contract* offers the general will as a remedy for the gross inequality that had developed unchecked. The general will, he thinks, provides some civil equality and strengthens the bonds between individuals within society. Particular wills may guide some pursuits of the individual, but when it comes to morality, the general will rules.

While this is an admittedly simplistic presentation of Rousseau's monumental point, we can nevertheless draw from it some insight regarding morality for social solidarity. For Durkheim, laws and morals increase as the division of labor progresses. As we saw, Rousseau made a similar observation—though with approbation rather than progress in mind—in his *Discourse on the Origin of Inequality Among Mankind*. Social solidarity marks the unity and the unity necessitates morality. Morality takes shape at least in part in response to the changing needs of the community. Durkheim explains the size and expanse of government based not on whether a society is unruly or not, "but rather because its growth is proportional to the progress of the division of labor, societies comprising more different organs the more intimately solidary they are" (Durkheim 1973, 110). Crime and immorality are indications of dissemblance from the majority (Durkheim 1973, 134; Doran 1996, 7–9).

Somewhat contrary to Durkheim, rational choice theorist Michael Hechter argues that solidarity is a function of individual members' dependence on the group (Hechter 1987). Whereas Durkheim begins with the society and proceeds to explain the individuation of its members, Hechter seems to begin with the individual and uses social solidarity as an indication of reliance among individuals. The less the dependence, the less the solidarity. If, for instance, a bus full of strangers gets stuck in the snow, then the social solidarity among the passengers changes. Their new situation requires a greater degree of interdependence and thus a heightened sense of solidarity results.

In Hechter's view, social solidarity further entails some requisite system of control. To maintain group cohesion, individual members must be given rules to follow and sanctions for noncompliance must be enforced (Hechter 1987, 52). The differences in degree of solidarity among groups might be due to differences in internalized norms, common individual interest, or rational choice (Hechter 1987, 8–10). It is clear that group membership affects the behavior of individuals, but as Hechter points out, some groups exercise more influence than others. What accounts for this difference is said to be "solidarity." Individual members abide by group standards of behavior because they are obligated to but this obligation varies among groups. Following Durkheim, Hechter argues that the extensiveness of "collective standards of conduct" depends on the group and "can be indicated by the proportion of private resources that each member is expected to *contribute* to collectively determined ends" (Hechter 1987, 17,18). Hechter describes solidarity this way: "The greater the average proportion of each member's private resources contributed to collective ends, the greater the solidarity of the group" (Hechter 1987, 18).

It seems clear, then, that sociologists, in particular, use "solidarity" as a descriptive term measuring the extent of "groupness" (Hechter 1987, 8; Durkheim 1973; see also Thome 1999 for a good sociological discussion of kinds of solidarity). But social solidarity, as we have seen, also presumes some sort of moral ties between the solidary members. According to Hechter, there are three main sociological approaches to solidarity: normative, functionalist, and structuralist. The normative perspective holds that social order arises from adherence to a set of norms much like a social contract. The functionalist perspective bases solidarity on the consequences of the association; that is, group outcomes are the causes or motivators for individual action. The structuralist perspective (in contrast to the functionalist and the normativist) holds that "individuals are seen to coalesce into solidary groups—such as collectively conscious classes or ethnic groups—by virtue of sharing common material interests. They learn of this commonality of interests as they interact with one another. But, in this view, solidarity does not arise merely from the existence and awareness of common interest. Instead, it must be forged in competition with the antagonistic interests of individuals in groups located elsewhere in the social structure" (Hechter 1987, 25).

This last component of the structuralist perspective is important. The solidary group takes shape in opposition to some other group. While Hechter does not argue that this other group is necessarily dominant, historical and literary invocations of "solidarity" are based on the dominant/subordinate (and thus solidary) group model. This sociological model also has the greatest crossover with political solidarity developed in this book, though the functionalist model also shares with political solidarity a teleological element that informs individual and collective action.

Social solidarity is by no means amoral. On the contrary, Durkheim, like Rousseau, clearly held that communal membership carries moral obligations.

In fact, one might argue that it is precisely morality that drives the articulations of social solidarity. Collectivity presumes morality and vice versa. More difficult is figuring out which came first: is it morality that compels human community or human community that requires morality? John Ladd uses the concept of solidarity to indicate the combination of political goods, social and economic goods, and psychological goods found in community, though not necessary or sufficient for the rich notion of community he articulates (Ladd 1998, 10, 19). He further argues that solidarity is instrumental to the attainment of other ends and notes that, as such, social solidarity might serve undesirable ends (e.g., Nazism). In order to avoid such ascriptions of solidarity and maintain community as a good, Ladd suggests that the notion of solidarity be qualified as an instrumental value to good ends (Ladd 1998, 11).

Max Scheler's principle of solidarity claims that every act or failure to act is social; an individual's moral responses carry a communal responsibility. Scheler calls this a moral solidarity. He presents four levels of solidarity. The four levels are based on the extent of commitment together with a form of identification. The first level, solidarity by contagion, is characterized by a mass movement in which the individual members are more or less swept along by the force of the movement. The events or actions of this group are nonvoluntary and the feelings aroused are based merely on imitation rather than understanding (Ibana 1989, 44; Scheler 1970). The second level, representable solidarity, is constituted by a "life-community" in which "each individual member . . . can 'represent' any other member of the group" (Ibana 1989, 44). According to Scheler, these first two levels are similar in that the individual member does not distinguish him- or herself from the group. The members of the representable solidarity share similar feelings and experiences. These provide the context for the community. Examples include families and tribes.

The third level of solidarity is "solidarity by interests" and the impetus for solidarity is the pursuit of individual members' desires, goals, or purposes. The social contract is offered as an example as it demonstrates individuals acting according to rational principles in order to gain their intended end. The final or highest level of solidarity for Scheler is "unrepresentable (or personalistic) solidarity" (Ibana 1989, 45; Doran 1996, 40–41). According to this level of solidarity, each individual is irreducible and serves a "unique part in the social whole" (Ibana 1989, 45). Thus, the highest form of solidarity blends the unique values of the individual with the unity of a group.

As Ibana presents these levels, the picture emerges of social reciprocity and interdependence—with a call for global solidarity in the end.

I suggested earlier that human solidarity might be considered a subcategory of one of the three other species of solidarity or it might itself be a species of solidarity. As a subcategory of social solidarity, human solidarity simply means that humans are united because of our shared humanity. But what counts as our humanity or who counts among the humans has historically been open for debate and a never-ending source of contention among political philosophers. If we are a human family or if we are united by shared humanity, then the strength of our bonds may be analyzed according to the criteria provided by Durkheim or Scheler.

Civic Solidarity

Civic solidarity is among the more recent developments in the use and analysis of the term "solidarity." In its broadest usage, it refers to the relationship between citizens within a political state (Kahane 1999; Stout 2004). More refined applications of civic solidarity pertain to the obligations the state as a collective has to each citizen; that is, by virtue of their membership in a political state, each citizen is obliged to all others citizens, and vice versa. Here a clear link to the tradition begun by Rousseau is also evident. The social bond of citizenship just means that one can expect certain protections from all others. (This is not to place civic solidarity in the social contract tradition but rather to show how Rousseau's particular imprint on political philosophy also evinces itself in the structure of civic solidarity.) The state is usually the vehicle through which those protections are issued. Civic solidarity targets those vulnerabilities that would inhibit or prevent a person from participation in the civic public. The aim is to utilize social policy to decrease the vulnerabilities of all individuals. Importantly, the justification for civic solidarity is based both on the rights of individuals and on the good of society. Civic solidarity presumes that when individuals lack the basic necessities, society as a whole suffers.

Solidarity in this sense of civic solidarity is a more common topic for discussion in Europe than in the United States. This may be due to a more entrenched history of socialism (solidarity is often cited as a socialist value), less of an emphasis on individualism, or simply just that solidarity as a cultural value appears more predominantly in Europe than in the United States. Regardless of the reason, it is to Europe that we ought then to turn. The European Union replaces "fraternity"—from the French Revolution's "Liberty, Equality, Fraternity"—with "solidarity" in the tripartite rallying call for "Security, Diversity, Solidarity." More important, within the Charter of Fundamental Rights of the European Union, which summarizes the "common values of the Member States," Chapter IV is dedicated to solidarity. The summary set of social rights protected under solidarity includes workers' rights, social security, healthcare, environmental protections, and consumer protections (EUROPA 2000). The Charter presents an overview of case law drawn from member states. The Charter is not legally binding though its value has been widely recognized for uniting in a single document the civil, political, social, and economic rights of the European Community.

Workers' rights range from access to information and placement services to the right of collective bargaining and just working conditions. Although the Charter often appeals to "Community law and national laws and practices," the broad outlines of workers' rights stipulated provide a framework grounded in human rights and the recognition that the right to work is an integral part of being fully human. Associated rights spelled out in the Charter include the right to leisure time and the right to maternity or parental leaves. Social security benefits, when physical health, age, or other factors inhibit the ability to work, are enumerated in the Charter as well.

The provisions for healthcare within the Charter are quite general in deference to national policies. Nevertheless, the Charter does stipulate that "everyone has the right to access to preventive health care" (EUROPA 2000). Again, something akin to a human rights approach is evident. Basic preventative healthcare is also a good for society as a whole insofar as it diminishes costly emergency care and tends to have a positive effect on overall well-being.

With regard to the environment, the Charter of Fundamental Rights of the European Union commits to improve the environment through policies framed by "the principle of sustainable development" (EUROPA 2000). Associated documents present quite detailed action plans, among other things to reduce pollution in all its forms (air, water, noise), to provide for a sustainable future, to reduce the risks from chemical products on the environment, and protect biodiversity.

Consumer protections, articulated in Article 38—the last article in the chapter on solidarity—range from the protection of health and safety to the right to adequate consumer education and information. Once again, in both the example of environmental protection and consumer protections, civic solidarity evinces a balance between the rights of the individual and the good of society.

Although the Charter does not have legal standing, its enumeration of rights is and ought to be upheld by the civil governments of the members of the European Community. The constitutive rights constitute a prime example of civic solidarity in action.

Civic solidarity, then, is the idea that society has an obligation to protect its members through programs that ensure that adequate basic needs are met. It is, as the European Union asserted, requisite community action. The principle of solidarity, in other words, is one of the moral ideals embodied in the welfare state—a state in which the interdependence of citizens is acknowledged. A welfare state is generally understood as a state wherein residents may make claims against the government for social protection in the form of basic needs, income, or insurance (Halldenius 1998, 335). A large literature on solidarity and the welfare state has emerged to discuss the origins and content of these obligations and to defend solidarity against the charge that the welfare state threatens individual autonomy and individual liberty. As Andrew Mason frames it, "the question [is] whether a welfare state, funded through compulsory taxation, can be an expression of genuine solidarity?" (Mason 2000, 28). Rousseau, of course, would counter with his argument that no one can be truly free if forced to be enslaved to another person, whether that be an employer, a master, or some other domineering figure. Through our mutual alienation of some rights to all others, we avoid being subject to the arbitrary or potentially tyrannical rule of any single other. The welfare state supports individual freedom insofar as it helps to keep some people from economic coercion, exploitation, or some other social vulnerability thereby facilitating their greater freedom within the state.

Bayertz explains that this understanding of solidarity was "invented" by Pierre Leroux to counter "compassion" and "charity." Solidarity, unlike charity, justifies an individual's claim to protection by the community (Bayertz 1999a, 23). Bayertz, however, further argues that this use of solidarity is somewhat euphemistic because "justice," as in just distribution of wealth, serves the same function. In defense of the use of solidarity here we need merely point out that justice focuses on the individual's claim against the community while solidarity shifts the focus to the communal obligation.

Kees Schuyt argues that civic solidarity in the form of the welfare state is actually just an organized form of social solidarity. Given that social solidarity includes "shared feelings, interests, risks, and responsibilities" (Schuyt 1998, 297; see also Boshammer and Kayb 1998, 382), the welfare state is just an example of shared risks on the social level. Schuyt reconceptualizes solidarity for this purpose by arguing that it means "nobody should drop below the level necessary for a decent existence in a free society" (Schuyt 1998, 298). Together with principles of social justice and universal employment, solidarity underlies the welfare state. But the moral principle of solidarity becomes transformed to an "administrative solidarity," according to Schuyt, and the result is a faceless bureaucracy established and maintained to address the material needs of individuals within society. Social bonds and their associated moral principles become obsolete within a system of administrative solidarity. In order to counter the "'anonymization' of responsibility" within the government, Schuyt proposes to localize responsibility, thereby localizing civic solidarity. Specifically, the responsibility for production, for individual actions, for allocating scarce commodities, and "for solidarity with persons who have landed in desperate circumstances through no fault of their own" (Schuyt 1998, 309–10) ought to revert back to the individual worker.

While the specifics of Schuyt's proposal may be morally or practically problematic for other reasons, the use of civic solidarity is indeed intriguing. Schuyt clearly ties civic solidarity to social solidarity in such a way that the bonds of social existence inform moral obligations to assistance. But an alternative model might be found within liberalism. Social solidarity need not be necessary, in other words, in order for civic solidarity to be present and morally obligatory. Lena Halldenius argues, contrary to Schuyt, that social solidarity is not required for political legitimacy and thus not required as a justification of the welfare state.

Halldenius points out that the very nature of the welfare state invites antagonistic interactions that counter, rather than foster, the bonds of social solidarity (1998, 335). If citizens can make claims against the government and if the government becomes the faceless administrative body Schuyt hypothesizes, then there is little incentive to cultivate social bonds or civic identification. Whereas Schuyt proposed a reinvestment in the localized communities that foster solidarity, Halldenius argues that social solidarity is not necessary and may even be undesirable. If dependent on social solidarity, she speculates, welfare claims would be linked to bonds of sentiment that may fail to motivate or turn out to be fickle (Halldenius 1998, 336). Halldenius replaces social solidarity with non-domination in order to legitimate an egalitarian welfare state. The result is a system of civic solidarity (i.e., the welfare state) that is detached from social solidarity. It is worth pointing out that civic solidarity differs from the civic virtue of solidarity trumpeted by numerous social theorists, including Michael Sandel. The two are certainly related—as are all solidarities discussed in this chapter—but the civic virtue of solidarity is better understood as the normative effects of social solidarity (Sandel 1996; Halldenius 1998, 338). It asks for or describes bonds between similarly located individuals. Civic solidarity more accurately describes the obligations of the state, society, or community, of which the individual is a contributing part, to protect individuals against vulnerabilities. As Halldenius says, "If the existence of solidarity (as part of civic virtue) is necessary for legitimate government, but the very notion of *civic* virtue presupposes a political community, it is possible that for solidarity to be fostered those very institutions that it is supposed to legitimate must already be established" (1998, 345f).

In addition to the welfare state, "solidarity" is used to mark universalized access to healthcare within a state or even beyond state boundaries. The link between healthcare and welfare might be made through an argument that individuals—even libertarians—do have an obligation to aid the infirm (see van Donselaar 1998). Solidarity is in fact one of the long-standing European bioethics and biolaw values; it is used *within* the concepts of dignity and vulnerability as part of the basic principles autonomy, dignity, integrity, and vulnerability (Sass 2001, 219). This set of principles serves as a powerful alternative to the principles articulated in the United States: autonomy, nonmaleficence, beneficence, and justice (Sass 2001, 219). Notice especially the contrast between integrity and vulnerability on the one hand and nonmaleficence and justice on the other. The patient is the focus of care within the European list of bioethics principles as it is the patient's integrity, dignity, and vulnerability at stake; but the care provider dominates the U.S. list; that is, the provider is instructed to do no harm and to do good and just actions. Sass also points out that "solidarity" understood as "justice" might be one of the principles rather than just part of one, as might "subsidiarity," given its robust history in European thought and tradition (2001, 221).

Another version of civic solidarity is the use of "solidarity" to indicate an obligation to aid distant peoples (Egonsson 1999) or global development policy. Such usage is more rare than the others but one could argue that at least some of the calls for solidarity from Catholic Social Teaching are instances of civic solidarity of this sort.

Within Catholic Social Teaching, Pope Paul VI describes the duty of human solidarity in *Populorum Progressio* (*On the Development of Peoples*): "the aid that the rich nations must give to developing countries" (*Populorum Progressio*, §44; see also Doran 1996). This obligation is part of a tripartite obligation that "stem[s] from a brotherhood that is at once human and supernatural": the duty of human solidarity, the duty of social justice (understood as "the rectification of inequitable trade relations between powerful nations and weak nations" [§44]), and the duty of universal charity ("the effort to bring about a world that is more human towards all men [*sic*]" [§44]). The duty of solidarity is unique in that it is presented as a requirement for relationships ranging from individual interpersonal interactions to nations interacting in a global community. The emphasis, however, is on the latter as more effective global operators.

Pope John Paul II in *Sollicitudo Rei Socialis* (*On Social Concern*) expands on this presentation of solidarity emphasizing the moral obligation it reveals. He refers to solidarity both as a "virtue" and as a "duty." This emphasizes the unity of thought and action, attitude and obligation, inherent in an understanding of solidarity.

The moral duty of solidarity explicated in *Sollicitudo Rei Socialis* (*On Social Concern*) is based on the empirical fact of interdependence among peoples. (Pope John Paul II also speaks about solidarity in *Laborem Exercens*. There, however, he focuses primarily on work and working people, saying, "Solidarity should always be present in places where there is social degradation of the worker, where there is exploitation and increasing areas of poverty" [*Laborem Exercens*, §8]. This particular use of "solidarity" is more akin to political solidarity than the civic solidarity of *Sollicitudo Rei Socialis*.) The interdependence cited in Catholic Social Teaching justifying the moral duty of civic solidarity is not merely economic. Indeed interdependence is also cultural, intellectual, technological, ecological, political, and simply human. As the encyclicals argue, our decisions and actions have an effect on other peoples regardless of whether or not they are considered in the decision-making process. For example, the values displayed in television produced in the United States affect the cultures in which it is shown. So too the resources used and/or abused in one nation or region affect another nation or region's access to those resources. Given such a condition of global interdependence, Pope John Paul II argues that both individuals and governments have the moral obligation, when making decisions, to take into account "this relationship of universality, this interdependence which exists between their conduct and the poverty and underdevelopment of so many millions of people" (*Sollicitudo Rei Socialis*, §9).

Not unlike Rousseau's understanding of the social bond, interdependence challenges moral agents to reexamine decision-making so as to consciously incorporate the real or potential impact of a decision on other people or peoples. According to Catholic Social Teaching, there is a sort of reciprocity between the individual and the group (something we will see in political solidarity as well, albeit in a slightly different form). When the fact of global interdependence is separated from its moral requirements, Pope John Paul II argues, the results are detrimental not only to the poorest or weakest countries/regions. Indeed, interdependence is such that the strong countries or regions also suffer from the underdevelopment of some. Thus, the motivating factor of both *Populorum Progressio* and *Sollicitudo Rei Socialis* is the true development of all peoples (see also Doran 1996, 200–201). This use of civic solidarity holds the international community and powerful nations responsible for providing for and protecting the most vulnerable populations in the world. I return to the interdependence of all peoples in the final chapter in order to contrast this understanding of the solidarity of humanity with other positions.

Civic solidarity is based on different motivations and marks a different form of unity than social solidarity, regardless at what level it appears. It entails positive duties, as do all forms of solidarity, and those duties largely pertain to how best to protect citizens against the vulnerabilities that would inhibit their ability to participate in civic life. Surely there are some social bonds between citizens as well, but the moral structure of civic solidarity does not emphasize these bonds so much as the bonds between citizens and the state. In that sense, of course, it is political, but "political solidarity" employs yet another normative structure and a broader notion of the "political" than merely state systems.

Political Solidarity

Political solidarity shifts the emphasis of solidarity. Instead of basing solidarity on varying notions of dependence and group control, the political conception of solidarity highlights individual conscience, commitment, group responsibility, and collective action.

Political solidarity, unlike social solidarity and civic solidarity, arises in response to a situation of injustice or oppression. Individuals make a conscious commitment to join with others in struggle to challenge a perceived injustice. A collective forms but it is unified not by shared attributes, location, or even shared interests. The unity is based on shared commitment to a cause. There is, in other words, an inherently oppositional nature to political solidarity as well as a mutually shared vision. The experience of the oppressed (or a particular oppressed social group, or even a particular instance of injustice) provides the content for the movement of political solidarity. For this reason, many who use the term have conflated the oppressed group with the solidary group. Sharing a common history of oppression is not, however, sufficient for solidarity; each individual in the solidary group must value an interpretation of the past and the present and share a vision for the future, regardless of whether each individual actually experienced the relevant history. The vision for the future is construed quite broadly, such as liberation from oppression or equitable distribution of rights and privileges, in order to allow diverse perspectives and diverse participants to become actively involved in the activity of political solidarity.

The collective of political solidarity is usually a smaller group acting in response to a larger group but it could also be a less powerful group (regardless of size) responding to a more powerful group (regardless of size). The solidary group may be long lasting or relatively short-lived. In other words, the collective that forms in response to injustice may attain its ends quite rapidly and then cease to exist or change forms; the goals may change and a new collective form, or a cause may span decades while the solidary collective experiences quite fluid membership. The collective may be strengthened as a cause becomes more pressing or urgent—perhaps radically affecting the life prospects of the oppressed and/or members of the solidary group. The collective that forms around a cause undergoes further changes as the numbers of oppressed involved rises or falls. So too when non-oppressed people participate in a struggle to end oppression, the nature of the collective changes slightly in response.

Political solidarity may also undergo other transformations that may not be as directly associated with the nature of the collective. The goal of the social movement may change or be subsumed into a larger project. For instance, a movement in opposition to oppression may turn into a revolution. Seemingly unrelated changes in social existence may make the solidarity movement obsolete. The solidary group may see the fruition of its efforts and cease to exist as political solidarity or it may seek other forms of praxis in an effort to keep alive the solidary group and the spirit of kinship it fostered. Or the solidary relation or parts of the collective may become formalized and a political party, organization, or association may develop.

Most accounts of collective responsibility focus on group liability (e.g., Feinberg 1970; Held 1970; May 1992; French 1972, 1992; McGary 1986). In at least this respect, political solidarity as collective responsibility is profoundly different. It is a form of overtly political group action marked by multiple moral commitments. Few have undertaken a systematic study of these ethico-political dimensions of solidarity (Bayertz 1999a is a notable exception), but a great deal of insight might be garnered from looking at political solidarity active in the feminist and racial justice movements, to take but two examples.

The oppositional nature of political solidarity is rich with positive moral content. Political solidarity is formed by the mutually undertaken obligations of individual members of a solidary group. Political solidarity entails multifaceted relations that inform many of the duties of political action as well as the duties to others. Any theory of political solidarity would necessarily include some sort of procedural ethics; more directed accounts of political solidarity, that is, accounts that target a particular form of oppression or injustice, might also include a much more developed account of substantive ethics. In general, however, an ethico-political theory of political solidarity offers guidelines for behavior and activity among members of a group and addresses the collective responsibility of the group acting as a whole.

Importantly, the moral content of political solidarity does not begin with impartiality or neutrality, as do most conceptions of ethics. On the contrary, context, situation, and experience provide the source and content of morality within political solidarity. Political solidarity must have "real people and real problems" as the starting point and concrete "human relationships" as the content (Ladd 1998, 7, 8). Ladd argues that the ideal of impartiality limits the sources of ethics for a community. He also notes the effects of social construction on community norms, practices, and relationships. These cautionary notes equally apply to the solidary group. Most of the moral content stems from the relationships that form out of mutually undertaken individual commitments. But the perceptions of injustice and oppression cannot help but be affected by long-standing communal norms. So too the tools used to combat oppressive practices will be mediated through preestablished understandings of appropriate responses to social ills. Oppositional politics might push the boundaries of cultural behavior norms and will most certainly challenge any it finds contribute to oppression, but even insurgents are influenced by those cultural norms. Women who spoke in public arguing for their political rights in the early to mid-nineteenth century were surely challenging some cultural norms that contributed to the silencing of women but also demonstrated others insofar as they used public speaking as a primary means of protest.

This book aims at articulating a particular theory of political solidarity by specifying the structure of the basic moral requirements involved in such a moral relation around a social movement. After a brief discussion of the normative contrasts between the three major forms of solidarity presented in this chapter and a brief caution against parasitical forms of solidarity, I offer a more developed theory of political solidarity in Chapter 2. Subsequent chapters unfurl the details and address some of the possible objections to the theory of political solidarity I articulate. The theory of political solidarity that I sketch offers some means of adjudicating between competing methods and ends of solidarity, and suggests some insight into how individuals and the collective acts as well.

Although usually discussed under the banner merely of "solidarity" rather than of "political solidarity," like other solidarities, a number of social philosophers have noted the existence of a particular form of solidarity that carries self-imposed moral requirements. Examples are discussed in the rest of this section. They are rightly categorized as political solidarity because of their oppositional nature, the unity based on an objective of liberation, and the implication of strong moral obligations as determining the nature of the solidary bonds (as opposed to the bonds formed through a similarity or identity of physical or geographical attributes, or the bonds protecting the vulnerable assumed within civil society). The logic of political solidarity, in other words, reverses the ordering between social bonds and moral obligations found in social solidarity and civic solidarity.

As I mentioned in the Introduction, Bayertz identifies four forms of solidarity and his third form matches what I am here calling political solidarity. He identifies it as a unity of interests aimed at liberation. Social movements such as the civil rights movement, the women's movement, and the labor rights movement are pertinent examples of solidarity in action (Bayertz 1999a, 16). Bayertz also notes that this particular use of solidarity recognizes its historical roots in socialism: "From its content, this form of solidarity has a *positive* component, which results from the goals which those involved are keen to realize with the help of their solidary actions" (1999a, 16). Furthermore, he argues that this type of solidarity "involves a commitment *against* an opponent, from whom positive goals must be wrung. This leads to a *negative* component . . . it is not only exclusive, in that it excludes particular individuals or groups, but adversative, in that it opposes particular individuals or groups" (Bayertz 1999a, 17; see also Dussel 2007).

Klaus Peter Rippe identifies what he calls "project-related solidarity" and describes it as based on a goal rather than on interpersonal relationships like that found in social solidarity. He uses the "solidarity with the leftists in Chile, with the Sandinistas in Nicaragua, with transport workers on strike in Paris, with children afflicted by cancer" as examples of project-related solidarity. A crucial difference between this form of solidarity and social solidarity, Rippe explains, is that "if those in need of help and those providing help actually ever meet, it is only as a *result* of the solidarity shown and not the *reason* for the solidarity" (1998, 357). Each individual elects to make "the concerns of another person or group, which faces a special plight, her own" (Rippe 1998, 357; see also Dean 1996, 31). Rippe further suggests that the concern displayed toward others must "fit" with the other concerns of the person demonstrating solidarity. Of course, solidary activity can effect a change in concerns and priorities among those involved; the point is that joining in solidarity affects the entire set of concerns an individual has: "The concerns of the assisted are therefore always related to the assistant's own interests, values or goals, or become so in the course of the solidarity process" (Rippe 1998, 358). This empathy of concerns is in fact one of the things that distinguishes solidarity from charity (Rippe 1998, 358).

Chandra Talpade Mohanty appears to employ the concept of political solidarity in at least some of her appeals to the term "solidarity." She defines it "in terms of mutuality, accountability, and the recognition of common interests as the basis for relationships among diverse communities. Rather than assuming an enforced commonality of oppression, the practice of solidarity foregrounds communities of people who have chosen to work and fight together" (Mohanty 2003, 7). She further asserts that diversity and difference ought to be recognized and respected in the building of alliances. She puts this understanding of solidarity to work later in her book when she defends the use of the terms "women of color" and "Third World women." Mohanty explains that the "term designates a political constituency, not a biological or even sociological one. . . . it is Third World women's oppositional political relations to sexist, racist, and imperialist structures that constitutes our potential commonality. Thus it is the *common context of struggles against specific exploitative structures and systems* that determines our potential political alliances" (2003, 49, emphasis in original). She explicitly rejects feminist arguments that assume "universal sisterhood on the basis of women's shared opposition to androcentrism" (Mohanty 2003, 112, see also 99). She later, however, appeals to "commonalities of experiences, histories, and identity as the basis for solidarity and in organizing Third World women workers transnationally" (Mohanty 2003, 167). The disparity—moving from struggles against structures to common experience—may be due to the fact that the articles collected in Mohanty's book were written over the course of ten years, but it may also be due to a slippage in her use of the term solidarity from political to social solidarity. As she explains in the final essay, a solidarity perspective in pedagogy "requires understanding the historical and experiential specificities and differences of women's lives as well as the historical and experiential connections between women from different national, racial, and cultural communities" (Mohanty 2003, 242). Oppositional politics seems to have given way to experiential commonality. Nevertheless, Mohanty clearly employs some notion of political solidarity in parts of her work.

Finally, Tommie Shelby identifies a solidarity that "depends on the political will of individuals to use whatever talents, resources, and influence they possess to push for social reform" (2005, 140). He describes this solidarity as "voluntary, nonhierarchical, and largely spontaneous" (Shelby 2005, 140–41). The cooperative activities of this "uncoordinated" group effect empowerment but do not assume unanimity in voice. Shelby also emphasizes the responsibilities of participants. He is, in other words, distinguishing solidarity of this sort from nonvoluntary solidarities that do not organize around a cooperative political project (Shelby 2005, 202; see also Blum 2007).

All four theorists—Bayertz, Rippe, Mohanty, and Shelby—recognize that there is something unique about the form of solidarity that emerges in opposition to oppression and injustice. The most notable element is perhaps that moral commitment provides the source of the solidarity. I have elected to call this "political solidarity" because of the substantial political constitution of the unity that forms. Here, political does not mean organized structures of governance, but instead refers to relations between peoples that have wide-ranging implications for social/political policy and practice.

Ethics and Social, Civic, or Political Solidarity

According to Durkheim, law and morality enunciate the "fundamental conditions of social solidarity": "Everything which is a source of solidarity is moral, everything which forces man to take account of other men is moral, everything which forces him to regulate his conduct through something other than the striving of his ego is moral and morality is as solid as these ties are numerous and strong" (1973, 136). Durkheim's point is that society is a necessary condition of morality and is moral itself. But his thoughts also highlight a distinguishing feature of the three species or forms of solidarity discussed in this chapter. Each has explicit and necessary moral import, but the three are very different in the source, structure, force, and content of the moral obligations entailed (see also Mason 2000, 28n30). In this chapter, I have laid out some of these differences, but I also aim to illuminate various bridges between some of the species of solidarity in this section. All three forms—social, civic, political—are, after all, forms of solidarity and thus share a lot more in common with one another than other forms of collective responsibility or political groupings. At times, a form of political solidarity transforms into social solidarity. The Solidarity movement of Poland, for instance, began as a form of political solidarity aimed at attaining the right to free trade unions but became a force that eventually unseated the dictatorial power of the Communist Party and eventually morphed into a social solidarity among Polish citizens. The storming of the Bastille that issued forth the French Revolution and eventually a new era in French society is another example of a social movement being transformed into another species of solidarity. Similarly, some forms of political solidarity may become civic solidarity once the urgency of response abates or the movement becomes recognized as a serious state concern. Political activists around the globe joined in solidarity to combat AIDS and the social and political conditions that exacerbated the pandemic in the late 1980s and 1990s. More recently, this form of political solidarity has become more formalized and now might better be understood under the rubric of civic solidarity: governments, international aid agencies, and pharmaceutical companies are now called to respond to the AIDS crisis in systematic ways that address the inequitable distribution of drugs and other healthcare resources.

One might also argue that social solidarity is merely a very weak version of the political conception of solidarity. Some theorists of solidarity do hold that social solidarity emerges out of social and political movements. Some accounts of Christian social ethics, for example, assume this relationship. The struggles to obtain liberation, it is argued, form bonds that strengthen in a localized setting. The community that forms consists of strong relations because of the shared experience of struggle. There are certainly some historical examples of social solidarity arising from political solidarity but there are also compelling reasons to argue that they should be kept at least theoretically separate. Social solidarity does not always emerge from political struggles and not all political struggles give birth to lasting social communities.

Bayertz suggests the opposite might be the case; that is, that political solidarity merely reveals an already existing social solidarity among humans:

> In so far as this feeling *nevertheless* emerges and activity is realized in practice, it seems reasonable to interpret this as the revelation of a readiness towards solidarity which is generally and fundamentally inherent in human nature. The solidarity practiced here and now in the battle for a just cause thus appears as the expression of a moral disposition which is incorruptible, even under the dominance of a capitalist profit motive or a patriarchal competitive attitude. To put it pointedly: the solidarity practiced here and now in the battle for a just cause appears as the trial sample of what human beings are capable of when social obstacles hampering the development of their moral strengths are removed. (Bayertz 1999a, 20)

Schuyt sees solidarity operating along a sort of continuum. Shared feelings and interests gradually expand the group. What begins in oppositional struggles (and shared experience of struggle) fosters more extensive feelings, stronger bonds, and mutual responsibilities. Insofar as any form of solidarity accounts for relations between members, it assumes moral obligations. The continuum model of solidarity assumes that the various forms of solidarity are merely different levels of moral relations between the members. But this also risks conflating social solidarity and political solidarity, which can lead to some troubling problems regarding who "counts" as a member of the solidary group, what might be considered consistent action within the solidarity relations, and who is granted epistemic privilege (topics I take up in later chapters of this book). Nevertheless, we can speculate that some instantiations of particular forms of solidarity will morph into others even if we reject the continuum model as a universal explanatory schema for all instantiations of solidarity. By looking at the three characteristics of all forms of solidarity, presented in the first section of this chapter, we can further highlight the different structures of social, civic, and political solidarity.

Solidarity, regardless of its form, mediates between the individual and the community. As should be evident from the descriptions above, each of the three basic forms approaches this relation differently. Social solidarity understands individuals as members of tribes, communities, or groups, based on shared attributes, experiences, histories, or locations. The group plays a relatively large role in shaping how the individual views the world and his or her place in it. That is, social solidarity, especially as Durkheim conceives it in its developing form, posits the ontological priority of group membership over individual identity. Morality issues from the preexisting bonds. In civic solidarity, individuals are members of civic society, which may be narrowly defined in terms of one's local government structure (as in "X lives in Radnor township"), numerous localities grouped together under a common umbrella ("X pays taxes to the state of Pennsylvania"), membership in an organized nation or state ("X is a member of the Lenape tribe" or "X is a citizen of the United States"), or participation in the international community. In all these levels, the individual and the community are mutually reliant in addressing the moral requirements of civic solidarity, though the onus usually falls on the formal communal structures to carry out the obligations. Political solidarity also marks a unique mediation of individual and community. In political solidarity the individual appears to have ontological priority over the community, but that priority is somewhat misleading. The conscious commitments of individuals create the unity of political solidarity. Ties to others become strengthened and affect the individual's identity, but he or she never loses individual identity and always contributes to the group identity. There is, in other words, a reciprocal relation between the individual and the group based on mutually undertaken commitments.

A brief look at human solidarity reveals the different natures of the unity in each of the three forms of solidarity as well. When we say that members of the human family are united, we usually have some sort of agenda in mind that makes that unity fall within social, civic, or political solidarity. The form of the unity varies for each, as do the moral relations. For social solidarity, the unity sustains community. Moral relations are between members of a community whether based on resemblances or division of labor, to use Durkheim's categorization. Moral obligations consist of those actions or inactions that sustain the community such as abiding by law, custom, and social mores to a large degree. As a subcategory of social solidarity, human solidarity would require moral responses to other humans in need based on our shared humanity. Civic solidarity, in contrast, aims more directly at strengthening civic society and ensuring the well-being of members of a civil community. Here, the obligation is to maintain a system of social protections (to provide for the least well-off locally or globally or to ensure adequate healthcare) but the responsibility rests more with the civic whole than with individual moral agents. The moral obligations are generally not spelled out beyond the duties the state has to particular individuals to provide the adequate necessities. We would talk of "human solidarity" as international civic solidarity—made more robust with an international governing body. This would connote obligations of the international community to protect and provide for the most vulnerable among us. In general, the vulnerable would be identified through national, geographic, or political groupings. We fulfill the obligations of civic solidarity because we reside in nations, states, and are part of the international community. Our location rather than our nature constitutes the basis for the solidary relation. Finally, as a subcategory of political solidarity, a worldwide collective response to injustice, while theoretically possible, involves a unified global effort at social critique and social transformation—global political solidarity. Such a universal effort may be necessary in response to pollution or disease that threatens all human beings. Of course, what is more commonly meant by global solidarity is a movement that spans the globe but does not necessarily involve all of humanity. Chapter 7 is a dedicated discussion of human solidarity and the challenge of global solidarity using genocide as a sort of case study for analyzing solidaristic responses.

Finally, all three forms of solidarity demonstrate the positive duties characteristic of solidarity per se. In social solidarity, our already existent communal bonds inform those duties. In civic solidarity they are presumed in the relation of citizens to the state apparatus. In political solidarity, by contrast, one of the primary moral duties precedes the social bonds and is informed by a commitment to a social justice cause; other duties stem from this commitment to a cause. The organizing logic of these three moral relations clearly differs.

Before leaving this section, I would like to pause to defend the distinctions I have drawn out here. It might be objected that given the amorphous nature of solidarities, the only things that may be said are general enough to apply to all forms of solidarities. In fact, the structure that I articulate offers three general elements of all forms—a unity relation entailing positive duties and mediating between the individual and the community or collective. As a way of defending the next level of classifications—social, civic, and political—I spend a little time looking at two influential writers on the topic of solidarity: Joel Feinberg and Larry May. Both have made invaluable contributions to social philosophy generally and the discussion of solidarity in particular. Joel Feinberg's 1968 essay on collective responsibility presents an argument for solidarity as a moral relation and Larry May's response (1996) modifies and furthers the theoretical development of solidarity as a moral relation. Taken together, these scholars set the stage for ever-more nuanced accounts of solidarity like the one I offer in this book.

Feinberg argues that solidarity entails three intertwined conditions. The first is that "a large *community of interest* among all the members, not merely a specific overlap of shared specialized interests" must exist (Feinberg 1970, 234). He explains *community of interest* by using the example of a father who, as part of his own interest in his well-being, includes the well-being of his family members. That is, the well-being of a spouse is a subset of the integrated interests of the other spouse. In order for a perfect community of interest to exist, the converse must also be true; that is, that the wife and children, in Feinberg's example, must have the well-being of the husband/father as a subset of their integrated interests: "A community of interest exists between two parties to the extent that each party's integrated set of interests contains as one of its components the integrated interest-set of the other" (Feinberg 1970, 234). Assuming that interests are construed rather broadly, such as the good of the community, this insight certainly holds for social solidarity but the integrated set of interests might be overstated for civic and political solidarity (cf. May 1996, 31). For civic solidarity, a relatively small subset of interests overlap between individuals in solidarity; that is, insofar as each of us has some interest in ensuring the well-being of others in the civic public, those interests overlap. That leaves, however, quite a substantial set of nonoverlapping interests. Similarly, for political solidarity, it is sufficient that only one interest overlap for there to be solidarity. Nevertheless, a weak version of Feinberg's point is that an important element of solidarity as collective responsibility is an overlap of some interest(s). No matter what its form, solidarity is a bond that is both individual and collective in its aim. Individual interest(s) and collective or communal interest(s) combine to create a unique moral relationship. That, in other words, is the unity that mediates between the individual and the community that I presented as elemental to all solidarities.

The second condition necessary for a group to have solidarity, according to Feinberg, is "bonds of sentiment directed toward common objects, or of reciprocal affection between the parties" (1970, 234). Notice that there are two types of "bonds of sentiment." The first is directed toward a common object and the second is reciprocal affection. Opposition to a common enemy and citizen welfare belong to the former and thus political solidarity and civic solidarity share bonds of sentiment "directed toward common objects," though, of course, the two species of solidarity are not directed at the same object. Reciprocal affection is found within social solidarity. Of course, reciprocal affection may also be found in political solidarity and perhaps even in civic solidarity, but for neither of those forms is reciprocal affection necessary to the bond of solidarity. In a similar vein, social solidarity may display bonds of sentiment directed at common ends, but they are not necessary to the relationship itself.

According to Feinberg, "Thirdly, solidarity is ordinarily a function of the degree to which the parties share a common lot, the extent to which their goods and harms are necessarily collective and indivisible" (1970, 234). May comments that the "common lot" is not a necessary condition but might serve to heighten feelings of solidarity. As he says, "having a common lot does not necessarily mean that goods or harms are collective and indivisible" (1996, 32). In other words, May wants to separate the parts of Feinberg's third condition. Whether or not sharing a common lot entails the collectivity and indivisibility of goods and harms may actually be a function not of solidarity in general but of certain forms of solidarities; that is, a characteristic of some though not all of the forms of solidarity rather than a characteristic about solidarity per se. Social solidarity, as we have seen, is strong or weak to the extent that individuals are interdependent. But Durkheim's mechanical solidarity appears to link the common lot tightly to the sharing of goods and harms within the community, and yet this is the weaker form of solidarity. Organic solidarity necessitates more differentiation, if also more interdependence, than mechanical solidarity but would also incorporate more divisibility of goods and harms. Civic solidarity, it might be argued, attempts to establish a mutually agreeable albeit limited common lot for all citizens in the form of welfare or healthcare. Goods and harms would not be either collective or indivisible in this case, though there may be some inverse correlation such that when one person's goods increase, another person experiences harm. This correlation could then be used to justify higher taxes on the wealthy to increase available social services, for instance.

Larry May discusses solidarity as linked to moral support, personal integrity, and security in his book *The Socially Responsive Self*. The chapter that focuses on solidarity begins by noting that solidarity has played a largely unacknowledged role in ethics, especially collectivist ethics. May argues that, "Solidarity must exist within a community before its moral demands are likely to be heeded by the members of a community" (1996, 28). As I have presented it, the ordering here holds for social solidarity but not for political solidarity because the latter sees the solidarity arise in response to a moral demand. The following five "overlapping threads" are descriptively present in solidarity according to May: "(1) conscious group identification, (2) bonds of sentiment, (3) interest in the group's well-being, (4) shared values and beliefs, and (5) readiness to show moral support" (1996, 44). Group identification can be as ambiguous as "shared commitment to the common good" (May 1996, 44) as might be found in social solidarity, but it could also be as precise as a commitment to respond in a particular way to a particular situation of injustice as is found in political solidarity. May adds "interdependence" to the bonds of sentiment that Feinberg cites as a necessary condition for solidarity. This addition is based on Durkheim's "organic solidarity" that arises from the division of labor. Replacing Feinberg's "integrated interest set," May claims that the relevant condition for solidarity is "that each member have an interest in the general well-being of the group, but not an interest in each of the things that the other member has an interest in" (May 1996, 31): hence, interdependent rather than integrated interest set. Although not his intent, May's refinement on the concept of "interest" with relation to solidarity tells us more about the various forms of solidarity rather than solidarity per se. Solidarity does involve some notion of shared interest; but social, civic, and political solidarity each require a different level of interest overlap as well as a set of interests, as we have seen. Although he does not discuss what precisely is covered by "shared values and beliefs," it is an important contribution to the discussion of the moral concept of solidarity. All three forms of solidarity rely on some element(s) of shared values and beliefs. They may be as extensive as cultural customs and law under social solidarity, as basic as a belief in minimal human rights as in civic solidarity, or as complex as the hope for liberation from unjust conditions as in political solidarity.

Finally, according to May, solidarity, in any of its forms, entails a willingness to lend moral support. Of course, this may or may not be moral support that one personally chooses. In fact, by looking at the various species of solidarity we can see differences in how lending support functions within the solidarity. In civic solidarity, lending moral support is probably best understood as paying taxes to support a welfare system or a system of universal healthcare. This "willingness" to lend support is a result of the obligation of civic solidarity, not a motivation for it. In social solidarity, lending moral support is a sign of the strength of ties that bind a community. If members of a group of people fail to lend support when needed, it indicates that they have very weak or nonexistent solidarity. Support and solidarity are symbiotic. In political solidarity, the willingness to lend moral support is the very motivation for the solidarity. Individuals make a personal commitment to help alleviate oppression or respond to injustice and the collective that forms is political solidarity. But here too the willingness to lend moral support is limited to the cause to which members have mutually committed. If it extends any further, we might argue that the participants in the movement have developed some degree of social solidarity through their shared experience.

As this discussion of Feinberg and May shows, solidarity is a very rich concept, but its richness could be enhanced even further if we pause to reflect on the differences in forms of moral relations covered by the concept. There is something truly special about solidarity. It carries a weight that community, camaraderie, association, and even friendship do not bear. But in order to understand the unique moral character of solidarity, we must not only pay attention to the similarities between solidarities; we must also heed the differences. The moral differences between social solidarity, civic solidarity, and political solidarity have for too long been obscured. Once we see the richness of the variety of species of solidarity, as well as the bridges that the species share, we can begin to map out theories of solidarity that, akin to theories of justice, promise to challenge our moral theorizing and enrich our understanding of the contributions of social philosophy.

Parasitical "Solidarity"

And then there are solidarities that are not really solidarities at all: the pretenders or posers, the parasites. By "parasitical solidarity," I mean that the term "solidarity" is used to connote a variety of feelings or relations that do not themselves count as full-fledged forms of solidarity because they often lack one or more of the key elements or because they are meant to appear as a form of solidarity only for rhetorical purposes. But these invocations of the term feed off of the various species of solidarity. The term is invoked to pay tribute to the ideal of "a non-individualistic, non-competitive, and non-exclusive" human relation (Steinvorth 1999, 29).

For instance, when solidarity is used to describe "similarity," as in the relationship between prisoners or between rapists, very likely there are no positive moral obligations and there may not even be a unity present. The term is used as a rhetorical device in cases like these in order to imply that there may be something more to the bond.

In a similar vein, though without the criminal overtones, when solidarity is used to stand in for sympathy, the rhetoric suggests that those expressing solidarity can or will respond in much richer ways than mere expressions of sympathy. Take, for instance, two countries that have both experienced acts of terrorism. While there might be a genuine relationship of social solidarity present between the victims of the bombings, and perhaps we could even make a case that social solidarity extends to all members of nations that have experienced terrorism and subsequently feel the ever-present fear of another attack, it is not clear that expressions of solidarity from leaders of those countries are anything more than expressions of mutual sympathy. The rhetoric of solidarity might be used to attempt to convey something much stronger, perhaps to convince a more reluctant country into joining forces with the more aggressive country in a coalition against terrorism. That is, by using "solidarity" rather than "sympathy" in the rhetoric of its public comments, one country might try to tie the people of another country to an official campaign against terror. By asserting a bond in this context, the leader attempts to ally the citizens of another country to him in a way that they may not choose. (President George W. Bush expressed "solidarity with the people of Spain" after the Madrid bombings in 2004. The question is whether that expression of solidarity was a genuine solidary moral commitment or an expression of sympathy that simultaneously served as a rhetorical tool to try to convince Spain—and perhaps others—to commit to U.S. policies and practices in combating terror. The point is not to question his feelings but to question the use of the concept of solidarity.)

Another common parasitical use of solidarity is as a stand-in for camaraderie. For instance, consider when a meat eater elects not to eat meat at a dinner with a vegetarian, when a smoker agrees to not to smoke around a friend in order to help the friend quit smoking, or when a woman takes her husband's surname. In each case, the actions are often described as acting in solidarity but are more fittingly described as acting out of camaraderie. Camaraderie certainly shares some common features with solidarity but it does not have the morally similar ties that solidarity entails. We might reasonably question the presence of a positive duty in the examples mentioned. An individual might elect not to eat meat out of a desire to respect a vegetarian friend's commitment to vegetarianism but there is no commitment to adopt a vegetarian lifestyle present. Similarly, while I might under different circumstances argue that smoking cessation is a positive duty, it is not clear that it is a positive duty of any form of solidarity. And taking someone's name might be publicly asserting a bond but that name-taking is not a solidary bond with positive moral duties though the marriage might be. Moreover, in these examples, solidarity does not mediate between an individual and a community—it does not alter the individual's self-identification significantly and contribute to a collective identity in any sustained manner.

In addition to sympathy, similarity, and camaraderie, parasitical uses of "solidarity" have included such meanings as peer pressure, mutual concern, and familial responsibility. These are all elements of some forms of solidarity but, standing alone, they do not constitute the moral relation of solidarity. Instead, they feed off of more developed conceptions of solidarity as a way to imply more content (here I am primarily interested in moral content) than is in fact present. Solidarity becomes drained of its moral content when parasitical uses predominate.

Conclusion

Some objections to solidarity as both concept and practice bear mention. One objection is that solidarity is a tool of socialism; anyone interested in any nonsocialist political theory thus ought to proceed with caution or simply turn back. But while solidarity has some socialist roots and certainly has been used as a tool of socialism, it is not itself an inherently socialist concept or practice. Dismissing it out of hand because of some parallels and applications within socialist theory seriously misunderstands both "solidarity" and "socialism."

Another objection might be that the term marks a feeling or sentiment and is thus the subject of psychologists rather than recognizing solidarity as a moral concept worthy of philosophical scrutiny. Two responses to this objection are in order. First, solidarity is a moral relation that certainly may involve feelings or sentiments but does not do so of necessity. Failing to see the moral content of the concept strips it of both its historical roots and its liberatory potential. Second, philosophers are wrong to dismiss a concept because it is perceived as a sentiment or feeling. Feminist ethics has made great strides in challenging traditional accounts of morality that drew a stark distinction between reason and feeling. Regardless of whether any particular form of solidarity marks a sentiment or feeling, sentiments or feelings themselves ought not to be so summarily disregarded. Moreover, reason does not stand in opposition to feeling; the two, if they can in fact be distinguished, work together more often than not.

The primary objection to solidarity—in whatever its form—is that it is anti-individualistic. Nicholas Capaldi forcefully rejects solidarity, which he aptly defines as that which "purports to describe the network of communal relationships from which we derive and that define who we are. It purports, as well, to prescribe our moral and political obligations to that network of communal relationships" (Capaldi 1999, 29; Heyd 2007 offers a similar argument regarding solidarity and global justice). Capaldi raises a number of objections that assume an oppositional relation between solidarity and individualism, including the claim that solidarity confuses deriving identity from a community with being identical with that community. It is worth pausing to consider Capaldi's criticisms briefly in part because while they are aimed at a social solidarity, they also pertain to the metaethical understanding of solidarity per se. In the first section of this chapter, I argued that one of the three primary features of solidarity was that it mediates a relation between the community and the individual. Only Durkheim's mechanical solidarity—a particularly strong communal notion of solidarity—might be faulted for not paying enough heed to individual agents. But Durkheim readily admits this and in fact builds it into the theory by emphasizing shared consciousness and resemblance in mechanical solidarity. It hardly bears mention that Durkheim also held that mechanical solidarity is a very primitive stage of society. He also argued that even mechanical solidarity, however, maintains some understanding of the importance of individual variation or uniqueness. Capaldi also chides solidarity for not providing "positive insight into moral and political obligations" (1999, 39). This is certainly true, but rather than being a drawback, it marks the strength of possibility for solidarity. And because solidarity is the mediation between individual and community and because there are no predetermined moral and political obligations, individuals in the solidary relation determine or shape the content of their solidarity and the moral force of their relation. This is especially true of political solidarity, but it is a feature of civic and social solidarity as well.

In this chapter I have described the different species of solidarity: social, civic, and political solidarity. I have also briefly discussed the parasitical "solidarity" in which an element of solidarity is mistaken for its whole and used as a rhetorical tool. All these relations are useful in lending conceptual clarity to a very important moral relation. But it is also worth noting the rhetorical force of maintaining the opaqueness of solidarity. Allowing the term "solidarity" to connote many different relations with multiple and overlapping moral obligations without clearly distinguishing between them, appears to assign more moral import to each usage than is usually warranted. This is especially true for parasitical uses that are not true instances of any form of solidarity, but it holds as well for the conflation of political, social, and civic solidarity. Interestingly, conflating social or civic with political also posits a common enemy. A social solidarity that is insular would then give rise to nationalistic tendencies that hamper multinational and international dialogue. A civic solidarity obscured by the structure of political solidarity that is simply labeled "solidarity" might take on interesting metaphorical guises such as a war on drugs or a war on poverty. Civil society becomes portrayed as the conquering hero of a common enemy rather than a social and political structure engaged in common action to protect citizen rights.

It should be obvious by now that I contend that the fluidity of meaning within solidarity is a mask that hides genuine moral obligations and commitments rather than enhancing them. The distinctions between forms of solidarity are more than descriptively revealing; they demonstrate the normative force of solidarity—genus and species—thereby challenging our accepted understandings of collective responsibility.

While I will continue to utilize the distinctions between social, civic, and political solidarity, fleshing out the theory of political solidarity I sketch in the next chapter compels much of the rest of this book. In the next chapter, I lay the groundwork for a theory of political solidarity and in Chapter 3 I present the moral relations as well as the primary moral obligations mandated by those relations. I thus leave social and civic solidarity largely behind until the final chapter. There, I will revisit the distinctions I laid out here as I explore the meanings and prospects for human and global solidarity.

TWO

Toward a Theory of Political Solidarity

In this chapter I take up a bit of the challenge left in the previous by sketching a theory of political solidarity, many of the details of which will be worked out more completely in subsequent chapters. No theory of political solidarity can be entirely complete, of course, because it takes a great deal of its content and means from the cause that inspired it. Political solidarity cannot be separated from a particular situation. Nevertheless, a broad outline that articulates a basic moral and political structure of the social movement can be presented and unpacked a bit. This chapter marks the beginning of my articulation of political solidarity. Political solidarity is an admirably complex moral relation, which, as others have noted, deserves much more attention than philosophers to this point have given it. Chapters 3–6 continue the exposition of a theory of political solidarity by dissecting some of the elements presented here and addressing some potential objections or problems.

Political solidarity is a unity of individuals each responding to a particular situation of injustice, oppression, social vulnerability, or tyranny. Each individual makes a conscious commitment to a cause. A number of things contribute to or motivate an individual's commitment to the sort of political engagement, social activism, and personal transformation compelled by political solidarity. An exhaustive list is impossible simply because that motivation is so personal. Anger, hope, sympathy, pity, fear, self-confidence, self-interest, friendship, and countless other feelings may contribute, as might a host of other intellectual factors, arguments, experiences, or perspectives. Perhaps injustice or oppression has reached such a pitch that some of the standard criteria for defense of a third party or assistance to those in need come into play. That is, if an individual or group of individuals is threatened with severe harm, violence, or death because of injustice or oppression, and if one is in a position to assist that group, one may feel compelled to do so. Political solidarity calls for sacrifices, so it is not undertaken lightly. Perhaps one has a unique ability to contribute to political solidarity. Individuals with unique talents, skills, or gifts might find that they are drawn into a movement through their own passion to practice the skill for the good of others or for social justice, or they might be compelled to act by friends, colleagues, or strangers who recognize that they have something important to contribute. They may even feel morally obligated to act because they possess particular talents, skills, and abilities depending on the particular exigency of the circumstances. Importantly, an individual usually attains a certain epistemic awareness of the injustice or oppression to be targeted. This might involve some element of consciousness-raising pertaining to the recognition of one's own part either in sustaining or perpetrating oppression or injustice, or even increased awareness of one's experience of oppression or injustice. By consciousness-raising, I do not mean that those united in solidarity share consciousness with one another. Political solidarity might entail some unity of vision for the future but does not require shared consciousness. Consciousness-raising for political solidarity is more individuated as each potential participant has a unique perspective on a situation given his or her own social situation, circumstance, or experience. Political power draws on and transforms that knowledge, helping to form the collective of individuals connected in struggle.

A Unity Mediating Between the Individual and the Community

The individual commitment to a cause in political solidarity shapes relationships with other members in the movement as well as beyond it and, depending on the nature of the political cause and the extent of the commitment, has the power to transform the individual's life and lifestyle as well. For those who suffer under oppression or injustice, joining with others for a collective cause can be an empowering experience. Empowerment in resisting and responding to one's own suffering can lead to empowerment in other areas of one's life as well. For those who do not suffer from the oppression or injustice but who nonetheless join in the struggles to end it, the personal transformation may start with seeing that one's actions have political import. Regardless of how one becomes involved in political solidarity, making the commitment to the cause puts one in relation with others similarly committed and in opposition to at least some others in society.

Depending on the nature of the cause committed to, taking a stance of political solidarity may require an individual to scrutinize his or her personal life for its political impact. One may be called on to represent herself, the cause, or the solidary movement in a public forum though voting, striking, waging protests, public speaking, letter writing, and other attempts to change social and political policy or relations. Moreover, even mundane actions might be included in the activities of political solidarity. Products purchased and consumed may either contribute to resistance efforts or support unjust social structures. In evaluating these personal choices, the individual lives out a commitment to solidarity and unites his or her actions with similar actions by others. If I oppose sweatshops or exploitative wages for workers, I will be consciously aware of how the products I use or the clothing I wear was produced and how the workers were treated. My choice not to buy clothes from a company that uses sweatshops or underpays workers in my own country or abroad is a political act of resistance. In a similar way, a personal commitment to political solidarity might require one to evaluate vocabularies, idioms, clichés, jokes, and language and communication patterns in order to avoid participating in oppressive practices. Objecting to the sexist joke, or revealing the English Common Law origins of the phrase "rule of thumb" to a class full of students, might be part of the activism of a political solidarity fighting sexism. n other words, sometimes individuals appear to act in isolation but their actions are actually in concert with the actions of many diverse others.

Sometimes coalitions between more organized groups form. Student groups, advocacy organizations, and women's organizations might work together to combat human trafficking. Individuals and groups also coalesce at various times during the social movement in order to accomplish particular tasks, offer social criticism, or help set the direction of the movement. For instance, a human rights lawyer may join forces with the groups mentioned above to help prosecute a known trafficker, or a politician may add her or his weight to the cause by drafting legislation that would make it more difficult for traffickers to operate in the United States. At the same time, the various organizations, groups, and individuals will likely also be pursuing other forms of activism or resistance for personal and social transformation in the name of the cause. Unless they have made the cause their career or vocation, they will also likely be pursuing other interests as well—some of these other interests may have some bearing on the movement of political solidarity, but some will be disconnected. Solidarity is a unity that mediates between the individual and the solidary community as well as the larger community. The range of resistance, protest, or oppositional actions varies tremendously from formal challenges to the law to conscious awareness of the political impact of personal decisions.

The cause or goal of political solidarity is broadly construed as justice or liberation, but social movements like political solidarity usually organize around a more concrete purpose as well. We can call these two layers of the goal or ends of political solidarity the formative and substantive ends. The formative ends, liberation or justice, serve as a sort of hopeful possibility for what collective action might accomplish if all the barriers that sustain oppression or injustice are removed. The substantive goals include all those specific barriers—such as gaining a just wage or fair working conditions, ending racial or domestic violence, removing the obstacles to full citizenship imposed on some people, bringing an end to the cultural or social exclusion felt by others, and so on. The substantive goal might be thought of as more concrete but it is not necessarily a short-term goal. Although the ends of political solidarity might be theoretically distinguishable into formative and substantive categories, they are really not separable within the moral relation itself. Each serves the other as the committed individuals form a collective to bring about social change.

Political solidarity arises in opposition to something; it is a movement for social change that may occur at many levels of social existence. The opposition that gives birth to political solidarity is an opposition to something that is human in origin. Natural disasters may inspire strong sentiments and even bonds of connection, but they do not inspire *political* solidarity. Political solidarity as I present it has a social justice content or aim; it opposes injustice, oppression, tyranny, and social vulnerabilities. (I defend this claim in Chapter 6.) While others may cast the net wider to include other forms of political organizing for social change, I focus on social justice in order to bring out the moral relations I see develop in political solidarity and to acknowledge some of the roots of the concept.

Perhaps more important, political solidarity is a response to human suffering. There must be some victims of injustice, oppression, tyranny, or social vulnerabilities. Although political solidarity organizes around social justice, the onus is on the actors—individually or collectively—to demonstrate that their cause serves justice. In taking a position alongside others in political solidarity, the individual takes a public stance that he or she believes to be just. In doing so, some attention to comparative justice must be paid. That is, the position should be weighed against other possible positions. Moreover, because it is a moral relation, the justice sought within political solidarity should heed the various obligations of the relations to others within and outside the solidary group. Of course, we are not always correct in our assessments for justice, and a theory of political solidarity has to acknowledge the possibility of error even while seeking to articulate the rubrics of the moral relations.

Injustice—or more specifically, social injustice—includes but is not limited to inequitable distribution of rights and privileges in society (unjust laws, oppressive social customs, dominant vocabularies that silence alternative perspectives, etc.), violations of human rights such as those found in the United Nations Universal Declaration of Human Rights, misuse or misapplications of otherwise just laws, physical harm or violence done to innocents or in gross abuse of the principles of retribution when done to criminals, and similar violations of justice. Oppression includes but is not limited to exploitation, exclusion from social and political structures, degradation (often though not solely related to group membership), violence, systematic humiliation, and countless other social phenomena used to abuse, marginalize, silence, or violate individuals and groups. Social vulnerabilities are those human-made structures or impediments that inhibit participation in civic life. Education, employment, healthcare, and consumer and environmental protections are among the most central areas wherein social vulnerabilities are found. Tyranny is the unjust rule of a state or society by a power, either in the hands of a single person or disbursed to a wider group or even the majority. Tyranny is, however, often opposed through revolution rather than political solidarity. With the exception of tyranny, Chapter 6 discusses each of these more thoroughly and defends the social justice orientation of political solidarity on both historical and principled grounds. Suffice it to say at this point that although political solidarity as I conceive it is social justice oriented, there are times when actors are mistaken about what counts as justice or social justice. The onus is on the participants within the movement to present publicly the arguments for the justness of their cause, that is, to subject their politically embraced stance to public scrutiny and criticism.

Political solidarity is a moral relation forming a unity, though it does not always look so unified. A small group of people may join together in political solidarity to address some injustice, or peoples in one nation may be in political solidarity with the peoples suffering injustice in another nation. A workers' union protesting unjust working conditions and the international struggle against violence against women both exhibit political solidarity. One is relatively small and can practice democratic decision-making among all of its participants. The other is quite large and diverse, made up of individuals acting more or less on their own, associations in coalition, formal international and intergovernmental organizations, and countless other actors. Democratic decision-making is virtually impossible in the latter group; but through cooperation, public acting, communication, empowerment, and other mechanisms within solidarity, activism in political solidarity occurs. Political solidarity does not, of necessity, require that those in solidarity know one another. For example, one may, through his or her daily lived experience, political commitments, interests and goals, be in solidarity with the peoples of distant countries or regions. The peoples in these distant countries or regions need not know this person or even know about him or her (though the knowledge of peoples joining in solidarity to struggle against the injustice a person or peoples suffer may provide a valuable support system). If the cause involves struggling for rights for children or the mentally ill, there may be few or no representatives from among the oppressed involved in the solidarity struggle. As Rippe suggests, "The addressee of this solidarity is sometimes completely unaware of the act of solidarity and may even lack the cognitive ability to develop a reciprocal relationship" (1998, 358). Alternatively, of course, the person or persons suffering from the injustice, oppression, or social vulnerability might join in the cause for justice and liberation.

Because political solidarity is a response to some injustice, oppression, or social vulnerability as I sketch it, there is another element. To be in solidarity with those who suffer is to work for social change to alter the conditions that create that suffering, but simultaneously those in solidarity may need to respond directly to the concrete needs of others and help to alleviate suffering. That is, political solidarity heeds a call for aid in multiple ways—the efforts of those people with the tools and means to assist others in distress might also be fulfilling the moral relation of political solidarity. Social and political changes come also through these acts that help to create the conditions for those who suffer to similarly stand in political solidarity.

The size of the solidary group is not as important as the commitments that brought the group together, the moral relationships that form as a result of those commitments, and the cause or aim that the group targets. Political solidarity may be a unity among people who all know one another or a widely disparate group that only loosely identifies or is identified as connected. Smaller, short-term struggles that bring about social change and larger, long-term struggles also fit under the banner of political solidarity insofar as the other elements of solidarity are present. Notice too that I am describing both the unity and the personal commitment as solidarity. That echoes a distinguishing characteristic of solidarity as both personal and communal; it also asks us to view solidarity as a moral relation out of a personal commitment.

In addition, as I have already intimated, it is important to note the distinction between the group of the oppressed and the solidary group. While it is often the case that the social movement called political solidarity begins through the activities of peoples who do directly suffer from oppression or injustice, it is not necessarily the case. Political solidarity rests on a commitment and not on the experience of oppression. Individuals who are not oppressed or do not suffer from injustice can and do join in political solidarity. So too not all peoples who suffer from a particular form of oppression or face a particular injustice will join in efforts to respond to it. Some may deny that they suffer from oppression or injustice, and some may be too weakened by the oppression to fight back.

Positive Duties of Political Solidarity

Political solidarity, as a form of collective responsibility, is unique in asserting that those who make the commitment to solidarity make a commitment that forces them to address issues that may not directly affect them and yet could simultaneously radically challenge other seemingly unrelated elements of their lifestyle. Political solidarity with the poverty stricken in Haiti, for example, may force a U.S. citizen to scrutinize U.S. policy on sugar subsidies and importation. Sugar was one of Haiti's primary exports, but as part of the U.S. sugar subsidies policy, a limit on the amount of sugar imported was instituted, striking a terrible blow to the sugar market of Haiti. A personal commitment to Haitians may, then, affect how one consumes sugar. Similarly, many people around the world do not have access to clean drinking water, but it is readily available and recklessly wasted in the United States. Simple changes, like planting a waterless lawn, taking fewer showers, or using an efficient clothes washer may be part of how someone acts on a solidary commitment to correcting the injustice in distributing this basic resource. These acts and their conscious connection to a cause one has already adopted help to connect activist responses and political solidarity movements. As bell hooks argues with regard to feminism defined as a movement to end sexist oppression, "Women must learn to accept responsibility for fighting oppressions that may not directly affect us as individuals. Feminist movement, like other radical movements in our society, suffers when individual concerns and priorities are the only reason for participation. When we show our concern for the collective, we strengthen our solidarity" (1984, 62).

Political solidarity entails positive duties. The particularity of the cause will inform most of the obligations participants undertake in making a commitment to solidarity. Nonetheless, among the broadly construed positive duties of every form of political solidarity are cooperation, social activism, and social criticism. Each of these duties arises because of a particular relation within political solidarity. The unity of members of the solidary group mandates cooperation. Within cooperation we count obligations of mutuality and reciprocity as well as obligations to communicate and the moral practice of consciousness-raising that leads to more authentic personal commitments and political empowerment. Because political solidarity is organized around a particular goal, identification of that goal and determination of the means to achieve it require dedicated and careful social criticism. Social criticism must be continual and must examine not only the dominant group or system but also the solidary group itself. The third duty, social activism, is required by the relation of the solidary group to the larger or more dominant group or society. A group that does not engage in active means to transform unjust conditions cannot rightly take on the name of political solidarity. Political solidarity is a social movement and as a social movement requires activism. I delve into the intricacies of these moral relations and incumbent obligations in the next chapter.

Thus, political solidarity is a committed unity of peoples on a range of interpersonal to social-political levels with a social justice goal of liberation of the oppressed, cessation of injustice, or protection against social vulnerabilities; it simultaneously fosters individual self-determination, empowerment, cooperative action, collective vision, and social criticism among those in solidarity. But not every instance of political solidarity and not every individual commitment to a solidary group can be measured using the same classification. Indeed, there are wide varieties within political solidarity. Clearly the context of struggle is the most informative, and there are compelling reasons to confine discussions of political solidarity to particular social movements in order to reflect the nuances of each movement. But there are also some compelling reasons to attempt a classification system that might provide a guide to the moral relationships and accompanying duties within political solidarity. Such a system would have to acknowledge the variances among the populations of solidary groups as well as the strength of the individual commitments in solidarity.

The Range and Extent of Political Solidarity

Unifying with others who make similar commitments to a cause, whether according to the motivation of their conscience, indignation, or the motivation of their social and material conditions, forms political solidarity. This interest ranges in extent and strength depending on the situation and the level of individual commitment as well as the communal movement. To explicate, we can categorize the relationships and commitments within political solidarity groups according to whether they are local, national, international, or global, and strong or weak or somewhere in between. Causes and commitments change, so in the background of this discussion constantly lurks the knowledge that the movement is only rarely monolithic. Solidary groups fluidly pursue sometimes shifting goals, but just as that has not stopped activists from seeing the unity of their cause or the coalition of their interests, so it should not keep us from making some theoretical arguments about political solidarity.

The range of participation determines whether the political solidarity is local, national, international, or global. Whether the solidarity is strong or weak depends on the extent of commitment or duty for the individual and the measure of power for the solidary group. Additionally, we might want to classify solidarity movements according to their specific aims. Political solidarity might target injustice, oppression, or social vulnerability. For instance, some group activism is aimed at challenging the legal, economic, and political systems within a larger community; some is aimed at unjust social practices or norms; and some is aimed at particular policies and practices of work or domestic life. No doubt there are others as well but these broad classifications get at the basic social justice roots of political solidarity.

A commitment to a cause in political solidarity brings with it a set of moral relations and associated moral duties. But not everyone elects to participate in the same way or to the same extent. That is, we might think of the commitment to solidarity as weak or strong (or somewhere in between). Any individual's allegiance to political solidarity is going to depend to a great extent on exigency. One's ability to commit to a cause is quite fluid and thus the duties that are entailed in the solidary relations will change in response to one's ability, available resources, hope, and commitment. An unmarried, childless college student will likely have more time and energy to devote to a cause than a working mother. Both elect to commit to a cause in political solidarity but they live out that commitment in different ways. Kevin Doran also suggests that the degrees of solidary commitment may be reflected in the manner that solidarity affects one's choices, even beyond those that directly pertain to the movement:

> It is possible to envisage solidarity simply as the attitude of the will on the basis of which a particular decision is taken and an action performed which represents the proper orientation of participation to the common good. In that sense one person might be described as being "in solidarity" with another person or persons. It would seem, however, that the fullest expression of solidarity is only to be seen when it has developed into a kind of skill or proficiency, so that it has become an aspect of the person's will and of his action in every situation. (1996, 156)

The commitment is considered "weak" if the individual in solidarity makes some efforts to act in a solidaristic manner but does not devote a majority of daily activity to the solidarity group. The individual still makes a commitment but it is not as extensive as that made by some others. The obligations of solidarity are no less binding merely because the extent of commitment for the individual is weaker; a weak commitment might allow for some variance among members in how willing and able they are to act. A weak political solidarity is in some respects closer to sympathy, with the important difference that solidarity requires positive duties like social activism. Political solidarity with others will necessarily transform the individual's existence, but the degree of that transformation or the extent to which the individual's lifestyle changes is indicative of the degree of solidary commitment. Urgency or exigency of the cause plays a crucial role here as individuals respond to oppression and injustice according to their particular set of abilities, situations, projects, and commitments.

If we use the example of support for a labor union to illustrate this element of political solidarity, then the individual who commits to solidarity would have to scrutinize his or her choices on a continual basis to determine whether a decision helps or hinders the cause of the labor union. Suppose a labor union that worked at a conglomeration of hotels within a major city was negotiating with an employer over wage increases and healthcare costs. An individual visiting the city who had made a commitment to political solidarity with the workers would have to determine the best ways both to support the union and to avoid benefiting the employer. This individual would likely boycott the hotels affected by the labor dispute. But this same individual might also be required to scrutinize the other corporate holdings of the employer to determine whether staying at another hotel, eating at a particular restaurant, shopping in a particular mall, frequenting a concert, or participating in citywide events would benefit the employer. The employer may have holdings far beyond the hotel and may sponsor events such as concerts, festivals, or fun runs. Attention to the political statements and requests of the union members, as well as critical reflection on one's own commitment in solidarity, would help to guide the actions of the nonunion individual who acts in solidarity with the union. Another example comes from the struggle against sexism. In making a commitment to political solidarity with women against sexist oppression, an individual might change some of her or his habits, language patterns, or social expectations. All of these are resistant behaviors of some sort, but solidarity also mandates examining relationships with others (both in and out of the solidary group) and the social structures that maintain oppression. It requires, in short, not just personal transformation but social transformation that is usually accomplished through political activism. bell hooks makes a similar point in her critique of the phrase "I am a feminist." As she explains, such a phrase employs either/or dichotomous thinking that marks a personal lifestyle choice but does not indicate a political commitment for social change. Instead, she proposes we replace the "I am" construction with "I advocate"; this shift indicates a personal commitment to a political movement for social change (1984, 25–31). Making a commitment to political solidarity means scrutinizing choices in order to determine the extent of one's involvement in oppression and determining all the possible means of resistance.

"Strong" solidarity, then, would be more encompassing of one's actions. The individual who commits to political solidarity in the strong sense would be compelled to examine the majority of his or her lifestyle choices in light of the solidarity commitment. Consuming certain products, frequenting certain establishments, or participating in certain events may be contrary to one's commitment. But a strong commitment would likely go even further and perhaps mean dedicating one's life to a cause. This might be accomplished through living among the oppressed while actively engaged in resistance and oppositional politics; or it might mean electing a career in advocacy on behalf of the oppressed. If my solidarity is strong, I might become one of the workers whose cause I have adopted and attempt to organize and use collective action against the employer. Alternatively, I might use my legal training to sue the company or my political skills to create legislation that would hinder the company's unjust practices. These would be in addition to boycotting a product.

Weak solidarity is no less morally compelling than strong solidarity, though the expression of it may make it appear as if that is the case. The commitment one makes to solidarity is personal and gauged according to such factors as ability, knowledge, experience, emotional impact, rational decision-making, and countless others. Both a strong commitment and a weak commitment involve consistent reflective action, but a weak solidary commitment does not involve transformations quite as radical in lifestyle or perhaps as much involvement in active protests (though activism of some sort is required). Notice, then, that in these examples, the weak commitment is still quite binding and can cause the individual to reflect quite profoundly on a number of life's choices, but the stronger commitment is more directly caught up in the fray of solidary activity. An important part of the challenge of political solidarity is to see one's actions or failures to act as affecting the social structure either positively or negatively. Personal choices are political—they might contribute to unjust practices or be the benefit of oppressive policies, or they might question, challenge, and even begin the toppling of those practices and policies. But solidarity is also more than merely the personal choices; it is also engaged political activism in concert with many others.

In addition to the personal commitments, the power of the political solidarity itself might be weak or strong and will likely fluctuate between the two as it advances toward its goal. Many of the controlling factors remain the same—the urgency of the cause and the abilities of the solidaristic participants will, by and large, determine the strength of the movement. But we also ought not to discount the more subtle forms of political activism in measuring strength. Activists of every sort have sought innovative and creative avenues for effecting social change. Protesting has not lost its power, but door-to-door organizing, e-mail campaigns, online petitions and blogs, civic organizations and lobbying, and even legislative initiatives have come to replace some of the in-your-face/in-your-street political activism. Moreover, some of the forms of oppression that inspired widespread public outcries in previous decades, have taken less overt forms that must be met with different, perhaps more subtle, approaches. Technology has also expanded the types of activism available. Think, for example, of the racism that inspired the civil rights movement, or the sexism that inspired feminist activism of the 1960s and 1970s. Racism and sexism still plague our social systems but they tend to have taken much less blatant or obvious forms in many parts of the United States. Social and political activism must adapt to address these changes.

The other qualifiers that help to describe the social movement of political solidarity pertain to how widespread the movement is. "Local political solidarity" describes a solidary group whose members probably know one another and probably communicate with one another on a regular basis. Members might hold meetings to determine the group agenda but that is not a requirement; the group might be formalized (i.e., set a group policy for membership), hold regular meetings, or have any sort of constitution or statement of policy, but it need not. If localized, the solidary group is established when a number of individuals collectively recognize some sort of injustice in their midst and decide to combat it. For example, a group of workers and concerned citizens might join together in solidarity in order to combat racism in the hiring and retaining of employees at a particular corporation, or a group of diverse citizens within a particular town or region might join in solidarity to change discriminatory laws or zoning ordinances. These may expand to encompass wider areas or populations. Similarly, multiple movements might coalesce to form a more national or even international movement either around the same cause or around a broader cause or goal. Members of a small community that relies on migrant workers to harvest the local produce might join in solidarity in an effort to obtain some adequate, even basic, healthcare and living conditions for the workers. It is easy to see how such a movement could gain momentum—especially given the economic reliance on the labor provided by the migrant workers—and perhaps become a statewide concern. Perhaps people in neighboring states either have similar concerns or adopt the concern once they become aware of the issues involved. Activists might take the issue to state legislators or their congressional representative, potentially bringing the issue to national awareness. Other activists might employ the civil legal system to bring suit against the farms that are negligent in their obligations to provide adequate housing. Workers and advocates might protest, strike, write letters to media outlets, and otherwise raise awareness for their cause. Individuals in distant states that do not rely on migrant workers might boycott producers and retailers that sell the goods harvested by the migrant workers, write their congressperson on behalf of the rights of the workers, or even protest a store or distribution center where the goods are processed and sold. So many levels of social existence are affected by social injustice. Through its reflective action and social criticism, political solidarity enacts social change by addressing multiple layers and levels of social life, bringing together people from diverse populations, and potentially expanding to encompass wider regions and more ambitious goals.

International political solidarity may take three forms: individuals across the globe may take up a cause together that spans the globe, individuals in one country or region may pledge solidarity with distant others, or nations or states may unify for a particular social justice aim. For individuals, the international scope of the cause spans national borders and may even challenge one's national identity. Whether the cause is located at a distance or affects individuals from all over the globe, the international unity and the personal commitment involved asks individuals to see themselves and their actions as having international and even global effects. This emphasizes the personal commitment that is involved but it also challenges national and cultural biases. There have been a number of international efforts of this sort (e.g., against female genital mutilation, apartheid, AIDS, international racism, etc.). Other examples of international solidarity are found when people in one country boycott the products of a multinational corporation because that corporation introduced potentially dangerous or even life-threatening products into another country. Solidarity among nations or between states may be seen in the commitment of domestic resources for an international cause or for a cause in a solidary country, as well as in the withholding of resources. For instance, economic sanctions in protest of a state's deplorable human rights record might be an action in solidarity with the people who suffer under the unjust regime. Of course, in order for this example to hold, a number of other conditions and obligations of political solidarity would also have to be met.

For the personal commitment to international political solidarity, individuals in solidarity might not, indeed, probably do not, know one another, though they may know *of* one another. For example, people in the United States may choose to be in solidarity with poor and politically repressed people of the Third World. The behavior and political activism of those in the United States would be affected by this solidarity. Notice that with this example, the people in the United States need not have any personal knowledge of or friendship with particular individuals in the Third World. It is sufficient that they have adequate knowledge of the situation and recognize it as being unjust. Poverty or an unjust political power might compel the person in the United States to adopt an attitude of solidarity; personal connections, friendships, or travel might also be a source of the political solidarity. Such personal international solidarity movements might also be recognized for the protests.

"Global solidarity" is sometimes used by theorists to mean a common humanity or unity of humans. Global solidarity, however, is distinct from human solidarity. Human solidarity is a subcategory of either social solidarity or civic solidarity depending on its motive and agenda. If a form of social solidarity, then it is a unity of humans based on their very humanity. It is, in other words, sufficient that one is human to be a member of human solidarity. Moral obligations are then based on one's humanity. If a form of civic solidarity, it is similarly structured, but the international community assumes the responsibility for protection of the world's vulnerable populations. Global solidarity, in contrast, is a subcategory of political solidarity. The uniting characteristic is not one's humanity but one's collective commitment to a cause with all others. For this reason, universal global solidarity would be very rare, if not impossible; but less encompassing examples of global solidarity are possible. I have more to say about global and international solidarity and human solidarity in Chapter 7.

It is also worth noting that individuals may have multiple commitments to different political solidarity causes. At times these too may conflict or cause one to confront a contradiction in one's actions or intentions. At other times, the multiplicity of movements to which an individual commits him- or herself provides a richness and deeper understanding to the social analysis, critique, and activism. It also contributes to coalition building. As individuals make connections between causes in their own lives through conscious reflection on social justice, they challenge social movements to do the same.

The classification of commitments is meant to allow for a richer discussion of the moral obligations of political solidarity not in order to provide any sort of criteria for judging individual commitment. On the contrary, I offer them merely to give a more detailed picture of the variety and possible scope of solidarity movements. These qualifiers may be combined to yield a number of varieties of political solidarity and, given that an individual's commitment likely will undergo some transformations, might wax or wane, or might combine with other commitments; and given that movements undergo similar vicissitudes, the qualifiers will likely change throughout the course of the solidarity experience. A weak local solidarity may transform into a strong local or even a strong international movement. A weak international commitment might change into a strong international one. Notice that the qualifiers apply both to the individual's commitment and the solidary group itself. This is part of how political solidarity mediates between the individual and the community—my own commitment may be measured, but it also affects the measure of the movement itself. The extent of the movement may be radically altered when a passionate individual from across national borders utilizes his or her charisma to arouse interest in a cause among his or her fellow nationals.

A worker who joins with his or her colleagues in attempting to form a labor union to facilitate bargaining with an employer engages in local solidarity. It is strong or weak according to how the solidarity commitment affects other aspects of his or her life. An academic who engages in political consciousness-raising and activism, and perhaps even offers financial support to people in another country who suffer from an injustice such as poverty or political repression, is likely to be engaged in weak international solidarity. But perhaps that same academic radically changes how he or she lives and what he or she consumes, challenges his or her own government's policies regarding the other nation, travels to the other nation for advocacy and consciousness-raising, and continually considers how to involve others in the efforts to oppose injustice. We might want to say that this is a strong commitment. There are no clear guidelines for determining the strength of one's commitment, and even the strongest of commitments might falter. Any line-drawing would necessarily be arbitrary and likely become pernicious within movements of political solidarity. Decision-making, distribution of resources, and participation in activities might become contentious were we to institutionalize any sort of divisions between solidary commitments. Nevertheless, if we wish to develop a theory of political solidarity, then the descriptive classifications of weak and strong might usefully assist our conceptions of the moral relationships and duties. So, with the crucial caveat that we not attempt to apply practically normative requirements to weak and strong solidarity, we can nevertheless employ them as useful tools in understanding the social movement of political solidarity.

Working for Social Change

Political solidarity involves activism but cannot be reduced to activism. It is a moral relation but has a political and sentimental side as well. It works for social changes and sometimes advocates something akin to complete revolution of a social system. But political solidarity also differs from revolution. Clearly there are some interesting similarities between revolution and solidarity; the similarities, however, should not be overemphasized. Revolution by nature detests the power structures and values that support a political system. It aims to destroy in large part the entire system in order to replace it with something new. Political solidarity, in contrast, usually tries to change some social systems or challenge some unjust laws; only rarely does it try to overthrow an entire legal system (cf. Walzer 1970, 36). Nor does political solidarity use violence to advance its cause, though, of course, violence may be part of other activist struggles for a similar cause (I say more about the role of violence in Chapter 3). In many cases, political solidarity sustains many of the important cultural values within the larger society of which it is a part. In fact, the social criticism that motivates and checks political solidarity often uses the social values of a society to demonstrate how a particular situation contradicts certain principles. The civil rights movement provides a vivid case in point. The practice of systematic degradation and exclusion of blacks from social and political participation contradicted the values of liberty and equality at the very heart of American society. The social critics and activists united in political solidarity targeted the unjust practices but did not rally for a complete overthrow of the political system (though, no doubt, some among the activists did). A similar case can be made for the women's liberation movement, the gay rights movement, and the disability rights movement, to name just a few important instances of political solidarity. But sometimes in challenging a social structure or fighting against injustice, political solidarity does aim to overthrow an entire system, as when a tyrannical regime seizes control of a country—perhaps even killing significant groups of ethnic minorities within its borders. While closer to revolution in that case, solidarity is still a unique moral relation that entails positive duties toward a cause as well as toward fellow participants in solidarity and nonparticipants in the wider society. Taking up arms against the tyrannical regime is not consistent with the principles of solidarity, though that is not to say that such actions are not sometimes justified by some other means. I say more about these elements of political solidarity in Chapters 3, 6, and 7. Given my focus, however, I do not present an argument for if or when military responses might be justified, nor do I think we ought to plunge into such a discussion lightly.

Political solidarity also differs from rebellion in that the latter usually lacks the committed moral action of solidarity. Rebellion usually uses relatively violent means and likely lacks the liberatory ends of solidarity. Political solidarity has a clear target and a clear end. Rebellion may have the target, though that is not a necessary requirement. Rebellion may, in other words, be rebellion for its own sake. As a social movement, political solidarity is never for its own sake but always for the sake of something else.

Finally, political solidarity is distinct from political organizations. Political organizations have a formal structure and status that political solidarity lacks. The structure generally includes rules for decision-making, goal setting, and membership. Decision-making within political solidarity is done in a loosely democratic manner when actions are determined collectively, and according to individual conscience when actions are personal. Many of the decisions regarding specific forms of activism, then, are left up to the individual members of the solidary group or to small coalitions within the movement. Membership is self-determined and does not rely on formal recognition of solidary ties. Both the formal organization and the social movement have relatively specific goals, but the nature of those goals is often quite diverse (though not necessarily so). A political organization will likely have a particular agenda with well-defined means for accomplishing its ends. The goals of political solidarity might be quite clearly spelled out, as in the case of women's suffrage or civil rights for blacks, or much vaguer, as in the case of liberation from poverty and oppression in Latin America. But, whereas the political organization likely has something of a united vision for an ideal goal or an idealistic (even utopian) vision of a just system, political solidarity is unity around a goal in opposition to injustice, oppression, tyranny, or social vulnerability. The vision of political solidarity is perhaps a shared vision of a future without the injustice but rarely or secondarily does it entail a map of the ideal political order.

Political solidarity can, of course, morph into a formalized political organization or association, or certain parts of the solidary group might form formal political bodies within the wider movement. The National Organization for Women (NOW) is an excellent example of this sort of transformation. While it never fully separates from the solidary group aiming at the liberation of women, NOW has become a separate political entity with clearly determined goals, structures, and decision-making mechanisms.

There are also other formal and informal advocacy structures, and some may be splinter groups from a larger social movement that falls under the umbrella concept of political solidarity. At times, some of these advocacy groups may even be at odds with each other within the wider solidarity movement. So too, given that solidarity is a moral relation with certain positive duties, not all activism for a cause will be consistent with it. The factions within feminism, for instance, or the radically different approaches to attaining civil rights, might be considered fully distinguishable and distinct solidarity movements or part of the same political solidarity, though perhaps construed more broadly. Attention to or articulation of the substantive and formative goals may move factions beyond confrontation toward workable coalitions. Nevertheless, disagreement about the means of obtaining the goals of liberation or cessation of injustice can factionalize solidarity. Some factions may even opt out, choosing instead to pursue their own means. Political solidarity is just one of the many possible struggles for liberation. Not every action undertaken in the service of liberation would or should be judged as appropriate for political solidarity. Social criticism within the solidary group provides a means of adjudicating between competing actions or methods while also keeping political solidarity focused on its ends.

Political solidarity is a collective venture. Solidarity mediates between the individual and the community, but both elements must be actively engaged. The collective that forms is composed of individuals, and the collective responsibility of political solidarity is more than just an aggregate of individual actors. We cannot fault an individual for failing to act on his or her own in the face of overwhelming oppression or injustice. Nevertheless, individual actors might be faulted for failing to act in particular ways within or with the collective in some situations. In Chapter 3, I discuss the moral relationships and the incumbent obligations that are implicitly accepted when an individual commits to a cause in political solidarity and when the collective itself acts.

Conclusion

Political solidarity, unlike its counterparts social and civic solidarity, marks a social movement engaged in activism to bring about social change for social justice. It is an inherently oppositional relationship undertaken because of its moral import. Political solidarity is an active, engaged, collective response to injustice or oppression. The unity that forms can affect an individual's life quite intensely. It is a challenge to change unjust conditions or bring about liberation. The group that forms in political solidarity seeks to transform social structures and unseat unjust systems of power. The group consists of individuals and at times more formal organizations or associations as well. Individuals shape the group but are also shaped by it, insofar as social criticism extends to other aspects of their lives. Of course, their activities in solidarity will also be transforming. Social solidarity, in contrast, is a social relationship that includes moral requirements, but those appear secondarily to the bond that creates it. Civic solidarity minimizes the bond to some extent and stresses the more formal social responsibility to protect others. In that sense, it is closer to political solidarity than social solidarity, but because the moral obligations of civic solidarity are often not personal commitments of individuals and because they often arise from membership in a political community, civic solidarity is distinct from political solidarity.

This chapter laid the groundwork for the theory of political solidarity that I develop further in Chapters 3–7. In each of those chapters I unpack many of the elements mentioned only briefly here. No theory of political solidarity, however, can be complete. It is a context-dependent m oral relation. The particularities of the social structures being opposed as well as the overall social situation will inform and shape each instance of political solidarity, and that relation will continue to change to meet new goals and address new or interdependent causes and concerns.

THREE

The Moral Relations and Obligations of Political Solidarity

Starting a social movement is no easy task. Often what appears as a spontaneous social movement has been decades in the making. The different commitments of the members of the solidary group account in part for the sustaining force of political solidarity. Some people will work diligently and systematically to chip away at what they perceive to be a system of oppression or injustice. Others will suddenly find themselves united by a passion for a cause or incensed by a current injustice. The unity that forms among actors might be close-knit and coherent or quite amorphous and fluid. Regardless of the diversity of commitments linking individual members and the power of the bond of the collective, political solidarity makes certain requirements on the participants. The content of the social movement will, of course, provide many of the specifics of these requirements, but the structure and purpose of political solidarity itself (as opposed to social and civic solidarity) reveal the outlines of the moral relationships and obligations that will be filled within the context of a particular injustice. This chapter examines the initial commitment to political solidarity and the moral relationships that form, as well as the requirements of those relationships. What I paint here in the broad brushstrokes of an outline receive their vivid colors within the particular social movements, contexts of injustice, and struggles against oppression.

An Individual's Commitment to Activity in Solidarity

How any particular individual gets involved in a social movement entails, at some moment, an active commitment. I say "active commitment" rather than conscious choice because there may in fact not be a conscious decision to become involved in a social movement. A commitment usually but not necessarily involves conscious choice, but we must be careful not to ascribe undue weight to rational decision-making within political solidarity. Certainly rational decision-making plays a role, and may play a primary role for some participants, but others will be compelled to commit due to other factors. Political solidarity may be motivated by any number of factors, such as feelings of indignation, experiences of oppression or injustice, desire to care for others who are suffering, or even employment situations. Those who join in solidarity may convince others to be similarly stimulated to act by the force of their arguments or feelings.

When injustice or oppression is recognized as such or when they reach an utterly intolerable level, the compulsion to respond can become quite forceful. That is why political solidarity often looks more or less spontaneous. Consider the Polish Solidarity movement for instance. More often than not, the events of August 1980 are used to mark the start of the movement, but Goodwyn (1991) offers compelling evidence that the movement can be traced back to the immediate post–World War II era. Indeed, Goodwyn challenges the notion that movements are spontaneous at all. The vague beginnings, he argues, are often obscured once the movement has momentum. Similarly, the movements for civil rights and women's liberation were decades—even centuries—in the making. But some movements really are spontaneous and the force of the collective passion carries the movement forward.

Political solidarity is a moral relation of a social movement that unites individuals because of their shared commitment to a cause or goal. While political organizations and other formal advocacy associations may share with solidarity many of the same structures and duties, there are some significant differences. The moral duties within formally organized political associations are better understood under the rubric of social or civic solidarity as they usually pertain to group cohesion or civic obligations. But perhaps more interesting is that because political solidarity entails a number of individuals collectively making personal commitments to a cause, a number of relations are presumed in the moral relation of political solidarity itself. A commitment to a cause establishes voluntary relations and obligations to that cause. The commitment is a sort of agreement to act in such a way that the pursuit of the cause or goal informs one's actions. But the commitment also informs other relations. A commitment to solidarity sets up a collective—a group that acts together, in concert, simultaneously, or consistently. Any individual who willingly takes on the commitment to solidarity also takes on a relation to others who similarly commit. More, the commitment to solidarity alters one's relationships with those who do not commit to solidarity. That is, by becoming part of a moral collective for social change, individual participants also publicly declare they are not a part of some other group or otherwise set themselves apart from aspects of the larger society. This is generally not a spatial dislocation (though it could be that) but rather a decree that one's commitment to a cause means that one will live in society in a different way.

The solidary group is a result of individual commitments (cf. Ladd 1998, 19), but the commitment is a multifaceted commitment that binds an individual not only to his or her own project but to a group of others similarly dedicated to a cause or project. One's identity shapes and is shaped by the solidary group. Although not speaking specifically of political solidarity, Thomas Hill implicitly articulates the relations that emerge from voluntary associations. "'Who one is' for moral purposes—e.g., a Nazi, a racist, a Christian, a humanist—is determined not simply by substantive contributions to various good or evil causes but to some extent by what and whom one associates oneself with, and in some contexts this depends importantly on the symbolic gestures one is prepared to make" (Hill 1979, 90). In other words, one's commitment to a cause, one's "associates" or fellow group members, and the relation between the group and the larger community or society all play a role in "'who one is' for moral purposes."

These three relationships describe any group participation that affects individual moral life. For political solidarity, however, they indicate (1) the relationship between members of the solidary group; (2) the relationship to the goal of the social movement; and (3) the relationship between both individual members and the solidary group and those not electing to participate in solidarity, or, in other words, the relation to nonmembers of the solidary group. The commitment to political solidarity—a commitment that often involves sacrifice, struggle, alienation, and effort—establishes these relations. The claim, then, is that political solidarity is not a single moral relation between members of a group but a set of at least three moral relations that are interdependent on one another. In addition, the diversity of individuals acting in solidarity provides important content to the moral relations of political solidarity.

Individuals transformed by the commitment to political solidarity reflect on actions differently than those not similarly affected. Consuming products becomes a political act when the solidarity commitment recognizes the impact of consumption on the lives and livelihoods of workers. Individuals who refuse to do things in the expected manner or take on new tasks act politically as they contribute to the collective project (Scholz 2007, 40). Of course, the particularities of the project determine the content of these and similar actions by the individual, but political solidarity of whatever sort entails these sorts of reflective personal actions. In political solidarity, ordinary actions become political actions when they are done in a reflective manner that actively engages the commitment to a cause that challenges or resists a system perceived to be unjust or oppressive.

As I have mentioned, consumerism serves as a good example of the means of individual resistance and activism in response to a commitment to a cause within a collective project of political solidarity. "Consumerism" has come to be understood as the use or consumption of resources, usually with the presumption that material goods bring happiness or satisfaction. A "culture of consumption" might result if consumerism becomes the focal point of social life. While not everyone goes to the extremes of consumerism, most people are consumers of some sort insofar as we seek to meet out basic necessities through the purchase of goods. At least some of us also engage in supplemental consumption of goods, services, and resources above and beyond our basic needs. How and what one consumes may seem like a personal choice, especially within the confines of a culture that puts a high premium on individual autonomy. But political solidarity challenges that idea by highlighting the connections between the production of what we consume and the social, political, environmental, and material conditions under which it is produced. A product sold cheaply in the United States may be available at that bargain price because the manufacturer uses child or sweatshop labor. Those motivated to join a political solidarity movement opposing poverty, child abuse, neocolonialism, or globalization, or in support of workers' rights or women's rights, on reflection, would see the boycott of the product as a political act. They might understand part of their personal responsibility within the solidarity action to consist in informed consumerism. Reflective consumerism is also a useful tool in educating and encouraging others to join a cause. When I stop to think that what I purchase may implicate me in the oppression of others, I begin to see my own responsibility in the success or failure of attempts to root out injustice. I can also reflect on how a small action on my part, when joined with similar small actions performed by others, can bring about social change. As this example illustrates, an individual's actions in response to an emerging social consciousness becomes political when joined with similar actions by others.

The nature of the commitment differs from other forms of commitment or choice within political decision-making. Classical liberal theory, for instance, views humans as autonomous, free individuals. Equality and liberty are ruling ideals as individuals pursue their own vision of the good life. Decisions are based on rational, self-interested deliberations and at least some relationships are formed through contracts. Certainly rational deliberation may motivate some to commit to political solidarity or to participate in certain activities consistent with political solidarity. But often action within solidarity is actually contrary to self-interest. So too, when solidarity becomes difficult, mundane, or hazardous, the nature of a rational choice means that one can simply opt out of solidarity. Classical liberalism emphasizes the effects of one's actions on one's self and self-interest or property. A commitment to social change, like what is found in solidarity, is, by definition, directed also toward the community. Solidarity is both a personal commitment and a social commitment. The merger of individualism and collectivism must keep sight of both the individual and the collective. Richard Rorty notes that when circumstances get oppressive and we risk getting lost or erased in the struggle, we seek "to get a reconfirmation of our own identities by articulating these in the presence of others" (1989, 185). Solidarity must have some mechanisms to reinvigorate individual commitment (and collective activity). This is especially true for situations that take decades or even centuries to change. Suffrage for women and civil rights for African Americans are two revealing examples. Both also, at times, involved very real physical danger for some social activists. Commitment to political solidarity must withstand these and other difficult challenges.

In contrast to the liberal autonomous choice based on rational decision-making, an existential commitment encompasses all aspects of an individual's existence and merges the individual's project with the projects of others. An existential commitment requires a dedication of the self, though not self-sacrifice, and a recognition of the individual's embeddedness within a community and social context. The cause, however, must never take a position over and against the individual.

An existentialist ethics requires a choice that is continually lived. The choice is for a project undertaken in freedom but is itself freedom. It is also worth pausing to note that the project any individual undertakes, while necessarily engaging the projects of others, might not be the precise project that that individual consciously chooses. Often our conscious choices are obscured or even mistaken as we pursue a project. The commitment to a project is nevertheless forceful—our own awareness or lack of awareness might be the limiting agent that hides our authentic commitments even from ourselves.

Simone de Beauvoir's *Ethics of Ambiguity* is perhaps the most sustained account of an existentialist social ethics. Elsewhere I have argued that Beauvoir's ethics is a solidarity ethics (Scholz 2005b), but it is useful also in the more specific case of political solidarity. The text begins with the question, "How could men, originally separated, get together?" (Beauvoir 1948a, 18). Beauvoir challenges the assumption that existentialism is an individualist ethics saying, "Man [sic] can find a justification of his own existence only in the existence of other men" (1948a, 72). A social movement cannot be merely a conglomeration of individual actors, and this is in part what distinguishes political solidarity from some other accounts of collective action. The existentialist ethics of Beauvoir provides one model for how we might approach the delicate balance between individual commitment on the one hand and group action on the other. One's own freedom is bound up with that of others such that "to will oneself free is to will others free" (1948a, 73). Although Beauvoir would extend this notion beyond social movements to everyday moral action, our focus on the moral parameters of political solidarity confines the discussion to moral relations and activities within social movements of political solidarity.

Perhaps because her ethics is aimed at all existents, Beauvoir makes the strong claim that each of us is caught up somehow in the struggle for liberation, but it is as individuals that we are so caught up: "Each is interested in the liberation of all, but as a separate existence engaged in his own projects" (Beauvoir 1948a, 112). Of course, we may be participating as oppressors or passive opponents to the liberation struggle rather than as liberators. Our freedoms interconnect: "For a freedom wills itself genuinely only by willing itself as an indefinite movement through the freedom of others; as soon as it withdraws into itself, it denies itself on behalf of some object which it prefers to itself" (1948a, 90). The oppressor or privileged individual might object that his or her ability to live in privilege is hindered on this account. Certainly that is the case but Beauvoir responds by again appealing to our interdependence. If we oppress or even if we fail to oppose tyranny in any of its forms, we not only hinder the freedom of others, we severely limit our own freedom. For this reason, she argues that "a freedom which is interested only in denying freedom must be denied; . . . to be free is not to have the power to do anything you like; it is to be able to surpass the given toward an open future; the existence of others as a freedom defines my situation and is even the condition of my own freedom" (1948a, 91; see also 1944, 112–14). The extension of the liberation struggle to all existents firmly places Beauvoir's solidarity ethics in the camp of global solidarity, which I discuss more fully in the final chapter.

Although Beauvoir's ethics encompasses more than a commitment to political solidarity would, it nevertheless offers an interesting model for what that commitment might look like. Take for example an individual's decision to join in political solidarity with the poor of Haiti. The decision cannot be undertaken in isolation but necessarily engages the lives and projects of the poor of Haiti, one's family and friends, one's social and political allegiances, and countless other interdependent relations. Does such a commitment mean one must live with the poor? Does it mean one lives like the poor? Perhaps it means that one continues to live as a middle-class American citizen aiding the poor of Haiti through activism, advocacy, fundraising, and education. What does an existential commitment to solidarity entail? The answer is particular for each individual, based on ability, needs, desires, and level of commitment. There will, of course, be differences between different individuals' commitments—some will make a strong commitment and others will make a weak commitment—as the last chapter explained. Any individual's commitment to political solidarity will be measured or determined by a number of factors, including the exigency of the cause; the skills, ability, and desires of the individual; the coherence of other commitments; and any additional personal compulsions. But regardless of the extent of one's commitment, the option to join in political solidarity is an adoption of moral obligations that have the potential to radically affect one's lifestyle and perhaps even all other significant moral choices. Beauvoir claims that "the oppressed is more totally engaged in the struggle than those who, though at one with him in rejecting his servitude, do not experience it; but also that, on the other hand, every man is affected by this struggle in so essential a way that he can not fulfill himself morally without taking part in it" (1948a, 88–89). She has turned the individual commitment to liberation into a moral requirement of existence itself. That is more inclusive than political solidarity, but her ethics offers a model for how the individual commitment to political solidarity is lived out. The existential choice is so embedded in who one is that abandoning the commitment is much more difficult. In effect, one becomes transformed by the commitment and activity of solidarity. Still, it is possible and at times necessary or even desirable for individuals to pull back or weaken their commitment to solidarity. These times allow for reflection on activism and a reorientation to goals while also opening avenues for additional social criticism. Any individual at any given time might have a multiplicity of interests, roles, relationships, and obligations that require his or her attention. A person might be a philosopher, a parent, and a spouse; that same person might be committed to feminism, environmentalism, and social justice. Each of these interests, roles, relationships, and obligations require time and commitment. They may and often do pull a person in varying directions. The ability to commit to a cause in political solidarity with others will both affect and be affected by the coherence of all these other commitments. It is possible, in other words, to integrate the commitment to political solidarity fairly completely into one's life, but the other commitments in one's life maintain their place and may at times pull one away from solidary action.

The initial commitment within political solidarity is multifaceted. Not only is it a commitment to a cause, but it is also a commitment to others and to society in general. That is, the commitment to solidarity is a commitment to form relations to a cause with others and work with these others to achieve the end that will bring about wider social change. The three primary relationships within political solidarity are (1) the relationship between members of the solidary group; (2) the relationship to the goal of the social movement; and (3) the relationship between both individual members and the solidary group and those not electing to participate in solidarity, or, in other words, the relation to nonmembers of the solidary group. Each of these relations within solidarity has positive duties. Although there are likely many others, I focus on the three primary duties of cooperation, social criticism, and nonviolent activism, which parallel the moral relationships of solidarity. Although I discuss these relations separately, they are in fact intertwined in such a way that to break faith within one of the relations adversely affects the others as well. That too is part of the nature of an existential commitment to solidarity.

Subsequent chapters delve into the issues raised here by exploring what it means to say that solidarity has a goal (Chapter 6) and the nature of the collective (Chapters 4 and 5).

Moral Sentiments

In the first chapter, I discussed what I called parasitical solidarity—that is, invocations of the term solidarity for what might at best be only a part of a genuine species of solidarity. Often, feelings or dispositions fall into this category. "Solidarity" might be used to describe the feeling of connectedness a person has with others who share a similar plight or with those for whom one has a high degree of empathy or sympathy in their situation. A few examples of this parasitical use are found when "solidarity" is used instead of sympathy, feelings of friendship, the spirit of camaraderie, and hope for a better future. I argued in Chapter 1 that when "solidarity" is used to stand in for these and other things that might be components of the genus or species of solidarity, it plays the rhetorical role of tapping into at least some of the other components of social, civic, or political solidarity.

What is missing from my account in Chapter 1 is the opposite of this: the fuller discussion of moral feelings as constitutive parts of the various species of solidarity. Among discussions of solidarity, social solidarity attracts the most attention and thus many of the moral feelings of solidarity pertain most clearly to it. But political solidarity does have at least one important moral feeling and that is *hope*. While I will argue that hope is necessary for political solidarity, it is the only moral feeling that I think is necessary. Other moral feelings may be necessary for other forms of solidarity—compassion, loyalty, or concern, for instance—but other feelings within political solidarity are dependent on the specific cause, the variety of relationships that form, and the means used to challenge injustice, oppression, tyranny, or social vulnerability.

Among some of the contingent feelings, we might find pride, shame, guilt, envy, indignation, and joy. We might feel collective pride in accomplishments that bring us closer to the libratory ideal. I might feel personal shame at failing to live up to my solidary commitment; or you might feel shame at my disavowal of the cause of our collective actions. We might feel collective guilt at our inability or failure to recognize the importance of some social practice in upholding the system we oppose. Some members of the solidary group might be envious of the abilities or privileges of others or envious of the privileges and power of the dominant group. People who are not directly affected by injustice or oppression might feel anger or indignation at the suffering of others with whom they join in solidarity. Or there may be feelings of personal or collective joy at accomplishment that may not even directly bear on the solidarity campaign. By no means is this an exhaustive list of the possible feelings or instantiations of feelings that abound within political solidarity. It does start us on a path to thinking more intently about the role of feelings within solidarity—both as an element and as a motivator—as well as the interconnections of feelings across the different species of solidarity.

Joel Feinberg argues that vicarious pride and shame are measures of group solidarity. He explains that solidarity is a necessary condition for vicarious feeling so this feeling should serve as an adequate index of solidarity (Feinberg 1970, 236). This "solidarity index," he demonstrates, might allow us to assess the extent of solidarity among different groups. Feinberg notes the greater extent of solidarity among American blacks as opposed to American whites; the former may even feel strong connection to their slave ancestors whereas white people in America tend to not have a corresponding feeling of connection with slaveholders. While Feinberg cautions that group solidarity is rather rare, his comments come in the context of solidarity as a form of collective responsibility. He does not distinguish between political solidarity and social solidarity, but one can argue that the distinction is implicit in how he sets up the solidarity index. That is, vicarious pride and shame allow us to appraise the extent of the bonds; the bonds themselves do not, it appears, cause the vicarious pride and shame. This direction of causality would lead us to believe that Feinberg has social solidarity in mind. Nevertheless, political solidarity may develop bonds with others that inspire vicarious pride and shame, but those feelings are contingent and not necessary to the relationship itself.

In his critique of Feinberg on solidarity, Larry May notes that while vicarious feelings may be present in solidarity, they are not necessary for solidarity. Instead, May argues, solidarity relies on the moral feeling of the bond. The feeling of the bond is based on a "willingness of the members to offer moral support to one another, even when they do not feel so deeply committed to one another's lives as to feel pride or shame through them. One may feel motivated to take responsibility for the other even though one disapproves of what the other is doing, thereby blocking any feelings of vicarious pride or shame. This is because in solidarity one can make at least two forms of identification: an identification with the other's behavior, and an identification with the other's characteristics" (May 1996, 32–33).

According to May, the bonds of sentiment in solidarity are moral; that is, when in solidarity, people feel motivated to come to each other's aid—responsibility and obligation (1996, 38). May relies on collective conscience to explain the other-directed feelings in solidarity and claims that it is "intertwined with feeling motivated to provide a member of one's group with moral support" (1996, 38). There are two dimensions of moral support according to May: "First, solidarity provides an impetus to various members of a group to feel motivated to go to the aid of fellow members who are in need. Second, and perhaps because of the first, solidarity also provides an impetus for a particular group member to feel motivated to overcome egoistic concerns in favor of concerns about the common good" (1996, 39).

May's position could fit any of the three main forms of solidarity but is only necessarily the case for social solidarity. What he describes is similar to the mutual concern captured in other accounts of social solidarity (e.g., Mason 2000, 27). Mutual concern is perhaps an ideal element of some versions of political solidarity but it is not a necessary moral feeling; the moral duty of mutuality, however, is. The difference here is subtle and not always that important; for a theoretical account of the moral duties within political solidarity, however, it is worth disclosing. The moral feeling of mutual concern extends to the whole person. When one of my fellows is in need, I am moved by mutual concern—a concern that assumes others might be so moved if I were suffering—to aid in alleviating that suffering. The moral duty of mutuality within political solidarity, developed more completely below, covers the reciprocity of our moral obligations mediated by the goal and our commitment to collective action. Notice, then, that the feeling of mutual concern encompasses more and assumes more about the relation between two people than the moral duty of mutuality. Only the latter, I argue, is necessary for political solidarity, but the former is found in greater or lesser degree in social solidarity.

Hope is the only necessary moral feeling for political solidarity. Political solidarity is primarily a movement of social change. Members strive to bring about liberation, create conditions free from oppression, and struggle for justice. These formative goals direct the substantive goals or concrete projects they undertake. Hope means that they believe the future can be better than the present. The moral sentiment of hope motivates activity within solidarity because it fosters the desire for the final ends or goals (substantive and formative) of political solidarity. Michael Walzer taps into moral sentiment when he identifies the common feature of social criticism as hope; criticism assumes that the future can be better than the present: "the critic must believe that the conduct of his fellows can conform more closely to a moral standard than it now does or that their self-understanding can be greater than it now is or that their institutions can be more justly organized than they now are" (1988, 17). Walzer assigns the social critic the task of "expressing the aspirations of his people" (1988, 229; see also 233). As I argue below, however, political solidarity calls all the participants to engage in social criticism of this sort. Hope keeps the movement alive, for without it there would be no reason to act collectively. Because the substantive end of solidarity is a realistically expected outcome, hope keeps the solidarity movement moving progressively rather than stagnating. Hope reconfirms our commitment to one another and to our purpose.

Moral feelings must, of course, move us to collective action. The key is to turn that moral feeling into concrete action, that is, to respond appropriately to situations of injustice in mutuality, or to maintain the moral feelings within political solidarity. May argues that it is the "felt commonality" among members of the group that motivates them to engage in "individual or collective action in support of one another" (1996, 38), but as I have shown, that assumes that the bond exists first. So May's account of solidarity is an account of social solidarity. In some cases, there is in fact at least a minimal connection between social solidarity and political solidarity. For instance, such a connection may be seen in those cases of political solidarity that emerge directly from or in reaction to experiences of oppression. If the solidary group is the same as the oppressed group, there may be no problem in conflating social solidarity and political solidarity; but given the overlapping and intersecting structures of oppression and privilege, such an equation of social and political solidarity becomes not only less feasible, but also less desirable.

In sum, hope is a necessary moral sentiment within political solidarity because each individual shares the belief that together they can create change. Hope helps to drive the movement and lays the groundwork for other sentiments to develop within the collective action and solidary group.

Relation Between Members

Political solidarity is not just a single moral relation but, as I have argued, entails three primary moral relations. These moral relations are interdependent with one another: each relation may be read through the other two. When most people think of solidarity, they think of a relation between people, in other words, a relation between those "in solidarity." As Hill describes in relation to symbolic protests, this is the relation between "one's associates." It is a moral relation because in solidarity, one assumes a moral role—that of solidaristic actor. I discuss some of the possible obligations of that role and relation in this section.

The commitment to solidarity is a mutual commitment: together, individuals commit to each other and to a project. Individuals need not know each other or care about each other prior to being united within the moral relations of solidarity. Their individual and collective commitments do, however, entail obligations to others in the solidary group. Each is, after all, committing him- or herself to all others in the collective project for social change. The commitment is a more or less explicit assumption of the obligations one has toward others in the effort to attain that goal. Three crucial aspects of the obligation to others within political solidarity are consciousness-raising, cooperation, and mutuality.

Consciousness-raising has a long history of effectiveness within social movements. It played a key role even before the women's movement made consciousness-raising an organized part of activism. Consciousness-raising is disseminating information among a variety of people, though it is often understood under the guise of demystifying the oppressed themselves. It can take any number of forms from public debate and discussion to support groups to direct confrontation. The main idea, in conjunction with the other elements of political solidarity, is to awaken not only an understanding of the oppression or injustice that is targeted but also to help to gain new perspectives on social structures in need of change and identify the values that will inspire the social movement or solidaristic activity. It is building awareness within oneself and others that there is a need for change. It is gathering information and obtaining knowledge so that one is well armed to commit to political solidarity. At times, consciousness-raising is also inciting emotions, such as hope for a better future, as I discussed in the previous section. Anger, along with hope, also can play a role in our joint activity. Effective consciousness-raising can provide that key piece of information that awakens a person's indignation or desire for change. Consciousness-raising is often understood to be an early part of an individual's participation in a social movement. It should also be understood as an ongoing part of that commitment; as cooperative activity heats up, consciousness-raising through information getting and social criticism (discussed in the next section) accompany it.

Cooperation connotes a joint activity that puts solidarity in the literature on collective responsibility. In doing so, however, we must avoid attributing too much agency to the group while also avoiding methodological individualism. The cooperative activity of political solidarity is both individual action and collective action simultaneously. Cooperation captures that balance because it calls forth individual input into group action as well as the dynamic of action done in concert with others, simultaneously, or as part of an overarching effort. Political solidarity challenges how moral theorists tend to discuss collective action primarily because the focus has traditionally been on whether groups could be held responsible for the actions of some or all of their members (e.g., French 1972), whether a group of individuals could be held responsible for failing to organize themselves into a formal organization with decision-making procedures (e.g., Held 1970), and whether the actions of the group are reducible to the actions of individuals.

There are essentially two types of collective action at work in solidarity. The first is the situation where multiple individuals see some action that ought to be taken and one or more of those individuals act in such a way that the whole group might be called responsible (and might benefit). The second is when the action taken must be a joint action; that is, only the combined/coordinated efforts of all members will result in the desired effect (cf. Bates 1971, 347). Regardless of the type of collective action, being in solidarity with others means that one is to some extent interdependent with others. They cooperate in such a manner as to avoid new systems or structures of dependence or domination/subordination: "The test of solidarity, the mark of a cooperative commonwealth, is mutual aid—the recognition of our fellow citizens, all of them, as men and women toward whom we have obligations by virtue of the fellowship" (Walzer 1998, 51). Additionally, the personal stance in support of a cause not only affects the individual's life but also lends support, honor, and legitimacy to the solidarity movement.

The Moral Relations and Obligations of Political Solidarity

When individuals join into political solidarity, they implicitly agree to act in accord with an end or goal—liberation from oppression, cessation of injustice, stopping of tyranny, or some other resistance activity. The individual does not, however, fold into the collective or otherwise give up autonomy in solidarity. Individuals within solidarity retain power of decision-making and critique within their own lives, as they live the commitment to solidarity and even through their participation in the group. As Robert Goodin argues, "Saying that the responsibility is a collective one does not exempt individuals from responsibility: it merely changes the character of their responsibilities. Individual members of the collectivities in question have a responsibility to cooperate in whatever schemes are organized to discharge collective responsibilities" (1985, 163, see also 164). So how can we understand the moral obligation of cooperation, and what requirements does it place on the individual participant? For some guidance in answering these questions, I turn to some of the literature on collective responsibility. Contrary to most accounts of collective responsibility that pertain to assigning responsibility when something goes wrong, political solidarity is obviously different. It aims to act collectively to produce a good, but it can, nevertheless, borrow substantially from discussions of cooperation, coordination, and communication found in the literature on collective responsibility.

Part of the cooperation and relative equality within the solidary group entails a shared responsibility. This shared responsibility, however, relies on a "working with" or "bringing together" among the participants in political solidarity. Individuals must work with one another to accomplish certain aims and, insofar as they do so (or fail to do so), might be held morally responsible for the group activity (or inactivity). Within solidarity, cooperation implies that others within the solidary group can count on you to participate when and where you are able. Of course, people do change their solidary commitments or opt out of activist responses, but the key here is that there is within the relationship between members of the solidary group an understanding of commitment to action that will draw on each person's talents and abilities; those talents and abilities in turn become strengthened by joining forces with others.

Peter French addresses this issue of individual responsibility or liability for group action or inaction in his work on collective responsibility. According to his account, collective power includes a "coordination allowance" (see also Hechter 1987, 34; Goodin 1985, 134–44; Held 1970, 475). The coordination allowance specifies that in order for a group to have the power to do something, each member or most members "must have information about what the others are likely to do to contribute to the desired event" (French 1992, 73). Solidarity, unlike other forms of collective responsibility, does not require such detailed specification of individual actions, but it does require that each individual consider his or her actions as part of a larger movement and act in such a way as to support or foster the solidary group aim. Individual group members exhibit various talents, resources, or strengths; among these will be found various types of power. For a group to have any collective action its individual members must coordinate their various individual types of power according to a mutually acceptable project. Individual actions must be consistent with group actions and interests. How they get that information and how they respond to it or act on it is part of the "coordination problem for groups." French further describes the coordination allowance: "If a group effort, no matter how feasible, is to be successfully undertaken, group members must come up with some way of letting each other know what each proposes to do in the circumstances. Minimal coordination sets the parameters on the lower end of the actualization of latent collective power" (1992, 73).

In his discussion, French deals with a small group (ten passengers of an overturned bus in need of righting), and hence it is relatively easy to see how coordination among group members occurs. With a larger group the case may not be so easily discernable. Political solidarity does not always require the sort of communication and coordination it would take to right a bus, but, in many respects, the tasks of the participants are much more important and have the potential to affect persons far beyond the solidary group. These factors do imply a coordination allowance not too dissimilar from French's. For political solidarity, the coordination allowance would be tied up with mutuality and the commitment to the goal. Each participant coordinates his or her actions in such a way that the social movement progresses. In other words, the requirements of coordination will be dependent on the aims and nature of the group. Global and local political solidarities require different manifestations of coordination among participants.

Because the group in political solidarity is formed around a particular goal—be it the formative goals of the cessation of injustice or oppressive conditions, or the more particular substantive goals of a cause—then we might say that group members have communicated their intentions merely in joining in solidarity. But that is rather unsatisfactory because it risks political solidarity being reduced to personal lifestyle choices rather than social and political movements to effect change. In global political solidarity situations, for instance, solidarity actors on the periphery (i.e., those who make only a weak commitment or are located at great distance from the center of the struggle) follow the actions of the actors in the center through news accounts, direct reports, travel, and other forms of information gathering. Those in the center might have a reciprocal exchange of information of the happenings among activists on the periphery but might also be unable to attain this information or even be unaware of these other activists. The center and the periphery are coordinated by their ability and information but they probably do not act in the same way. The solidaristic activity is activity in concert toward achieving the same end—and in that sense is collective activity—but it may not be the same forms or manifestations of activity.

Local political solidarity, as in the case of a student protest or labor union action, faces fewer obstacles to coordinating activities and communicating aims, but it may still encounter some problems. Individual members actually can meet to discuss their goals and strategies for achieving their objectives. The coordination problems are minimized with the face-to-face discussions but the momentum of the movement may rise and fall with the personalities that come forward.

Within both local and global political solidarity, each individual has a certain power to affect change. The coordination of these powers and the mutuality between participants constitutes cooperation. Individual power ranges widely, from the power not to consume a product made by a company that engages in unjust treatment of employees to leading the struggle through the courage and force of one's rhetorical ability, from participating in a public event to arguing against an unjust law within the court system, and from writing letters advocating the release of unjustly held prisoners to fasting in a public manner to raise awareness of an unjust economic distribution. Of course, these are just a few of the examples of personal power engaged in political solidarity. Each is much more powerful when united with the actions of others similarly committed to a cause.

French suggests that power within collective responsibility is a combination of ability and intentional action. He explains, "When a person has power with respect to a particular occurrence or event, there is some intentional action (or actions) that person can perform at the appropriate time that will insure that the event will occur and that there is some intentional action (or actions) that same person can perform that will prevent the event from occurring" (French 1992, 71). An additional element to French's account of collective responsibility is the "power distribution principle," which holds that "a person has some power with respect to a task if a group of which that person is a nondispensable member has collective power with respect to the task" (1992, 75). A nondispensable member is one whose opposition to a task would alter the outcome; that is, that member is necessary to the completion of the task. Thus, an individual who has the power to effect some outcome might be held morally responsible for not doing so.

In relation to group membership, French claims that an individual has a moral responsibility to understand the place he or she occupies and level of respect he or she commands within the group (1992, 78). An individual member of a group may not have the power to achieve the outcome on his or her own but may wield significant influence to create a critical mass within the group. That critical mass, then, does have enough power to achieve the outcome. Given that people within a group tend to secure their allegiance to other group members who command respect, it follows, according to French, that those individual group members whose social station commands respect have an individual responsibility with regard to the overall group action or inaction within a given situation. French uses the example of a nun on a bus with nine other passengers. The bus tips on its side and no individual passenger has the power to right it, but the nun may have enough social station to rally enough passengers to form critical mass and right the bus. She is responsible for the group action or inaction insofar as she uses her social station and commanded respect accordingly. Notice that French relies on what he calls the "rational person test"; that is, "Any rational person in the circumstances should recognize the reasonable course of action and try to communicate it to the group" (1992, 78).

Obviously, French's example pertains to a small group wherein communication among the members is quite simple. With the large, diverse group found in political solidarity, communication may take on very different forms that complicate the coordination of the various group members or subgroups. Nonetheless, French's account is important because it clearly illustrates the connection of power, responsibility, and communication. These three elements overlap in the specific attribute of the relations between members in political solidarity: empowerment. Committing to solidarity is committing to listen to the needs of others, to ask what those needs are and how you might be able to help address them, to articulate one's own needs, and to help others find the tools needed to communicate and meet their own needs. Each of us has the power and responsibility to help one another. Communication, in particular communication through listening aimed at identifying the other's needs and recognizing how each of us can help without reinventing the structures of domination or oppression within our efforts to help, combines with power and responsibility for empowerment. Empowerment in political solidarity, however, never leaves the empowered individual alone in his or her role or agency in resisting oppression of injustice. Ann Ferguson makes a similar argument with regard to empowerment, albeit linking it more strongly with those who suffer injustice or oppression than I do here. Empowerment movements, she says, must be "part of an indigenous social movement" so as to ensure that the movement speaks for the people it purports to represent. She also argues that there must be "some political way for individuals and groups within the social movement to negotiate conflicts of interest within the movement" (Ferguson 2005, 13).

Robert Goodin explains collective responsibility and the affirmation of an individual's power within the group according to two principles. The first, the Principle of Group Responsibility, states, "If A's interests are vulnerable to the actions and choices of a group of individual's, either disjunctively or conjunctively, then that group has a special responsibility to (a) organize (formally or informally) and (b) implement a scheme for coordinated action by members of the group such that A's interests will be protected as well as they can be by the group, consistently with the group's other responsibilities" (Goodin 1985, 136). The second principle, the Principle of Individual Responsibility, affirms an individual's participation within the group and ability to influence group decision but does not emphasize unique ability or contribution from the individual:

> If B is a member of a group that is responsible, under the Principle of Group Responsibility, for protecting A's interests, then B has a special responsibility: (a) to see to it, so far as he is able, that the group organizes a collective scheme of action such that it protects A's interests as well as it can, consistently with the group's other responsibilities; and (b) to discharge fully and effectively the responsibilities allocated to him under any such scheme that might be organized, insofar as doing so is consistent with his other moral responsibilities, provided the scheme protects A's interests better than none at all. (Goodin 1985, 139)

Goodin's principles, like French's, are useful in thinking about the cooperative activity of political solidarity. We should be careful, however, to avoid reducing group moral responsibility to individual responsibility in discussing political solidarity. The solidary collective is more than the aggregate of its members. Mutuality between members bolsters any individual's power and ability while also obviating some of the individual responsibility for action or inaction.

Virginia Held offers a suggestive account of collective responsibility that encompasses some of the elements of political solidarity I have been discussing, but she does not quite get the balance between individual and collective that political solidarity captures. Held argues that a random collection of individuals may be held morally responsible for not acting (depending on the information available; that is, whether it is clear to a reasonable person what action ought to be taken), or barring that, for not forming into an organized collective, however loosely organized, to make the decisions required for action: "If a reasonable person judges that the overthrow of an existing political system is an action that is obviously called for, he may perhaps consider himself morally responsible for the failure of the random collection of which he is a member to perform this action. If he thinks some action to change an existing political system is obviously called for, but is not clear about which action, he may consider himself morally responsible for the failure of the random collection of which he is a member to perform the quite different action of transforming itself into a group capable of arriving at decisions on such questions" (Held 1970, 480).

Suppose, for example, that a particular individual within solidarity displays a talent or skill in navigating legal discourse or crafting legal arguments. Suppose further that the solidarity movement is aimed at achieving equal legal rights for a portion of the overall population previously denied (formally or informally) those equal legal rights (call them the oppressed group). The individual participant in question has the power to use his or her knowledge of legal discourse to help educate others in the solidary group who do not have a similar knowledge and to assist in the negotiation with the society as a whole to communicate the need for liberation and reversal of injustice. Having the power to do so, the participant with knowledge of legal discourse would be morally irresponsible not to assist in some way, however minimal.

As is evident from this discussion of French, Goodin, and Held, collective responsibility usually pertains to assigning blame for failure to act. In political solidarity, there may be some of that sort of assigning of responsibility, especially if a coordinated effort fails because of negligence or irresponsibility within the collective. But mostly, political solidarity requires a concerted effort to work with others to alleviate some oppression or injustice and, given the intransigency of both, blame laying plays a very insignificant part. Instead, members owe each other a continued commitment to the cause that also affects their relationships with each other. In other words, part of the collective responsibility of political solidarity is to ensure that personal relationships between members reflect and maintain the aspirations for justice that inspire the cause itself. The particular cause of political solidarity will have the most to say about the nature of relationships within the solidary group; for instance, a democratic movement in opposition to some form of tyranny would not want to replicate tyrannical relationships within the group. The values of democracy should be infused through the means the group uses to directly address the injustice as well as through the relations among all the members.

Cooperation does rely on shared responsibility, but for the purposes of a movement in political solidarity, the shared activity is more to the point. The activity to transform unjust social structures and challenge oppressive systems and persons relies on the positive cooperation and mutual support of all members of the solidary group, even those who might otherwise be considered as having relatively lower levels of power within the group. It is to this role of mutuality and support within the cooperative activity that I now turn.

The individual member's commitment to the solidarity cause requires a mutual engagement with others. This mutuality means that even seemingly trivial actions bear on the success of the project (cf. Ibana 1989, 48). Our interpersonal relations with other individuals (regardless of whether they are committed to the solidarity cause) reflect our level of commitment and contribute to the attainment of the goal. Bayertz explains the mutuality of political solidarity saying, "A fundamental equality exists between those involved, giving them the *mutual* right to expect help as it may be required" (1999a, 19). Mutuality might mean that the interests of others enters into my own practical reasoning in noninstrumental ways (Mason 2000, 27), that our fates interconnect such that our triumphs, joys, and hardships in relation to the cause are shared (cf. Crocker 1977), that each of us is bound to respond to all others in a reciprocal fashion (Ladd 1998; Thome 1999, 126), or some combination of these. Political solidarity may display a variety of manifestations of mutuality at any given time.

According to Lawrence Crocker, "People like the feeling of being part of a team where all members sink or rise together and equally" (1977, 263). Characterizing political solidarity as a team risks misrepresenting the types of bonds that form but does represent the sense of mutuality present within the loose, amorphous collective. Political solidarity fosters a sort of team spirit by tying together those interests and fates that pertain to the goal that unites the members. Setbacks in the social movement affect everyone who is committed to the cause; so too the joy of triumphs ripples through the entire movement. In spite of this mutuality, often individuals or smaller pockets within the solidary group bear the brunt of any harm or directly influence a particular outcome. Aggregating all the noticed triumphs, as well as those personal transformations that cannot be calculated, reveals the social movement's power and potential.

Mutuality, it might seem, opposes "free riders" (i.e., those who benefit from solidary struggles but who do not themselves participate) (Bayertz 1999a, 18). But solidarity is not a closed system or insular organization. The struggles for liberation are undertaken in mutuality, and the mutuality of the group does carry special privileges as well as special responsibilities. But the results of a political solidarity movement ought to be shared much more broadly than the solidary group. Liberation from oppression or cessation of injustice cannot themselves be doled out only to those who actually participated in the struggle to accomplish them.

John Ladd argues that "mutualism is implied by the idea of community" and has three facets (1998, 15). The first is that "interactions and relations between individuals within a community are characteristically manifold and many-sided" (Ladd 1998, 15). The second is equality; and the third facet of mutualism is the fact that responses are "vague, flexible, and open-ended" because of their reliance on context, situation, and ability. In other words, individuals respond to particular needs based on their own particular abilities and needs, as well as based on the assistance of others and the exigencies of the situation (Ladd 1998, 17). Ladd's remarks are useful for political solidarity, in spite of the fact that there is no formal community in the sense that he articulates. The relations between those who commit to political solidarity vary quite dramatically. While their lives will at times intertwine in important and meaningful ways through activism and assistance, often the personal transformation accompanied by feelings of hope shared with others constitutes the extent of the interconnections between individuals. But, as we have seen, the relationships also affect one another through less direct methods. Consuming products made in sweatshops three thousand miles away is contrary to a worker's own solidarity commitment aimed at better working conditions locally. If we come to see the campaigns for workers' rights as united under the banner of political solidarity, we also recognize that this breach of commitment affects the relationships between workers. Relationships within solidarity are multifaceted, complex, and often (but not necessarily) indirect; they are full of ever-new challenges as the cause that inspires the movement grows, transfigures, becomes fulfilled, or even disappears. Our responses to the sufferings and needs of others within solidarity, as we have seen, are mediated by the goal of the movement as well as by our own abilities and those with whom we join in solidarity. They are vague and open-ended, but they are also rooted and required in the commitment that brings us together in the first place.

Mutuality also means that those who commit to political solidarity commit to *ask*. They ask others in solidarity how they might help, how the collective action ought to proceed, what values are most important in informing the solidarity activity, and what about this particular form of injustice or oppression is most troubling. In political solidarity, as opposed to social solidarity, *need* forms the basis of the movement—need for justice, need for liberation, or need for protection. Within the other two forms of solidarity, need may signal weakness (Mason 2000, 31), but in political solidarity, our mutuality targets the needs of others and our activism attempts to address those needs in concrete ways. In small groups, mutual concern may appear more demanding than in larger groups (Mason 2000, 40), but a better interpretation for political solidarity is that the manner in which our needs are expressed and our mutuality addresses them changes to accommodate the relative distance between solidary actors. The demands of mutuality remain the same; the methods used within our reciprocal relationships vary.

As Ada Maria Isasi-Diaz asserts, solidarity entails the two interdependent elements of mutuality and praxis (Isasi-Diaz 1990, 33). These two elements replace charity and demand a real social connection with the sufferers of injustice even if some of them do not join in the social movement to overthrow it. Charity is usually one-sided, but mutuality assumes participants in solidarity are "working with" rather than "working for" those who suffer injustice or oppression. This is similar to what María Lugones describes as part of "world" traveling. Lugones contrasts the "loving perception" with the "arrogant perception" and argues that arrogant love entails domination, deception, "parasitism," and abuse. Loving perception, on the other hand, requires the independence of the perceivers; it is not based on parasitism. Loving perception also requires "world" traveling: perceivers travel to another's world as a means of identifying with them; that is, they attempt to see themselves and others through the perspective of the other (Lugones 1987, 17). Mutuality demands a non-arrogant perception of the other's needs as we listen and ask what we can do.

Of course, there may be times when our obligations to members within solidarity or to the oppressed conflict. In his discussion of the vulnerability model of morality, Goodin offers the following criteria for use when obligations to vulnerable parties conflict: "We must determine: (1) how strongly that party's interest's would be affected by our alternative actions and choices; and (2) whether or not he would be able to find other sources of assistance/protection if we failed him" (1985, 119). Although suggestive, Goodin's approach appears to assume a rather limited ability to respond. The possible vastness and diversity of the moral relation of political solidarity might meet the challenges of conflicting obligations quite differently. I take up this question in greater detail in Chapter 6.

Mutuality, because it emphasizes the activity of each person, is contingent on the commitment of those persons. Each individual must be the source of his or her own decisions and activities within the context of interdependent communities and varying social conditions. It is only then that true solidarity is possible (see also Anderson 1991, 112). Individual uniqueness contributes to rather than detracts from political solidarity. One way to ensure the balance between individual and community within group activity is to allow for social criticism. Because it is a social and political ethic, solidarity requires honest and diligent social criticism directed at both society as a whole and at the solidarity movement itself.

Relation to the Goal

The second primary relation is the commitment to a specified goal. This obligation is particularly manifest when an individual opts into the group or opts to leave the solidary group or otherwise cease his or her activism on behalf of the goal of any specific solidarity movement. At other times, the relation to the goal serves both as the justification and aim of political activism and as a mediating force within the solidary group. That is, an individual's activities and the group's activities are mediated by the final goal of solidarity. Of course, substantive goals in political solidarity are more or less amorphous. Projects change as goals are achieved or as needs change.

Although it is often overlooked in favor of the bond itself or even in favor of group conformity, it is the cause or goal that creates the social movement and compels individuals to join in solidarity. As we have seen, among types of groups, political solidarity is among those least likely to call for conformity (although perhaps among those most likely to call for agreement in vision). The final goal serves as a guide throughout the solidarity process. As Sandra Bartky comments, "The moral worth of collective action is a function of its specific ends and of the means employed to realize these ends" (2002, 75). Individual relations, that is, relations between individuals in solidarity and with those who are not involved in the solidarity movement, become altered according to one's conscious avowal of a cause. This goal mediation, however, must also allow for some change if that becomes necessary.

Among other things, what this relation to the final goal illustrates is that the means of solidarity may vary even within a single movement or cause, but they must engage the end. This helps to avoid the potential hazard of activists working at cross-purposes and may help obviate the potential problem of activists inadvertently working contrary to their overt purpose. To some extent, both of these are unavoidable in political solidarity, but maintaining the relation to the goal perhaps can alleviate or circumvent at least some of the pitfalls.

The goal of political solidarity may in some sense be idealistic—it is the hope for a brighter, better future, a future without at least some form of oppression or injustice. Moral ideals that guide action and mediate some interpersonal relations are implied in the fact that I am calling the relation to the goal a moral relation. Michael Walzer argues that obligations to ideals also oblige us to others; even after we renounce those ideals we must consider how our actions affect those who remain committed to them (1970, 6–7). Among other things, he argues that the social critic is challenging because he or she uses the values espoused by a society or group in critiquing it (1987, 42, 65, 89). I think we can also argue that the social critic uses different values—values that he or she thinks are more just—in critiquing the dominant group or society that he or she opposes. Social criticism is the primary means by which the relationship to the goal is carried out, and it is the primary duty of that relationship. The stance of the social critic is not that of detached observer or social enemy but rather that of skeptical idealist. The critic "finds a warrant for critical engagement in the idealism, even if it is a hypocritical idealism, of the actually existing moral world" (Walzer 1987, 61).

Social criticism evaluates social practices such as customs, language, laws, social mores, and religious and cultural rituals; it examines the values that support such social practices (Walzer 1987, 42, 65, 89). The three primary interrelated functions of social criticism are (a) to critique a society or social practice according to the society's espoused values or to question those values entirely; (b) to awaken feelings in response to value inconsistencies; and (c) to use (a) and (b) to establish communities of resistance for collective action (Scholz 2003b). Social criticism will often reject outright the values it identifies as problematic and replace them with new values to ensure liberation. At other times, the values themselves are worthy of defense but the social practices that arise from or around them are problematic.

Walzer describes social criticism as taking many forms: "Political censure, moral indictment, skeptical question, satiric comment, angry prophecy, utopian speculation" (1988, 9). "The primary or natural language of criticism is that of the folk; the best critics simply take hold of that language and raise it to a new pitch of intensity and argumentative power—like Luther in his pamphlets or Marx in *The Communist Manifesto*" (Walzer 1988, 9).

Social criticism, which examines the consistency or coherency of values, functions to ensure the unity of vision while simultaneously maintaining the validity of individual thought: "At its root, however, criticism is always moral in character, whether it is focused on individuals or political and social structures. . . . The special role of the critic is to describe what is wrong in ways that suggest remedy" (Walzer 1988, 9–10). Criticism not rooted in moral value is merely complaint. Equally important, however, is the diversity of moral values that may inspire and undergird political solidarity. The most far-reaching moral values within political solidarity are liberation and justice, but other moral values also penetrate social activism in important ways. This is where the particularity of social activism in the form of political solidarity asserts its importance. Each cause, each solidary group, will have particular aspirations and draw on particular moral values to achieve them. Any attempt to codify that process underestimates the importance of context in articulating political solidarities.

Although the goal of solidarity unifies and mediates the relations within the group, it does not and ought not to silence any of the members. Nothing in solidarity opposes dissent (cf. Bernstein 1989, 203). In fact, social criticism in political solidarity is twofold: The first is in part the justification of the group itself. That is, social criticism awakens some individuals to the injustice or oppression present in their midst. It holds oppressors and architects of injustice accountable. It also holds the rest of us, those of us who silently benefit from a system of injustice or oppression, accountable for our silence. This new consciousness compels some to respond in a collective manner, that is, to commit to political solidarity: "One of the chief tasks of social criticism is to give them their proper name, to say that *this* is tyranny—whenever religious or cultural associations perpetuate longstanding oppressive practices (the denial of education to their women members, for example); or whenever the company of men and women who control the market or the state dominate all the other distributive spheres; or whenever all the groups, or the strongest among them, adopt exclusionist policies, denying the everyday opportunities of social life to immigrants or blacks or Jews or any set of stereotyped and degraded others" (Walzer 1998, 52). The second function of social criticism relevant here is *within* solidarity movements. There are three elements to this form of social criticism. The first pertains to the means of political solidarity. Individual participants in solidarity must continually provide a critical role aimed at advancing toward the goal and the means used to achieve it. In other words, social criticism ensures that the ends of solidarity are not used to justify any and every means to achieve it.

Secondly, social criticism within political solidarity examines the various values that the solidary group draws upon. Suppose, for instance, that those in political solidarity claim that the values of the oppressed are or ought to be used to critique the dominant regime. Effective social criticism usefully demonstrates the conflicts in values and interests among the oppressed (Walzer 1988, 227). Differing values may yield opposing means to liberation. Social criticism can be used to examine the differences, highlight commonalities, and help the overall social movement move beyond the ideological conflicts that block effective social change. The social critic within a movement of political solidarity might suggest avenues of compatibility between two differing perspectives or ideologies. Two perspectives that seem to be completely at odds might find common ground on some third issue or approach. Moreover, the social critic might question whether there are other alternatives or other dangers or both about which we can agree. In addition, the social critic within the social movement could helpfully suggest the pitfalls of an ideological divide within the movement and look for mutually agreeable means of proceeding. Perhaps the movement will split, but it is equally plausible that their agreement about the overall goal of liberation will encourage those in political solidarity to see the possibilities and potentialities of a combination of their various approaches. Perhaps because it is something of an umbrella term and perhaps because it is oppositional in nature (opposing some injustice or oppression), political solidarity can accommodate some amount of disagreements among members that more formal social movements may not.

The other element of criticism within political solidarity is to continue the criticism if the new regime issued in under political solidarity fails or is worse than the old regime (Walzer 1988, 227). Describing the critic as hero, Walzer comments on the "doubly heroic." The social critic "criticizes the powerful and then he criticizes the others, the members of the complaining public—because they get the complaint wrong or don't complain loudly enough or only complain and never act or act recklessly and ineffectively" (Walzer 1988, 12).

Together with the elements of cooperation, social criticism also allows for individual input into the group process. As Goodin explains,

> No one ... is entitled to assume that the cooperative scheme is working perfectly. While the primary responsibility of everyone within such a scheme may be to discharge his own special responsibilities under it, each person also bears certain residual responsibilities under the scheme. One of these is the responsibility to monitor the workings of the scheme to make sure that everyone who is vulnerable is in fact being protected. Another is to lobby for the adjustment, reorganization, or replacement of schemes that prove deficient in that respect. Depending on the circumstances yet another may be to provide interim relief to those who would otherwise go unprotected until the lobbying effort succeeded. (Goodin 1985, 140–41)

One might say that solidarity resolves the tension between individual autonomy and group participation through the activities of social criticism and cooperation (cf. Walzer 1970, 195–202). As Walzer argues, "People experience solidarity separately and differently" (1998, 51; see also 1988, 231). Rather than being a weakness to an ethics, the variety of experiences of solidarity within a single movement lend to the strength of personal commitment. They also demonstrate the need for the critic to be embedded and involved in a situation rather than aiming at neutrality, impartiality, and detached objectivity.

Although Walzer does not clearly distinguish between the oppressed group and the solidary group, he claims that "the best possible movement of the oppressed requires the best possible criticism, dispassionate, tireless, utterly honest" (1970, 71–72). He charges intellectuals with the obligation to criticize. But this criticism must be well-founded; the critic must have proper standing. The critic should be neither committed to a party or other authority nor completely detached from all others (Walzer 1988, 237). The affiliated critic fails because he or she lacks the independence that would allow for honest social criticism. A critic who is utterly detached demonstrates bad faith by failing to recognize the possibilities for change: "For it is not just the feelings of the others, but their situation, ideology, arguments, and choices, that must be imaginatively entered into and intellectually joined. The possibility of doing this, for all the difficulties involved and the likely failures, establishes the right of criticism" (Walzer 1970, 73). One need not, however, be from among the oppressed to criticize the social conditions that result in oppression. In a later work, Walzer discusses two models of criticism. The first is "that the people are the instruments of social criticism" (1988, 25). This is the Marxian view of the critic as the head of the movement while the proletariat constitutes the body. The second model, and the one he claims as his own, places the social critic within the movement of the masses: "The people are the subjects of criticism: the revolt of the masses is the mobilization of common complaint. . . . the critic participates in an enterprise that is no longer his alone; he agitates, teaches, counsels, challenges, protests *from within*" (Walzer 1988, 26, emphasis in original).

Social criticism in political solidarity ensures that individual ideas are contributed and the movement does not subsume the participants: "Every man has his own revolution. Even when he joins with others in a party or movement, he does not wholly surrender his own sense of what a revolution is. Rather, he and his comrades together commit themselves to an idea they all share, and that idea must exercise some control over their future actions and obligations" (Walzer 1970, 181). Moreover, each participant in a social movement will likely also be involved in a number of other movements. Such diversity of experience and commitment carries the potential of enriching any given moral relation of political solidarity. Walzer calls for an increase in the number of associational ties, claiming that by providing more opportunities for individual participation, individuals will have a "growing sense of their own effectiveness" and be "our best protection against the parochialism of the groups in which they participate" (1994, 189–90).

But the critic and social criticism is also mediated by the other two moral relations within political solidarity, namely, the relation to other participants and the relation to those outside the solidary group. That mediation, as Walzer aptly points out, challenges solidary actors to understand that their actions toward one cause might be beneficial or detrimental toward another. So too the enemies one has today may be allies tomorrow:

> For criticism will never shake the world unless it is directed against specific features of the world that other people besides the critic recognize as wrongful, oppressive, brutal, or unjust. So the critic must be loyal to the others, to all those men and women for whom a different regime will make a difference. He cannot disregard their interests any more than he can, simply, grossly, repudiate their values. He is in opposition here, and here, and here; he is never in absolute opposition. (Walzer 1988, 237)

Relation to Nonmembers in the Larger Society, the Dominant Group, and Other Oppressed Persons

The third moral relation is the relation between the solidary group, either taken as a whole or as individual members, and the larger society or community. To some extent, of course, I have already presented an important aspect of political solidarity's relation to the larger society or dominant group: social criticism that is directed at identifying and critiquing some element of the dominant society or group. But there is more to this relation than just social criticism, and that is what I aim to uncover in this section.

The relation between solidary members and nonmembers can be broken down into a number of different but interconnected relations. The differences are due in part to the status of nonmembers. Oppressors or architects of injustice will have a different relation to the solidary group and its members than those who, while not part of the resistance movement nor directly responsible for oppression and injustice, are privileged because of the unjust situation. The relation to nonmembers may be a relation between individuals or a relation between groups or states; it might be characterized by anything from respect and indifference to disdain and animosity. Because political solidarity is necessarily oppositional, there will also likely be a fair degree of distrust or suspicion within any or all of the various types of relationships covered in this category. Finally, what about the relation between the solidary group and those oppressed who do not (or have not yet) committed to political solidarity? What about all those individuals and groups who suffer injustice but for whatever reason do not participate in the movement to change their situation? They may not see their situation as unjust, the logic of oppression may have silenced them, or they might lack the material means that would afford them the time and energy to resist. For any number of reasons, some among the oppressed will opt against participating in political solidarity. What is the relation between the solidary group and these others? What obligations animate that relationship?

Some might argue that the tension or opposition of political solidarity is in fact a severing of relations with the larger society or dominant group. Indeed there is some truth to this as the solidary group may overtly reject some of the values of the dominant group and in doing so set itself apart from that group, which it faults as oppressive. But political solidarity is not solely a response to oppressive practices wherein there is a clearly identified or identifiable oppressor. Oppression and injustice might be systemic and might even arise from explicit attempts to create a system of justice or fairness for all of society (Scholz 1995). So too, many of the individuals who join in political solidarity will be from among the privileged classes or groups and, in the case of systematic oppression, may even be from the group of oppressors. To say that there is no relation between the resisters and the others fails adequately to take account of the wide variety of participants within political solidarity and grossly underestimates the moral obligation of those in solidarity to all others. Often the literature on solidarity emphasizes the bonds and moral ties between those in solidarity. Given the unique oppositional nature of political solidarity, however, particular relations are formed that force a recognition of the moral dimensions and requirements between the solidary group, individually and collectively, and the larger society or dominant group.

The multiple moral demands of these relations constitute both the resistance to oppression and the activism for a libratory ideal at the heart of political solidarity. Of course, the original commitment to political solidarity might be weak or strong at any given point. Both, however, display multiple strategies for resisting injustice as well as numerous ways of working for the common goal of liberation. Lugones (2003) and Adrienne Rich (1986) both use an example of women quietly refusing some element of patriarchally prescribed housework as a form of resistance. Marx and Engels called for a much more overt form of resistance when they called on workers of the world to unite and overthrow their capitalist oppressors. Gandhi's satyagraha movement falls somewhere in the middle. What unites all the various forms of resistance, those mentioned as well as countless others, is both the personal transformation and the political challenge. Lugones describes resistance as operating under a different logic than subservience. The resister cannot and does not have servile intentions while the oppressed is perceived to be acting under the logic of oppression (Lugones 2003, 13). Moreover, she argues that resistance ought not to be understood merely as reaction; it is "response—thoughtful, often complex, devious, insightful response, insightful into the very intricacies of the structure of what is being resisted" (Lugones 2003, 29).

Three of the responsibilities entailed in this relation are (1) act according to conscience, (2) negotiate in good faith, and (3) act in a morally coherent manner with regard to the ends of solidarity and the existence of the larger community of which the solidary group is a part. Each of these plays a role in resistance and activism within social movements. I will also argue that the structure of political solidarity requires a rejection of violence as a means of activism in political solidarity.

At least part of resistance involves doing some of the same activities one usually does but in a different way. These might include the more subtle forms of resistance that have their nascence in a shift from compliant thinking to oppositional thinking. Engaging in oppositional thinking is reacting against a practice or system of practices to disavow the practices of daily life perceived to be unjust. For those who are oppressed, this could include refusing to see oneself as the oppressor prescribes. Paulo Freire's notion of internalized oppression demonstrates the need for resistance of this sort. If the oppressed have internalized oppression or have adopted the oppressive consciousness, then they measure themselves according to the oppressive look. He or she sees him or herself as an object in the world of another. One has come to adopt uncritically the consciousness of the oppressors; I see myself as "naturally" inferior because that is how the oppressors see me. Resistance as a shift in thinking rejects these perceptions. Accordingly, some of the same activities I usually perform may take on new, libratory meanings when I resist the oppressor's consciousness.

Resistance might also involve doing some different activities in the same way. For example, one effective means of resisting oppression is when the oppressed refuse the role they have been given and perform the activities they are usually excluded from performing. Rosa Parks sitting in the front of the bus, other black civil rights activists sitting in the whites-only sections of restaurants, women applying for admission in men-only clubs: these are just a few instances of doing different things (activities usually excluding the oppressed as part of their oppression) in the same way (the same as oppressors usually do those activities).

Resistance necessarily changes communal relations as well as the relations among those in political solidarity. Resistance confronts the violence of an oppressive or unjust system by creating strategies to cope while effectively working for social change. These strategies change our chosen communities as well as our involuntary communities (Lugones 2003, 186).

I have already alluded to the fact that activism, concrete activity, is a constitutive obligation in a solidarity ethics. But activism cannot be for its own sake. It must be enlightened by social criticism and enlivened by the multifaceted relations among members in solidarity. This sort of reflective action within solidarity is often called praxis in order to distinguish it from other forms of practical activity or resistance. Praxis is reflective action in mutuality aimed at liberation of all peoples.

Activism occurs on multiple levels and takes countless forms. One important aspect of activism is the change in personal behavior that occurs when an individual adopts a cause according to conscience. This personal transformation becomes a form of activism when its effects are publicly manifest such that it challenges the thoughts and behaviors of others. Boycotts, protests and marches, and public forums and symposiums exposing injustice or oppression exemplify some of the most common forms of activism.

Activism that earns the name of "grassroots activism" usually takes the form of either door-to-door canvassing or activism that emerges from the bases, that is, from those who are most directly affected by the oppression or injustice. Door-to-door canvassing links consciousness-raising with activism for social change. Advocates for a cause expend energy and efforts talking with others in an instructive, educative manner. The object, of course, is always to convince others to dedicate their own efforts and energies to the cause, but canvassing has the added duty of connecting solidary members and nonmembers in such a way that the specifics of political solidarity are conveyed. Hearing about a social movement from an advocate in a face-to-face manner carries the benefit of making the cause personal for those who are unfamiliar with it. Grassroots activism of this sort can also help to keep the activist responsible and accountable for his or her actions. A personal connection, perhaps even a personal relationship with one's neighbors or friends who are not involved in a social movement, facilitates more civil dialogue for change. When opposition is expressed under the guise of a cause rather than through the particular actions and words of individuals, it is easier to avoid hearing what is said. Door-to-door canvassing puts a face to the oppressive, privileged, or complacent individual as well as the advocate for the cause. Of course, door-to-door canvassing is not without its flaws. In the United States, where people are less schooled in civic discourse and where the home is thought of as private, the appearance of an individual espousing certain political views at one's door might be an unwelcome sight. Nevertheless, talking with people about issues builds recognition for the issue itself, potentially adding a diversity of new perspectives to the issue as canvassers learn from those they speak with as well; it also connects individuals who might otherwise have little or no reason to see themselves as tied together. In his extensive history of the Polish Solidarity movement, Lawrence Goodwyn argues that "protest moves from idea to action when it becomes social—that is, when it is organized so that people are acting rather than writing or talking about acting" (1991, xvii). Grassroots activism, such as door-to-door canvassing among those not already convinced of the efficacy of a cause, moves the actors from talking among themselves to acting for social change.

Electronic communication has of late replaced some door-to-door efforts to participate in movements for social change. Much of the electronic activity is best understood as consciousness-raising rather than activism per se. E-mail, blogs, online petitions, and informational and polemical web sites all carry the educative function of grassroots activism but fall short of requiring either the personal transformation or interpersonal connections that I used in characterizing grassroots activism through door-to-door canvassing. Goodwyn claims that "people who object to one or more features of the received cultures in which they live—most people—but who also cannot be observed doing anything about it are routinely described as 'apathetic.' . . . To become real—that is, to become historical actors—apathetic people, it is presumed, need their consciousness raised" (1991, xx). Cyber protestors surely do something in signing online petitions, reading blogs, and forwarding e-mails and thus cannot be considered apathetic people, but what they do is exchange information and discuss ideas. At times, this will reach beyond the self-selected audience, as when an advocacy e-mail gets forwarded to a known opponent, but without the face-to-face discussion there is no responsibility on the sender's side to make a personal connection and no responsibility on the receiver's end to read the e-mail or act on it (other than putting it in the trash, of course). Still, if the various forms of information dissemination available are used effectively, they can be important tools in promulgating a position and raising awareness about an issue or cause.

In addition to door-to-door canvassing and cyber consciousness-raising, grassroots activism of this sort might entail protests. Indeed, protests also play a crucial role in the other major form of grassroots activism, that is, from the ground up. Protests are generally of two sorts: immediate and symbolic. Immediate protests are direct responses to an unjust action or event and are usually aimed at halting an immediate practice. I chose the term "immediate" because the protests have an urgency about them. Often they are spontaneous rallies and, for many participants, they may spark or enflame a commitment to more sustained praxis in political solidarity. I follow Thomas Hill with the use of the term "symbolic protest" (1979). Symbolic protest certainly has its benefits, and participants often feel a sense of social importance in participating in the protest at the time. The urgency found in immediate protest, however, is not present in symbolic protest. Symbolic protests raise awareness, articulate demands, and pull participants in political solidarity together for concrete action, but they are not designed to stand between oppressors and oppressed or halt an immediate injustice the way an immediate protest would.

Activism that starts with those who suffer from oppression, injustice, or tyranny, and, through their efforts, expands to include others—some of whom will not be directly affected by the oppression—highlights what is perceived and experienced as the most egregious parts of oppression; this sort of activism might even suggest strategies for overcoming them. By coming from the situation of oppression or injustice, this form of activism can reveal crucial elements of the experience of those who suffer.

The multiple aspects of oppression and injustice complicate liberation struggles. Suppression and oppression must be abolished by adopting the tactic of opportunity and efficiency. Each person's individual situation guides their participation. Nevertheless, in any liberation struggle one may experience any number of antinomies. In order to fight for the liberation of some, we inevitably do disservice to others either by our inattention to their plight or more directly by further entrenching oppressive practices while we seek liberation. Many social movements provide troubling examples of such antinomies. For instance, the nineteenth-century women's movement, led by bourgeois white women in the United States, sacrificed the personhood of black women in an effort to advance the cause for "all" (read "white, educated, middle-class") women. Similarly, efforts to obtain remuneration for women who regularly perform housework simultaneously function to cement gendered divisions of labor. Following Maurice Merleau-Ponty, Sonia Kruks (2001) refers to this problem as the problem of "dirty hands" accompanying much political action. Failing to act may make one culpable, but acting is also fraught with potential moral problems. One's actions might yield an unforeseen harm. Feminist advocates against domestic violence argued for a mandatory-arrest policy in some jurisdictions. This policy, however, often worked against women as much as it worked in their behalf. Rather than avoid these sorts of paradoxes by not acting, we must continue to act but be ever cognizant of the potentially hazardous outcomes of our actions and engage in careful social criticism to try to foresee the problems before they occur.

A related issue, and certainly one that falls in the range of activism, is the question of violence within the moral relation of political solidarity. Is it ever appropriate to employ violent means to attain a goal in a movement of political solidarity that aims at ending oppression and injustice? Is there a difference between violent activism and violent resistance for social change? Can violence be justified on the grounds of political solidarity? Although arguments based on idealized principles of political solidarity might be offered, and I will offer some in the rest of this chapter, it should be kept in mind that the practical realities of oppression and political solidarity challenge even the most encompassing of theories. Complex situations of oppression and the solidaristic movements for liberation that arise in response to them pose numerous challenges that defy easy explanations or pat answers to questions like these.

Oppression is often directly or indirectly physically violent, and some have described it as a form of violence because oppression affects the consciousness of those victimized by it. Iris Young argues that violence is one of the "five faces of oppression," and Freire argues that both the oppressed and the oppressor are infected by the violence of oppressive consciousness (Young 1990; Freire 1968). Using violence to confront and topple unjust and oppressive systems would seem to be an almost natural reaction under such conditions. Like nonviolent resistance, violence is sometimes used by individuals, groups, organizations, or mobs—after all, activists will employ a wide variety of methods in their effort to bring about social change. But it is important to remember that resistance may be practiced both within the relations of political solidarity and outside of it. The question is whether, as a moral relation, political solidarity precludes some of the methods used by resisters and activists.

At times, some of the more conventional tactics of activists are perceived to be violent by those people whose lives are challenged or disrupted in the activism. Protests, blockades, letter campaigns, and posters and leaflets that disrupt business or identify racist or sexist practices within businesses might be considered harmful insofar as they carry the potential of diminishing the business prospects or upset the status quo. Properly speaking, however, the activist methods listed are not what is meant by "violence" in asking whether it is ever justified in political solidarity. Rather, by violence is meant the intentional infliction of physical harm or injury to another person or property. Disruption of business or personal confrontation and embarrassment do not count as violence but instead not only can but in many cases probably should be used as tools to bring about social change. The question of violence for political solidarity, then, is whether physical injury to members of the oppressor group or serious damage to their property is compatible with the form of unity understood as political solidarity (see also Scholz 2007).

Activism is a tool and an obligation of political solidarity, but an important part of what makes that relation different from other activist campaigns and what makes the activism in political solidarity different from activism practiced under other guises is the critical reflection on the relationships in and out of the solidary group with an eye toward achieving a particular goal. While violence might be a part of some activist struggles, it is inconsistent with the form of group unity in liberation struggles that involves the complex relations of political solidarity. In the rest of this chapter, I look at the effects of violent methods on the three primary moral relations found in political solidarity and address some possible objections to the prohibition against violence in political solidarity.

Conclusion

Activity within solidarity movements, according to the duties of social criticism I have discussed in this chapter, must be measured against or in accordance with both the substantive and the formative goal of political solidarity. Not all means to achieve these goals will be justified. Oppression, tyranny, and injustice frequently employ intentional and direct violence as a means to sustain themselves, and if it is to oppose the dominant values and logic at the heart of oppressive or unjust practices, political solidarity must take seriously that opposition. If the nature of political solidarity is a struggle for liberation in opposition to a system or group that uses violence, then in opposing violence, political solidarity cannot in principle utilize violent means. The struggle against oppressive systems would not grant legitimacy to the value or logic of violence in the liberation struggle because it is a value of the oppressor system. To utilize violence, political solidarity risks recreating some of the system of injustice, oppression, or tyranny within the movement or the new regime it seeks to establish. In a similar vein, I discuss in Chapter 7 the use of just war. Kevin Doran (1996) argues that the violence of war is contrary to solidarity per se because the logic of war is division—in contrast to the logic of solidarity as unity. In contrast, May (2007) presents some cases wherein military intervention might be justified, but it is important to note that he uses the moral rubric of social solidarity as the basis for articulating an obligation to distant others in his argument. The oppositional nature of political solidarity, together with the social criticism emerging from the obligations participants have toward their collective goal and the unity of cause, alters justificatory tools and yields a different assessment of the role of violence.

In some movements of political solidarity, the social change that is sought is within a social and political system that is otherwise acceptable. For instance, when full rights of citizenship are denied some members of the community on the basis of some oppressive identity, those who commit to political solidarity might aim to challenge the exclusion and gain access to those rights within the structures of the system. Utilizing violence on the social, legal, and political structures to which one aims to gain rightful access could be counterproductive as it both appears to desire and destroy those structures simultaneously (Walzer 1970, 61). The aims of the solidarity group risk being misrepresented and the relation to the goal of political solidarity appears to be violated when violence is used against the legal and political system that currently grants rights to some while depriving the oppressed group. The means of political solidarity within a society must take into consideration the effects on a social and legal system to which access is sought.

In addition, within the solidary group itself, the use of violent methods to effect social change poses serious challenges as well. As we have seen, the relationship between members forms the unity of solidarity and entails co-operation and mutuality. At times, of course, members will disagree and actions may even conflict or be misguided attempts to attain the ends of political solidarity. Nevertheless, the relationships between participants are important and serve as another rule by which actions ought to be measured. Cooperation, mutuality, and communication mean that in acting one considers whether his or her actions could be agreed to by others in the group or whether one's actions might tear at the unity that is political solidarity. Destructive militant responses to oppression risk not only alienating some members of the movement who do not support the use of violence but also puts the very unity itself into jeopardy as participants acknowledge their inability to cooperate with such tactics. An activist tool that has the potential to undermine the movement by splintering the unity of solidarity is contrary to the obligations of mutuality and cooperation.

Violent activism used by actors in political solidarity also contradicts the duty to those outside the solidary group. Members of a privileged or oppressor class, and others outside the solidary group, might be or become allies, potential or realized members in the political solidarity campaign (Walzer 1970, 67). Participants in political solidarity have an obligation to communicate with those who will be affected by social change or who are responsible for the unjust conditions; there is an implicit obligation to educate others regarding the cause and explain the opposition. A similar argument may be made regarding the need to negotiate in good faith with the openness or willingness to compromise. According to Walzer, "Rebels can never deny to their opponents the recognition they themselves seek" (1970, 41). Violent forms of activism, however, preclude meaningful communication or education and thus violate the obligation to others. The move to violence closes channels of communication that might draw allies into the movement.

One objection to my argument is that it might also rule out other forms of confrontation or radical displays insofar as such actions would cut off possible avenues of communication with the larger society one wishes to change. By restricting "violence" to violent activism understood as the intentional infliction of physical harm or injury, however, I allow other forms of activism that may be quite socially disruptive. Protests, boycotts, pickets, blogging, and other forms of activism are some of the possible means by which the solidary group spreads its message and brings injustice to light in the social sphere. In contrast to Young (2001), who draws a distinction between protests and democratic deliberation, I view protests and nonviolent confrontation as compatible with democratic deliberation; confrontation (even militant nonviolent confrontation) names a problem and demands recognition through public debates and discussions.

Another objection arises out of the nature of nonviolent activism itself. Some have argued that a movement needs at least some violent resistance—perpetrated perhaps by those outside the movement itself—in order to make effective use of nonviolent activism (Tyson 2004, 68–72). For instance, it has been suggested that Gandhi's satyagraha movement and King's civil rights movement succeeded in using nonviolence *because* oppressors were taunted into using violence against the protestors. In such a situation, the nonviolent activists appear to hold the higher moral ground, but their position is ensured by those outside the movement willing to use violence. Timothy Tyson wryly suggests that Martin Luther King's nonviolent resistance benefited from the "'nonviolent' rocks, bricks, and bottles" thrown at police by those outside the Southern Christian Leadership Conference (SCLC), which spurred the segregationists to attack King and his followers violently (2004, 70). But the problem with this objection is that the nonviolent response followed the violence of oppression. Nonviolence does not need violent allies; the violence of oppression provides the stage on which the nonviolent resistance may be displayed.

One of the most important objections is that nonviolent activism requires an already-established subjectivity or recognition within the larger society. Internalized inferiority or the social degradation of oppression, it might be argued, keeps resisters from seeing alternatives to violent action. As Frantz Fanon argued, violence might be seen as the way to reclaim one's status as a human agent in a society bent on domination (Fanon 1952, 1963; Tyson 2004, ch. 7). In response, recall that political solidarity is based on an individual commitment. Individuals who join with others to struggle for liberation or combat an injustice exercise agency in that very political commitment. Subjectivity is, at least to some extent, reclaimed logically prior to any decision about activist methods. Tyson also hints that nonviolent activism may be the purview of the wealthier or elite classes, which seemingly have more time to both plot against and endure systems of oppression.

Of course, political solidarity is not the only form of group unity in these struggles nor is it always found in liberation struggles; other groups and organizations may form without the commitment to relationships within the group, beyond the group, and to the formative as well as the substantive goal. While the relations of political solidarity and the duties associated with those relations might rule out violent forms of activism as a possible means to effect social change, other liberation struggles might find other means of justifying violence. For instance, might violence be justified on the basis of self-defense?

In *The Wretched of the Earth* (1963), Fanon presents a moving call to arms, justifying violence or the use of force to resist colonialism, thereby freeing the colonized from the psychological damage inflicted by the colonizers. In *Pedagogy of the Oppressed* (1968), Freire also discusses violence, arguing that it never begins with the oppressed but also not denying that the oppressed might use it. Neither Fanon nor Freire explicitly address the normative requirements of political solidarity; both speak instead of resistance to oppression or individual and collective self-defense. Freire speaks of liberation struggles divided into two phases: "In the first, the oppressed unveil the world of oppression and through the praxis commit themselves to its transformation. In the second stage, in which the reality of oppression has already been transformed, this pedagogy ceases to belong to the oppressed and becomes a pedagogy of all people in the process of permanent liberation" (1968, 36). The distinction between resisting oppression and joining in political solidarity may not always be evident in the individual lives of activists or the structures of particular movements. Nevertheless, moral justifications can and do often hinge on just such a distinction. Resistance to oppression may take many forms: it might be part of the activism within political solidarity but it also might be a form of self-defense or defense of another outside the moral relations of political solidarity. A principle of self-defense might be used to justify resistance, even violent resistance, when the violence of oppression directly threatens the existence of oneself or another. But the principle of self-defense here is a justificatory structure outside the moral relations of political solidarity. Walzer also points out that "self-defense and mutual defense are also limiting principles. They apply within the immediate context of violence and not more generally" (1970, 64). So self-defense might justify some instances of the use of violence—as when an oppressor is caught in the act of brutalizing someone—but as a strategy for the political solidarity movement, it violates the principles on which the movement is based. What this reveals is that the commitment to solidarity may at times conflict with the principle of self-defense. Political solidarity itself is incompatible with physically violent forms of activism and resistance, but activists may confront the choice between using violence in self-defense and respecting the relationships of political solidarity (Scholz 2007, 48–51). Just as those who practice civil disobedience must weigh the costs of breaking an unjust law against the damage to the rule of law, so too must those who act in resistance to oppression weigh the cost of using violence in self-defense against the damage to the unity of political solidarity. Walzer argues that we can issue neither praise nor blame when the oppressed employ spontaneous violence or violent resistance in self-defense (1970, ch. 3). We can, however, examine what sort of value we put on the moral relations of political solidarity and decide whether employing violent methods is worth sacrificing those relations.

FOUR

The Solidary Collective

Solidarity is a moral relation that creates a unity among peoples, but how does that unity come about and what is the precise nature of the unity that distinguishes solidarity from "community," "society," "organization," "association," or "party"? Ontologically and morally, the solidary group differs from these others and some might even question its status as a group altogether. I argue that we can continue to call that which forms for political solidarity a group or collective in spite of the fact that it does not resemble other types of groups united around a common identity, shared attribute, common history, or communal experience.

Solidarity may be counted among the forms of collective action but each individual makes a personal commitment; solidarity, as a moral concept, includes prescriptions for both individual and collective moral action. Among these commitments is the moral relationship with others and the duties entailed in that relationship. I discussed the moral aspects of that relationship in the previous chapter. The social and ontological aspects of the relations that form the solidary group are worth pausing to consider here. Interest in voluntary associations, cosmopolitanism, civic participation, and solidarity is burgeoning in the philosophical literature, and with good reason. Globalization in business and entertainment, innovative global communication systems, gross international crises in human rights, transnational environmental hazards, and the widening gap between the rich and the poor around the world, among other international and global issues, all conspire to diminish or erase the importance of national borders for civic participation. Involvement in political life takes a new shape and addresses alternative dimensions of social existence, both new and old. The family, the club, the workplace, and the world itself become the loci for politics. Coupled with this is an ever-increasing confidence in the power of collective action to bring about social and structural change.

Political solidarity, which arguably has been present and active in social arrangements for centuries, becomes recognized as a powerful tool for political involvement as well as a worthy topic of study for scholars as one of the many forms of voluntary association through which an individual both shapes him- or herself and contributes to the shaping of society.

In this chapter, I examine what it means to call political solidarity a voluntary association or, more precisely, a form of collective action, by focusing on the group itself. The chapter is divided into four main sections. The first section discusses how a solidary group differs from other types of groups. With particular attention to the moral differences, I compare and contrast the solidary group with other groups common in social activism or social change, namely, organizations, associations, parties, collectives, and communities. I also distinguish solidarity from society. The theory of political solidarity, as a political or social theory, does not aim at constructing a society and ought not to be confused with those types of social and political theory that set out to articulate the just society, such as social contract theory. The second section examines the relation between the solidary group and the oppressed group. As I have already intimated, these groups are distinct, though their membership may overlap. Most articulations of solidarity conflate these two groups (and for rather compelling reasons), but, as I will show, there are both moral and ontological reasons for understanding them as separate and distinct.

Social and political activism to bring about social change rarely occurs in isolated pockets. Activists are often involved in multiple causes and their efforts at times overlap and at other times contradict. The third section of this chapter offers some consideration of the moral issues that arise when political solidarities interconnect, overlap, and contradict.

The final section of the chapter considers the relationship between democracy and solidarity by looking at decision-making within solidarity activity and the solidary group. I bypass the larger question of whether participation in political solidarity is a form of civic participation because I presume that it is. I also presume that such activity is a right of democratic societies and indeed a human right. Michael Walzer is correct when he says that "in a democratic society, action-in-common is better than withdrawal and solitude, tumult is better than passivity, shared purposes (even when we don't approve) are better than private listlessness" (1994, 188–89). Instead of arguing that political solidarity is a constituent part of democracy, I look at the converse: whether democracy is a part of political solidarity. This gets taken up again in the next chapter, which looks at some of the obstacles to and issues of participation and equality within solidary groups.

Collectives, Associations, Organizations, and Other Groups for Social Change

Forms of unity among peoples abound. Some forms have clear moral requirements embedded in the very relation, but others are merely descriptive categories that help distinguish one form of unity from another. Some have formal decision-making structures while others are groups by ascription with no clear ties between members that would call for decision-making. Some have long-standing, deeply rooted ties, and others are quite short-lived, united for a brief encounter or task. Of the myriad forms of unity that might be classified, categorized, and analyzed, solidarity retains a unique and unrivaled stance largely because of the moral obligations inherent in it, but also because of the multiplicity of ends, aims, feelings, and relations evoked by the term. Chapter 1 offered an account of three broadly construed species of solidarity, and Chapter 2 illustrated some of the various forms of unity that might form under the banner of political solidarity. One of the primary distinguishing characteristics of solidarity is that it implies equality and reciprocity, whereas mere unity may entail domination (cf. Lugones 1987). Unity might be structured by some mutuality but might also rely on elements of control, force, or coercion. In this section, I distinguish political solidarity from other forms of unity that have social change as a more or less explicit aim or end. In the case of each of these, the distinctions are not meant to be sharp or mutually exclusive. On the contrary, solidarity often or even usually involves a multiplicity of other unions under its broad category heading. Political solidarity might consist of free-floating individuals, informal friendship groups, formal social justice organizations or associations, and national political parties, all at once or individually and incrementally.

Recall the categories of political solidarity I offered in Chapter 2: weak and strong, local, national, and international. By and large, these categories are determined by an individual's commitment but they also describe a group. A group of worker's acting collectively to change the conditions at the factory where they work is a strong local movement. Other individuals may join in solidarity with the workers by not crossing picket lines or by boycotting the company's product until conditions are adequately addressed. Still others, say nonunion workers in different jobs at the same factory, may join the strikers. (And, of course, some workers will opt not to protest, that is, not to join in solidarity.) Each of the actors in solidarity will experience varied levels of commitment, but together they perform collective action. That, then, is what I mean by the solidary group: All those people who self-identify as members in solidarity to bring about change for social justice.

But another example instructively illustrates the difficulty of discussing the theoretical structure of the "solidary group." Consider, for instance, the issue of fair trade chocolate or coffee. A middle-class woman in the United States may commit her resources and strengths to the project of ensuring just wages for workers through her support of fair trade products. Indeed, she may be so committed that she buys, eats, and drinks only fair trade products when they are available. We describe her actions as being in solidarity with fair trade farmers in Central America. Her commitment is weak or strong just as the farmer's commitment is weak or strong. The question is: Do they form a unity? And the answer for political solidarity is "Yes, of course they do." Their actions, in spite of the distance between them, make them co-participants in political solidarity oriented around bringing about a change for social justice in trade. They act individually, but their individual actions, as well as the individual actions of countless others, contribute to collective action. But how do we describe their unity, collective, or solidary group? Clearly, it lacks central organizational structure, strong emotive bonds between participants, and collective decision-making methods. But this, like the workers and their supporters, is an example of political solidarity; their unity is a solidary group.

Earlier, I argued, with Kurt Bayertz, that political solidarity is an oppositional politics. One solution to the question of how to characterize the solidary group or specify the unity is to define the group negatively as the group of people against some practice, system, or structure they perceive to be unjust. Alternatively, we might offer a loose characterization of the group that highlights the unique unities of solidarity while it also belies the lack of formal structure. Here, it might be worth examining some of the alternative forms of unity or natures of social bonds, such as camaraderie, organization and association, crowd, and party. Political solidarity cannot be entirely reduced to or adequately explained by any of these other forms of unity. Similarly, the types of unities I discuss do not exclude one another either—members of organizations might experience camaraderie, or they might not. Comrades might form organizations, or they might not. The point in delving into these various forms of unity is to bring out the unique characteristics of solidarity, in part through examining what solidarity is not.

Camaraderie, a form of unity generally less affiliated with social change than others, distinguishes itself from solidarity through the nature of the bonds and the moral expectations they determine. Those who share camaraderie with each other share a friendship, which is very often the source of the camaraderie. Individuals may share some common interests, just as friends may share likes and dislikes. Some more formal organizations like fraternities and sororities, athletic teams, book clubs, or gangs, and some less formal gatherings like the folks who meet at the local coffee shop each morning to discuss politics and the weather, engage in camaraderie. Camaraderie is mutually supportive, but the mutual support of each individual is motivated by friendship. The relationship is not mediated by any sort of shared aim or end, especially one oriented around justice or liberation. Friends of this sort come to each other's aid, but often camaraderie lacks the critical judgment that would require one to confront or challenge an unjust action. A gang of thieves or drug dealers may enjoy camaraderie. So too might the men at a law firm or the women at a university. Enjoying camaraderie does not make the relation just. Camaraderie might also be exclusive (though, of course, it need not be). Camaraderie does not carry the moral requirement that one try to stop one of their members from perpetrating an immoral or unjust action. In fact, as my examples of camaraderie ought to illustrate, camaraderie itself may be organized around illegal or immoral activity.

But camaraderie, like solidarity, does entail positive duties to another, and it is a unity that has the potential to transform individual consciousness. It is also the case that individuals who join in solidarity may develop or share a camaraderie with each other. The crucial differences between political solidarity and camaraderie seem to be the emphasis of the former on social justice, the limitation of the latter to include only those people one can actually know and with whom one has interactions, and the social criticism informed by a commitment to a cause mandated by political solidarity.

Organizations and associations have formal structures with decision-making procedures, membership policies or criteria, and often clearly defined agendas or goals. Often, organizations also develop formal relationships with institutional structures of the larger society. The AARP (American Association of Retired Persons) and the NAACP (National Association for the Advancement of Colored People), for instance, both have formal lobbying relationships with the legislative branch of the U.S. government. These sorts of relationships would require the larger social institutional structure to recognize the organization in some widely accepted fashion. Smaller organizations or associations, like a neighborhood commission or a playgroup for toddlers, may also have some relationship to the larger social institutional structure but are less likely to. In either case, however, such a relationship is not a necessary condition of being an organization per se, though recognition by the larger social institutional structure may be a requirement of some organizations or associations depending on their nature.

A party, like an organization or an association, probably has a formalized structure with membership criteria (even if only minimally that a person must declare their party affiliation) and stated agenda. What makes parties distinct is that they are factions of some larger group, organization, or society. Political parties are the obvious example, but one could also imagine factions within large institutions or organizations such as universities or labor unions.

Michael Hechter distinguishes "*crowds* (which have no membership criteria); *social categories* (in which criteria are defined for those people who are *not* involved in the activity); and *corporations* (which are defined by ownership rights, rather than by joint participation in activities)" (1987, 16). Political solidarity, on the other hand, creates a group of sorts out of the individuals who make personal commitments to a similar cause and to other similarly committed individuals. Hechter's list is interesting because it shifts the focus from the purpose of the groups he mentions to the membership criteria or categories.

The term community tends to get used as a sort of catchall term for any type of unity. It is not inappropriate or wrong to use it for solidarity, though the community that forms for solidarity should, I think, be considered as unique in itself. Communities may or may not have unifying traits or close ties with one another. Think, for example, of a "community of scholars." It might be the case that such a phrase implies that the scholars all know one another, share in some common or even overlapping interests, and engage in mutually helpful and morally sustaining relationships. The term might, however, also simply mean a reference group, as when one describes all philosophers as a community of scholars. This example demonstrates the varying usage and meaning of the term community. The solidary community does have some shared interests that develop out of their mutual commitment to a cause. Some solidaristic movements are also tight-knit groups that share other overlapping interests or concerns; some, however, are more like reference groups. The person who steadfastly buys fair trade coffee out of a commitment to solidarity is engaged in a political act and helps to constitute a solidary community with all other fair-trade-only coffee drinkers. They likely do not necessarily, however, share other overlapping interests that would otherwise constitute communal identity. Their identity as a community rests in the notion that they are distinct from coffee drinkers who, through lack of critical awareness, lack of concern, apathy, or convenience, drink coffee that is not fairly traded.

Collectives, like communities, are difficult to pin down. At times the term means something along the lines of a commune while at other times it appears as a random mixing of people who simply happen to be associated in some way. In the former model, a collective would have fairly strict guidelines for membership and participation, which could include structures for moral and social interaction. In the latter, looser understanding of collective, there are no such rules.

Virginia Held tries to strike a middle ground with her characterization of collective as entailing some form of decision-making structure. She defines a "random collection of individuals" as a group of persons distinct from the "set of all persons" but "lacking a decision method" (Held 1970, 471). Random collections of individuals, as opposed to collectives, might be called a group but they do not have an organizational structure that would provide for decision-making and facilitate the collective acting on decisions. Held contrasts random collections with "organized groups" or "collectivities." These latter are distinguishable by their membership characteristics "but especially by . . . possession of a decision method for action" (1970, 471). So, whereas the passengers on a public bus are a random collection, the members of a military troop are an organized group or collectivity.

But requiring a decision-making procedure or method of action may swing the characterization of collective too far toward a formal organization. Consider, for instance, the problem of collective responsibility. When moral theorists discuss collective responsibility, they rarely discuss the decision-making procedures or method of action. The bulk of the literature on collective responsibility actually pertains to a collectivity's failure to act. Often the examples pertain to random associations of people—the disparate and separated people who witness a gang rape from their apartment buildings for instance. At best, decision-making is done on an individual basis but their collective inaction defines them as a collective. Of course, collectivities also do describe things like the group of bus passengers who work together to right a bus, described in the previous chapter. Solidarity seems to fall somewhere in between—where decision-making is often individual but the decisions themselves, and in particular the decisions to act, constitute the collective.

In opposition to Held, Sonia Kruks explains that "collectives" are individuals "serialized, atomized, isolated, and placed in competition with each other." "Groups," on the other hand, "involve organized and conscious nodes of resistance of various kinds (ranging from union activity, to spontaneous participation in brief acts of sabotage, to attempted revolution)" (Kruks 2001, 122).

Accounts of group ontology and dynamic abound, and, like communities and collectives, these accounts of "groups" rarely result in consensus primarily because groups themselves come in so many different shapes and sizes with so many different purposes or aims. Jean-Paul Sartre famously provides an analysis of groups as well as the process they undergo in folding into one another in his *Critique of Dialectical Reason* (1991 [1960]). The four types of groups Sartre describes affect the self-identity and exterior identity of each individual differently. Seriality denotes the group related by pure alterity; individuals are collected by their passive experience of habit. "Groups in fusion" have a clear project; groups in fusion fold into pledge groups that are organized around clearly defined functions. The fourth type of group, institutional groups, take on a life of their own in that the project of the institutional group ends up opposing the self-actualization of the members of the group. The orientation of groups in fusion and pledge groups makes them most applicable to political solidarity. These two groups organize around a goal but affirm the individuality or uniqueness of contributors. The pledge group is slightly more formal than most examples of political solidarity, though if one were to loosen the understanding of pledge, then the commitment individuals make to political solidarity may stand in for the more formal pledge.

The group that forms in political solidarity comes close to fitting what Iris Young calls a "social group." She distinguishes social groups from aggregates and associations in her *Justice and the Politics of Difference* (1990). An association is a "formally organized institution, such as a club, corporation, political party, church, college, or union" (Young 1990, 44) and an aggregate is a "classification of persons according to some attribute" without necessarily experiencing a shared sense of identity. Social groups, according to Young, are non-substantial entities that "exist only in relation to other groups" (1990, 46). Of course, the solidary group does exist in relation to other groups, but the personal commitment to identify and act in solidaristic ways, rather than purely opposition, makes the solidary group different from just any social group.

In spite of the differences among the accounts of communities, groups, and collectives, we can see that all three tend to be relatively fluid, membership might be ascriptive or self-determined, and there may or may not be formal decision-making structures. Although not terribly definitive, that is precisely the sort of openness or ambiguity that an account of political solidarity requires.

Political solidarity can result in a collective, a community, or a group depending on the strength of the cause and the extent of the solidary relation. I use "collective" and "group" interchangeably in part because I want to emphasize solidarity's place in the literature on collective responsibility and in part because I want to acknowledge the wide variety of relations that form under the banner of political solidarity. Only rarely do I use "community," and that is restricted to cases where I am discussing the relations between participants in solidarity. The particular instantiation of political solidarity would determine the more specific nature of the group, whether there are decision-making mechanisms, and how inclusive the group may become.

Individuals who join in political solidarity make a personal as well as an ethical and political commitment. For this reason, joining in or committing to the struggles of political solidarity is self-determined. Moreover, an individual's participation in solidaristic activity waxes and wanes according to personal ability, commitment, proximity, and numerous other contingent factors. These variables account for the strong and weak determinations discussed in Chapter 2, but groups undergo similar changes in size and intensity. Exigency and urgency additionally affect the group's status, strength, and activity. It is important to note that solidary groups are much more than the aggregate of their constituent members. It is the public, collective action—multiple people acting in concert and openly—that effects social change.

In local solidarity, that is, in movements of political solidarity that are localized and relatively small, the solidary group may resemble an association or may transform into a formal association with explicit membership criteria, decision-making structures, and agendas. Prior to such a transformation, however, even a local political solidary group exhibits the fluidity and radical individual input of all political solidarity movements. As the solidarity movement gains momentum or expands its membership, the resemblance to an association may be lost. It could also be formalized—perhaps even losing its role or status in political solidarity. At times, it may look more like a crowd or even a mob, but the moral relations to others united for the cause keep political solidarity from becoming mob action. This is not, of course, to deny that some members who claim allegiance to a cause might utilize violent or immoral means to attempt to advance that cause but it is to say that when such tools are employed, they are done so outside the moral bounds of political solidarity.

The unity of political solidarity based on individual participation in a group in order to achieve a particular goal, purpose, or common interest makes it similar to some recent discussions of civic participation. This is similar to what others have called cosmopolitanism: "If cosmopolitanism can be casual about community building and community maintenance and tends to seek voluntary affiliations of wide compass, pluralism promotes affiliations on the narrower grounds of shared history and is more quick to see reasons for drawing boundaries between communities" (Hollinger 1995, 85–86; see also 36–38). Hollinger further characterizes cosmopolitanism as favoring voluntary affiliations and claims that it "promotes multiple identities, emphasizes the dynamic and changing character of many groups, and is responsive to the potential for creating new cultural combinations" (1995, 3–4). Solidarity is not itself an example of cosmopolitanism, though it might be one of the voluntary affiliations; because of its emphasis on social justice and the moral imperatives that accompany such a commitment, however, it is unlike other voluntary affiliations. Political solidarity is a moral relation formed by individual commitments to a cause and acted out in a wide variety of personal and social measures, rather than something akin to the joining of a club or bowling league.

Thus, the group that forms in political solidarity is somewhere between an organized group and a random collection of individuals. We call it a group because there is a unity of purpose that connects the members but, in some forms of political solidarity such as international political solidarity, there may be very little contact between and among group members.

In addition, within any given solidarity movement, there may be pockets of more tightly knit groups or even formal organizations. Political solidarity may be a common cause that unites multiple organizations, associations, parties, and groups. The National Organization for Women, for instance, may be called a participant in the political solidarity that is the feminist movement, and even something like the Congressional Black Caucus may be a participant in political solidarity to end racism. That these subgroupings draw on more established traditions, rules, or relations does not detract from political solidarity. On the contrary, the group for political solidarity is probably best characterized by involvement in a collective project. How one subsequently participates in that collective project can vary over time, according to means, and even cease altogether.

The group that forms when individuals jointly recognize their mutual commitment to a cause is something more than a random collection of individuals but may not necessarily meet the qualifications for an organized collective. The more localized the solidarity movement, the more likely there will be a decision-making structure (formal or informal). As the solidarity movement extends, the feasibility and opportunity for formal or informal mechanisms of group decision-making lessen. Instead, there may or may not be subgroups that focus on a particular activity within social activism or relate to one another according to their own interest and identity within the solidarity movement.

For the purposes of brevity, I continue to use "solidary group" or "collective" to indicate the loosely organized, voluntary group capable of joint action in solidarity. One final consideration pertains to those who opt not to join in political solidarity either through choice, inability, or lack of adequate knowledge. Surely there will be individuals who suffer from some form of injustice, for example, who do nothing to alter their situation. And yet, if the activities of the solidary group are successful, that system of injustice will be overturned. The individual who did nothing thereby benefits from the actions of other individuals who joined in solidarity to challenge the injustice. The results of many political solidarity movements are non-excludable public goods. Although only some individuals work to achieve them, many more individuals enjoy their use. The good is generally not a limitable good. (Of course, there are some exceptions, as when political solidarity forms around the substantive goal to support just wages for farmers. Presumably it is the farmers who receive the benefits of the movement if it is successful.)

It is worth noting that solidarity challenges another widely accepted assumption about individual and group action. Hechter notes that "truly rational actors will *not* join a group to pursue common ends when, without participating, they can reap the benefit of other people's activity in obtaining them" (1987, 27). Political solidarity demonstrates that rational actors can and will join a group even if they can reap the benefits of the activities without participating because solidarity situates the individual in a wider political context and among interdependent others. The interdependency, as I show in the subsequent section, is a result of a different understanding of subjectivity and, one might argue, a different notion of rationality. In brief, political solidarity is a wholly different moral and political relation that demands at least a partial rethinking of some of our more traditional concepts.

The Oppressed Group and the Solidary Group

There is something importantly different between the solidarity of a small town and the solidarity that unites individual workers in their collective efforts to win free unions or just wages. Similarly, the solidarity that victims of domestic abuse might share with each other is not equivalent to the solidarity of a social activist movement aimed at changing a culture of abuse. In both cases, the initial sense of solidarity marks the bonds of a community united by some shared characteristic or similarity (social solidarity), while the second sort of solidarity indicates political activism aimed at social change (political solidarity).

At some level, this example and the distinction between social and political solidarities harkens back to the question: How does solidarity start? What sets social activism in motion? Solidarity may be attributed to any number of possible sources. The oppressed and vulnerable may reach the point when they can no longer tolerate unjust treatment; intellectuals and activists may examine their consciences and uncover indignation at the injustice done to themselves or others; some new instance of oppression or injustice may tip the scales; tensions may erupt; or any combination of these and other causal factors may come into play.

The initial articulation of political solidarity and subsequent development of the concept emphasized the element of individual commitment in forming the solidary group and creating the movement for social change. A crucial assumption hides in this element, an assumption that I now wish to defend. The theory of political solidarity assumes that the oppressed group is distinct from the solidary group. This fact both serves as a supposition of the individual commitment, insofar as it is the commitment rather than oppressed group identity that determines participation in political solidarity, and it also results in a wider, more inclusive understanding of political solidarity, insofar as former oppressors and those people privileged by oppression have the opportunity to join in solidarity. I first look at some of the approaches to solidarity that start with the oppressed group; namely, those that posit shared consciousness, identity, or experience as the basis for solidarity. After examining the strengths and weaknesses of these approaches, I suggest that political solidarity is best theoretically understood, if not always practically evident, as creating a distinct group from the group of the oppressed. Of course, with any movement to address injustice or oppression, there will be significant overlap between the two social groups—the oppressed and the solidary: any given individual might be a member of both groups. It should be remembered that "group" here does not mean an exclusionary relationship between certain peoples but rather a fluid social category; it should also be remembered that each individual is a member of multiple groups—both through voluntary affiliation and external prescription.

Most accounts of solidarity for social change do not draw a clear distinction between the oppressed group and the solidary group: a distinction, I argue, on which political solidarity rests. When the identity of shared experience of oppression marks the solidary group, the oppressed group is assumed to be the group of political solidarity. Another way to think about this is that political solidarity becomes conflated with social solidarity. In spite of my disavowal of it, this presumption of shared experience nevertheless has many merits worthy of consideration. The strength of the group cohesion found in shared experience or shared identity might lend itself to very effective social action. The exclusion of others as well as the potential for overdetermination of identity and similar problems, however, make this model for a theory of political solidarity untenable.

The accounts of solidarity that do ground it in the identity, experience, or consciousness of the oppressed conflate social solidarity with political solidarity. That is, they conceptualize the solidary group as the same as the oppressed group. I look briefly at shared consciousness, identity, and shared experience or history to show the problems that accrue with such a conflation. If these do mark solidarity among the oppressed, it is a social solidarity; but it is important to note that the oppressed group might be marked as oppressed without sharing any sort of solidarity.

A shared sense of social identity may be constituted by biological conditions that distinguish one group from another, social status, political commitments, lifestyles, geographical locations, or simply that those in the group share the same experience of oppression. Paulo Freire, for example, discusses shared experiences of oppression as a unifying function in group formation (1968). And, in her essay "Feminism and Modern Friendship: Dislocating the Community," Marilyn Friedman mentions the possibility of sharing a common oppression as providing the basis of a community of choice, that is, communities in which we "*relocate* and *renegotiate* the various constituents of our identities" (1992, 95, emphasis in original). As Iris Young says, "Our identities are defined in relation to how others identify us, and they do so in terms of groups which are always already associated with specific attributes, stereotypes, and norms" (1990, 46). While it is not always the case that the identity an individual obtains via his or her externally prescribed association with a particular social group is oppressive, the tendency is in this direction.

Some theorists base the notion of solidarity for social change on shared consciousness arising out of victimization. Shared consciousness means two things. First, it refers to the shaping of individuals' consciousnesses by oppression. In other words, those who have similar experience of oppression will likely have developed similar or "shared" consciousness of their identity, power, potential, and nature. I am here folding into this prong of shared consciousness such things as "internalized oppression" and "oppressor consciousness" as they are relevantly similar for this discussion. While there is no clear consensus on the matter of oppressed shared consciousness, it is widely believed that people who are continually excluded from active participation in social existence or are consistently told they are inferior will come to believe these "facts" as true. They may also hold that it is impossible to change the structures that sustain the oppressed consciousness—if those structures are even recognized.

The second meaning of shared consciousness, and more useful for theorizing about solidarity, is the shared consciousness that comes when oppressed peoples recognize their victimization as a contingent fact. Consciousness-raising helps others with similar experiences of oppression reveal the contingent nature of oppression and perhaps begin to strategize for change. Larry May succinctly describes this coming-to-awareness: "For Marxists and other social theorists, solidarity necessarily involves the oppressed's overcoming false consciousness and recognizing how the oppressor class treats the oppressed class" (1996, 37). According to this thinking, solidarity happens because individuals who are victimized by the same situation of injustice begin to express their victimization; as others express or reveal their own accounts of victimization, realization of a shared experience—shared consciousness—develops. Shared consciousness, it is believed, allows groups to form and provides the impetus and power for collective action to change a social situation.

While this account of shared consciousness has some merits, especially in its power to identify oppressive structures deep down, there appears to be a gap between having the consciousness and acting to change the social structures that sustain oppression. One can certainly be aware of one's oppressed status, lack of liberty, or victimization by injustice, and still take no steps to change the situation.

A slight variation on this second use of "shared consciousness" focuses on the unity of interests. Rather than shared knowledge or understanding, Robert Ware argues that class interests are the object of consciousness (rather than part of it). Consciousness, after all, does not give rise to organization—unity does. More specifically, unity of interest guides movement organization (Ware 1983, 264). Ware's point supports a theoretical, if not also a practical, distinction between the oppressed group and the solidary group insofar as shared knowledge and understanding varies from interests. This is precisely my current aim, though I diverge from Ware insofar as I hold that the group that forms in political solidarity need not have shared interests in any strong sense of the term but rather have an aim or goal that different individuals and organizations support for varying reasons or motivations. I also ague that the ends of political solidarity need not be tied directly to one's own experience of injustice or oppression.

Oppression is widely acknowledged as a group-based phenomenon; one is victimized precisely because one is a member of a particular group. Young's discussion of oppression captures the significant aspect of how an individual's membership in a social group marks him or her as oppressed. To begin with, a distinction may be made between oppressive group identity and positive group identity. The former does not provide for the ontological primacy of the individual. That is, the individual is defined by, and his or her reality is determined according to his or her membership in a social group. The ontological primacy of the group determines that a person belonging to a particular social group may be described by the attribute that a social group has been assigned according to how others perceive or define the group. The individual has no input into his or her own self-identity. Instead, identity is constituted from the attributes or characteristics perceived to be inherent in group membership. In other words, if the individual is defined by and her or his reality determined according to group membership, then the group membership is ontologically prior to the individual qua individual, that is, qua able to authentically participate in self-identity formation. Thus the individual, insofar as she or he is identified as a member of the group, is oppressed. Young offers the following as a possible definition of oppression: "Oppression consists in systematic institutional processes which prevent some people from learning and using satisfying and expansive skills in socially recognized settings, or institutionalized social processes which inhibit people's ability to play and communicate with others or to express their feelings and perspective on social life in contexts where others can listen" (1990, 38).

Others similarly analyze oppression as a group-based phenomenon. This fact, coupled with the fact that solidarity is a group-based phenomenon, has led many people to assume a tighter identity between the two groups than is necessarily the case. As Sandra Bartky says for the solidarity among women, "One is victimized as a woman, as one among many. In the realization that others are made to suffer in the same way I am made to suffer lies the beginning of a sense of solidarity with other victims" (1990, 15). And later she uses oppressive "body rituals" and confession of sufferings as a basis for political solidarity (2002, 23, 64). Of course the realization Bartky speaks of may be one of the forces—and in some cases the most important force—that compels an individual to join in political solidarity, that is, to commit to action for social change. But if shared victimization results in any sort of group unity, it results in social solidarity, not political solidarity. Equating oppressed group identity (and the social solidarity that may arise because of it) with the solidary group of political solidarity cannot explain why all oppressed peoples do not join in solidarity, why some privileged and oppressor peoples do join in, and how subjective activity for liberation is even possible.

It would be remiss, however, to fail to notice the positive potential of identity. A realization of shared identity might be the launching point for more engaged political action. Identity may be understood also as the cultural connections or "modes of expression whereby we define ourselves, including the 'languages' of art, of gesture, of love, and the like" (Taylor 1992, 32). Each of these might serve as powerful motivators for the commitment of political solidarity.

In a similar vein, some have used the phrase "solidarity of the oppressed," as in racial solidarity or class solidarity, to indicate a shared place in society that may be accompanied by a shared experience but need not be. The presumption is that those who occupy a similar place, status, or role in society will stick together and defend each other. May presents it thus:

> [S]olidarity is more than group identity felt by individuals from the participant perspective. Individual group members need to understand how others perceive and treat them in order to understand their true interests and to be most likely to identify with one another sufficiently to feel motivated to come to one another's aid. Solidarity involves a moral dimension, namely, willingness of the members of a group to engage in individual or collective action so as to aid fellow group members. (1996, 37)

That shared place and the moral duties that issue from it serves as a compelling example of social solidarity's moral relations. Jean Harvey (2007) develops a similar conception of the morally rich relations between commembers of an oppressed group. Her account, which she calls "moral solidarity," revolves around what she calls "empathetic understanding" between actors. That understanding captures at least some of what May refers to in the quotation above when he speaks both of understanding how someone is perceived or treated as well as that person's interests.

In many ways, identity-based appeals to solidarity reach back to familial models, that is, conceptions of solidarity that liken the solidary community to a family. Such a notion is distinctly centered in social solidarity where the community or communal bonds exist prior to any decision to act. It might, for instance, be presumed that racial solidarity requires members of the same race to join hands to throw off oppression. Of course, "racial solidarity" might also apply to non-oppressed peoples; white segregationists in the United States often cited racial solidarity as the motive for maintaining the unjust Jim Crow system. That is an appeal to social solidarity albeit a weak form; that is, the segregationists hoped that they could draw on the bonds of commonality with other whites to uphold a system that directly benefited them.

Other examples of the conflation of social and political solidarity, in addition to shared consciousness, shared prescribed identity, and shared experience or location, might also be found. May, for instance, argues that "in solidarity one can make at least two forms of identification: an identification with the other's behavior, and an identification with the other's characteristics" (1996, 33). Behavior can include any number of personal, social, or cultural practices. The identification with others through these practices, however, need not result in all those so identified acting together for social change. And in his discussion of rational choice solidarity theory, Michael Hechter argues that "solidary groups are most likely to emerge when demanded goods are not attainable from the state or in the market" (1987, 177). He further explains this in relation to solidary groups based on race or class by saying: "To the degree that the allocation of goods is discriminatory, solidary groups are likely to form among those individuals so affected. This explains why discrimination will sometimes be the ostensible basis for solidarity" (Hechter 1987, 177). In this case, it is not an identity claim but an experiential claim that may or may not affect any particular individual's self-identity or externally perceived identity.

There are three main reasons not to use identity ascription as the basis for political solidarity membership. The first reason is that it limits the membership of the social movement to only those individuals who, often because of some non-chosen attribute or characteristic, are ascribed a particular identity. Moreover, strong emphasis on group identity risks contradicting solidarity insofar as individual freedom and uniqueness is lost. Oppressive group prescription might motivate any particular individual to take action, but it does not necessarily mean that one will take action. Social change requires collective efforts; if movements for social change are described or circumscribed by oppressed group identity, then concerned or indignant nonmembers are excluded. In addition, more compelling reasons also favor varied group membership for achieving the goals of solidarity. I mention some of these briefly here and explore the issue in more depth in the following chapter. Groups that are based on commitment should be stronger than groups based on identity because their members have made a personal moral commitment to the focus of the group. Additionally, a solidary group that includes individuals not subject to the injustice that is the particular interest of the group might better be able to communicate with others who do not readily agree with the cause. Individuals who do not share the experience of oppression offer the social movement support and social criticism insofar as they commit to the struggle to end that oppression.

The second limitation to theoretical accounts that conflate the oppressed group with the group of political solidarity is that the oppressed identity is not so easy to pin down or identify. Although his focus is on assigning responsibility to collectives for actions or omissions, Stanley Bates argues that if we were to make identity (as I am using it here) the basis of assigning collective or group responsibility, then we would have to define the identity sufficiently narrow enough to avoid including those individuals who clearly do not share in responsibility. To quote his example: "Perhaps we should say something like 'mature, rational white Americans who know what the racial situation is, and who either take actions to perpetuate or worsen it, or who fail to take actions to alleviate it' bear the moral responsibility for the situation" (Bates 1971, 348). Alison Bailey (2000), in her analysis of race traitors (whites who renounce the privilege of their race), similarly emphasizes traitorous activities rather than identities or locations. We ought not to rely on externally prescribed identities or shared consciousness of oppression as the basis for collective action in solidarity because that will require us to narrowly specify the identity and exclude valuable members from participation. Similarly, we avoid at least some moral responsibility for sexism and racism insofar as we divorce ourselves from sexist and racist circles and argue against their practices (see especially Bates 1971, 348; McGary 1986; Bailey 2000). Such a move, however, requires an active choice and a continuing commitment; in identity-based solidarity, the oppressor would also be identity based and, it seems, it would be impossible for a member of the oppressor class or caste to throw off that status and join with those who struggle against oppression.

bell hooks supports this point when she contrasts solidarity with "sisterhood." Sisterhood was a movement or rallying cry in the early feminist movement. It encouraged women to focus on their shared weaknesses by joining consciousness-raising groups to discuss their sufferings. Sisterhood predominantly attracted white, middle-class, educated women concerned about their experiences of sexism. It provided a forum for women to come together to discuss those things that were previously thought "unspeakable." Women shared their experiences of wife battery; marital, date, acquaintance, and stranger rape; poor working conditions and low wages for women; general feelings of exclusion in home, workplace, politics, and society at large; feelings of being constrained by prescriptions of beauty, intellect, and power; and numerous health-related issues. Although this approach certainly has some notable strengths, among which is the bringing to public discussion those things that had previously been left unchallenged, there are also some notable weaknesses. The sisterhood approach assumes a common experience of oppression for all women, thereby obfuscating the many differences among women. As hooks explains, "The idea of 'common oppression' was a false and corrupt platform disguising and mystifying the true nature of women's varied and complex social reality. Women are divided by sexist attitudes, racism, class privilege, and a host of other prejudices" (1984, 44).

The third reason not to use identity prescription/ascription as the sole basis of solidarity is that these identities are often the basis of oppression, and oppression itself may make solidarity an impossibility. A person may be unaware of the myriad oppressive identity prescriptions that affect him or her. Through oppressive identity prescriptions, self-deception or bad faith, or lack of adequate knowledge of the group, an individual may not perceive him- or herself as a political agent. Or the external prescriptions may bar individuals from fully exercising their rights; indeed they may, on the basis of prescriptive identity, be denied some rights that are crucial to challenging and changing their oppressive situation. The personal recognition—according to conscience not shared consciousness—that something is unjust compels an individual to participate in social activism. María Lugones hits on this point, calling it a problem of subjectivity, in her work on colonization. As she explains, Marx's conception of revolutionary action among the working classes fails to provide an explanation for how and why resistance to capitalism begins:

> Marx also conveys clearly that proletarians must organize in the workplace against capital. He gives great importance to class struggle and the production of class consciousness. But, given his account of the logic of capitalism, I do not see how that is subjectively possible. I need to understand the subjective mechanisms of its possibility. If class consciousness is to be produced through necessities of particular unstable structures rather than through the subjects' exercises of their agency, such production is uninformative from the point of view advanced here. (Lugones 2003, 54)

This is not to deny that there may be some moral obligations among members of social groups categorized by identity. Rather the point is that the bonds that form among the oppressed are examples of social solidarity. These bonds may even require active measures to aid others if one is able: "Shared suffering is a powerful bond among men [sic] and seems to entail—though I cannot specify the method of entailment—very strong positive obligations of mutual assistance" (Walzer 1970, 160). Political solidarity only emerges when a number of individuals, many of whom will likely be those same people who suffer, commit to some form of action that transforms the lives of the individuals involved, aims to bring about social and structural change, and entails various positive collective and individual duties. This is not to deny that political solidarity can and does flow out of the social solidarity of the oppressed at times. But not everyone who shares a similarly oppressed condition, or even everyone whose consciousness is raised to the point of recognizing that condition as contingent, will engage in activism to change or challenge the oppression. As we have seen, political solidarity also creates bonds between participants that may extend beyond their mutual commitment to a cause. In that sense, one might also understand the way that social solidarity can and does flow out of political solidarity. May suggests this, saying, "Indeed, Marx was quite correct, in my view, when he said that a revolutionary class must develop 'radical chains' if it is to be successful. These chains or bonds are characterized by a mutuality of interest that is conjoined with a mutual willingness to offer support to one another. The bonds that so often persist even as self-interests change" (1996, 30). Although May makes "willingness to offer support to one another" appear to be a factor for success in solidarity campaigns, it is not clear that that mutual support necessarily extends beyond the interests that participants share in joining solidarity. Marx certainly posited a shared consciousness (or social solidarity) as a requirement for the revolutionary activity, and May could be appealing to that as well; but my point is that social solidarity is not a necessary prerequisite for political solidarity and that political solidarity could be a source of the future social solidary bonds. When the mutual willingness to aid others extends beyond the political goals of the group (implicitly and explicitly), it may be the case that political solidarity has transformed into social solidarity even if or even while it still entertains a political solidarity faction, element, or focus.

Thus some forms of group identity might connote stasis and prescription while voluntary membership or affiliation entails flexible, dynamic social interactions (cf. Hollinger 1995, 6–7). Negative group identity relies on the ontological priority of the group in identity formation; positive group identity, by emphasizing the importance of self-determination, requires the ontological primacy of the individual-within-community. Positive group identity grants the individual responsibility in defining her or his identity: both how she or he regards herself or himself *and* how others regard her or him at any given time. It is, in other words, a constant process of critical recreation or remaking within a fluid social context.

Political solidarity shifts the emphasis for the group from the traits in common to the collective action. In a sense, this flips the logic of the accounts discussed above. Instead of group consciousness causing the collective action, collective action in political solidarity causes group consciousness. This does not deny that some group consciousness among the oppressed occurs; it merely transforms our understanding of the relation between that group consciousness and the consciousness, if there is one, of the participants in solidarity. Once an individual undertakes the commitment to a cause with others, he or she sees him- or herself as part of something bigger—they become the solidary group. Collective project, rather than common fate, sets solidarity apart from oppression and the solidary group apart from the oppressed group (see also McGary 1986, 160).

Commitment is an individual's formal or informal pledge or promise to a collective cause. Commitment transforms reciprocity in interpersonal relations to a reciprocal relation with the cause and the group. Social consciousness, to borrow from Howard McGary, not shared consciousness, characterizes the solidary group. The group does not take on a separate existence but exists through individual commitment (see also Scholz 2005b, 54) and yet the group nonetheless transcends the mere aggregation of its parts.

What motivates that commitment varies for each participant in solidarity. Oppressed identity may be the impetus for at least some participants. I argue that the crucial point is that we not assume that there is an identity or even a necessary correspondence between the *oppressed group* and the *solidary group*. That correspondence may be an element of individual participation. A common feature, fate, or experience may compel some individuals to make a choice to struggle to change their situation or attempt to end the oppressive systems/structures to which they are subject. In other words, simply because a variety of individuals share a certain common feature or fate—a common identity—it is not the case that they will engage in political solidarity, though we can describe their connection as a form of social solidarity.

Political solidarity emphasizes shared strengths, collective commitment, and mutual acceptance of the burdens involved in social change. As "victims" we are not required to assume responsibility for confronting complexity of experience. Political solidarity requires that we define our own terms and not rely on the terms of the dominant ideology. In order to critique social status, values, and political beliefs, individuals must realize their collective power to alter social conditions. This can be accomplished only if we forcefully move beyond considerations of victimhood. In addition to emphasizing shared strengths, political solidarity affords the opportunity to critique the solidary group. Such social criticism, as I argued in the previous chapter, is an obligation of solidarity because it helps maintain the motivation for the solidarity movement and provides critical reflection on the means of achieving the goal of the movement. It also instructively scrutinizes the implicit membership criteria that may inadvertently bar some potential allies from participation. In the example of the solidarity of women, hooks demonstrates how social criticism allows us to see the way in which sexism teaches women womenhating and how racism among women serves as a barrier to group cohesion. For instance, social criticism of racism within the women's movement might reveal the contradiction black women might face in deciding whether to join a movement they view as exploitative and exclusionary (hooks 1984, 50).

McGary uses the distinction between group identification and solidarity in the manner I describe here. Solidarity requires some notion of shared commitment. He illustrates this point with an example citing the interest Californians from Beverly Hills and Californians from Watts share in "efforts to prevent needed water from being routed to some other state" (McGary 1986, 160). In this example, all the group members share the group identity of Californian, but it is only the shared commitment to a political agenda that unites them in political solidarity: "Strong group identifications have served as a source of self-esteem and as a foundation for cultures. Solidarity, unlike group identification, requires a level of political and social consciousness" (McCary 1986, 160).

Of course, the implication is that political solidarity enables anyone, including those who benefit from the oppression of others, to join in solidarity to topple oppressive systems or structures. In fact, former oppressors and others who renounce their privilege may have important contributions to make to political solidarity if they are able genuinely to abandon systems of domination and privilege. I take up this particular issue of the participation of the socially privileged in the subsequent chapter. For the purpose of this chapter, by inserting a conceptual distinction between the solidary group and the oppressed group—and by implication between political solidarity and social solidarity—I have expanded the potential membership of the solidary group beyond those people who actually experience oppression or injustice. Related to this expansion, the benefits of political solidarity extend far beyond those who immediately participate in the social movement.

The benefits (if they are to be had) of collective action to bring about social change accrue not only to those who protest, boycott, sit-in, write letters, or otherwise act to resist systems of domination, injustice, and oppression. Women who do not participate in feminist activism nonetheless benefit from the accomplishments of the feminist movement. All workers benefit from the actions of those engaged in political solidarity to make working conditions safer or obtain a more just wage. Similar claims may be advanced for every social justice movement. Moreover, society as a whole benefits as political solidarity aids in justice efforts. All these "free riders" or beneficiaries of at least some movements of political solidarity might find themselves inspired to participate in other similar movements. Political solidarity must remain open to allow for diverse membership and ever-changing group dynamics.

The opposite is also the case: political solidarity, as a cooperative venture, is not necessarily for the mutual advantage of its constituent members. Historically, movements of political solidarity and the individual participants often meet disdain, hostility, and even violence as a response to their activities. These burdens, unlike the benefits, however, are generally not shared equally, nor do they extend beyond the group, although violence in response to social activism does reap effects for society at large. This reality often discourages participation—especially participation by those who are already vulnerable. Support from the non-vulnerable can bolster a group's resolve and may even help to insulate it from some of the potentially damaging reaction from the larger society.

Political solidarity is the quintessential example of collective moral action in part because it demonstrates that collective action is much more than the sum of individual action—that solidarity activity is irreducible to individuals' actions. As Thomas Hill argues with regard to protests, "The underlying idea is that any decent self-respecting person has more to offer individuals (and groups, causes, and so on) than whatever effective action he can take on their behalf. He can also give it 'honor,' credit, and acclaim; and he does this not just by explicit praise but by identifying himself publicly with those individuals (groups, causes, and so on)" (1979, 98).

Each individual commits to solidarity and at times the commitment may be weak or strong. The strength of individual commitment, the exigency of the cause, the urgency of the struggle, and the inspiration of others united in solidarity help to define the group. In political solidarity, as opposed to social and civic solidarity, the goal or cause is instrumental in the measure of group cohesion rather than the bonds between members. This is not to say that members in political solidarity do not share a bond—they do but it is primarily a bond to the cause that subsequently brings individuals together for collective action.

The individuals that form a group based on a cause may have little in common with one another aside from the cause. The moral commitment precedes any sort of group membership. There is, in other words, a significant subjective principle for group solidarity. Individual agents must assume some responsibility for their futures and see their projects as interconnected with the projects of others. According to the standards of voluntary group affiliation, it is the individuals themselves who determine whether they are group members; external prescriptions of group membership are not relevant to the determination. Kruks makes this point in developing an existentialist feminist politics (and rejecting a postmodern conception of subjectivity). Kruks explains:

> For example, although shifts in the discursive field certainly enabled the civil rights movement to articulate demands that would not previously have been possible, there still remains that moment when each individual rider actually does—or does not—get off the bus, when each potential demonstrator actually leaves for the demonstration or decides to stay home. For the resistance to catch on, something more than the relevant discursive shifts (analogous to what Marxists used to call the correct objective conditions?) is necessary. This, among other reasons, is why metanarratives of history are inadequate: change is mediated through the actions of individual agents who are not passive vehicles. (Kruks 2001, 12)

Elsewhere I argue for a conception of subjectivity that is relational, interdependent, embodied, and political (Scholz 2005a). This conception fits the subjectivity of solidarity as well. Instead of the isolated individual acting out of self-interest, political solidarity presupposes individuals who recognize that their actions are interconnected and interdependent with the actions and inactions of others. In addition, political solidarity requires the individual to see actions as politicized. An important first step is to claim subjectivity for oneself, that is, to see oneself as an agent rather than a victim. The shift from oppressed group identity to solidary group identity aids in accomplishing that. The other aspects of subjectivity challenge traditional liberal notions of autonomy, rationality, and individuality with what I take to be richer notions, drawn from feminist literature, that emphasize our interdependence and social context in acting for change. Interdependent subjects are challenged to see their actions as coalescing, intersecting, and even contradicting with the actions of others. Particular actions thereby take on heightened meaning; so too relationships with others help define who we are as actors or agents in solidarity. Politicization, or recognizing the many social influences that come into play in individual relations and value formation, affects one's decision-making in political solidarity as well as the decision-making of the solidary group.

Up to this point, I have been speaking as if any given individual is a participant in one movement for political solidarity. While that lends to the ease of discussion, it rarely reflects reality. Individuals who participate in political solidarity are often involved in multiple movements, committed to multiple causes, and often even see their various efforts as interconnected. Solidaristic activity has wide reverberations as well as unintended effects. Although membership in one movement does not necessarily implicate one in or with another, part of the task of social criticism is to identify when one's actions might be at cross-purposes with those of another social movement.

Interconnections and Contradictions Between Political Solidarities

Many scholars have attempted to address social theory's ability to accommodate difference while maintaining some conception of group solidarity. For instance, some recent feminist theory grapples with the recognition that women do not share similar experiences of oppression. Nor do women prioritize sexism as oppression in the same way. Racism, colonialism, imperialism, ageism, and other forms of oppression complicate attempts to combat oppression as a unified phenomenon (see hooks 1984 and Huntington 1997, among others). Clearly these differences pose some challenges for social solidarity, though they are not insurmountable challenges. Differences also challenge political solidarity and invite some interesting responses. Moreover, individuals often commit to multiple causes, many of which cohere with one another but some of which may at times conflict. Although I touch on some of the challenges that diversity poses for political solidarity, my main focus in this section concerns the interconnections of political solidarities, not the interconnections of oppressions (which others have quite eloquently addressed).

Three related issues pertain to the intersecting of political solidarities. The first is the way social movements might inadvertently (and sometimes purposefully) exclude, dominate, or even oppress others. The second is how to ameliorate potentially exclusionary practices. The third, more positive, is the way political solidarities might coalesce as they see their respective projects blending, intermixing, or in fact leading to the same end or goal. The interrelation of these three is important. Movements of political solidarity must scrutinize their practices. Chapter 3 presented the obligations of social criticism within political solidarity. There, I focused on how the aim of the movement shapes or informs social criticism. Here too the aim or goal informs social criticism, but the issues of difference and diversity challenge us to see that end of political solidarity as instrumental to many more of our social relations. At times, of course, that also means that movements for social change will contradict each other. Participants in political solidarity must be equipped to deal with such an eventuality, even if it means abandoning one's goal.

María Lugones describes what she calls "pure communities" and "impure communities." No oppressed group is a pure community and no solidary group is a pure community either. A pure community would be a cleanly demarcated group with identifiable characteristics that denote the group as oppressed or oppressor, vulnerable or powerful, subordinate or dominant. Impure communities, on the other hand, involve both oppressing and resisting activities and members. The pure communities, "atomistic, homogenous, autonomous, bounded, fixed entities," obscure subjects' participation in "oppressive or resistant practices" (Lugones 2003, 200–201). The point, of course, is that pure communities do not exist, and the impurities can come from multiple sources; activities within groups also change such that what appeared to advance liberation one moment might feed domination the next. Recognizing the impurity of groups helps us—as individuals and as a group—to own the myriad ways that we might act to support domination, privilege, and oppression even as we work to alleviate or redress it.

Historically, examples of political solidarity demonstrate sometimes-troubling instances of exclusion. The U.S. women's movement in the nineteenth century, arguably arising from the activism for abolition, intentionally abandoned their allegiance to fight racism ostensibly in order to better concentrate their efforts to attain rights for women. The socialist movement in the eighteenth and nineteenth century, whether intentionally or not, frequently distinguished itself from the struggles to attain women's rights and often excluded women from positions of power or participation in decision-making. More recently, the feminisms of the 1960s and 1970s have been roundly criticized for assuming that all women experience oppression in the way that middle-class white women do. So, whether it is a feminist movement that excludes women of color and poor women, an antiracism or workers' rights movement that marginalizes women, or any number of other movements for social change that fail to reflect on and reorganize so as not to reproduce oppressive ideologies and practices within its midst, political solidarity becomes seriously marred and perhaps so internally inconsistent as to be counterproductive.

Intersectionality proposes one way to address this problem in political solidarity. Intersectionality is the position that oppressions intersect; racism, sexism, and classism blend in different ways for different social groups. While a middle-class white woman might view inequality in the workplace as the most manifest form of her oppression, a lower-class woman might cite her inability to obtain adequate housing (and in a decent school district for her children) as the most manifest form of her oppression. The key is that intersectionality attempts to understand the multiple oppressions that might afflict any particular individual, thereby making her or his experience different from those who may experience only one type of oppression. Domestic violence advocacy provides a revealing case in point. Without an awareness of intersectionality, domestic violence advocates might focus on getting a woman out of her abusive relationship and "standing on her own two feet" again. But, as Kimberlé Crenshaw argues, that traditional domestic violence discourse overlooks the way racism and classism affect not only a woman's experience of the violence but also her desires for overcoming it (1997; Hirschmann 1997, 201). "Standing on one's own" may not even be a value held by every victim of domestic violence. Family relations, including the abusive relation, may take a higher priority than is assumed by the phrase. Economic conditions may make it difficult for some women to see alternatives to abusive relationships. In a related manner, Uma Narayan (1995) asks us to be attentive to such things as immigrant status, which may contribute to women's situation of impeded liberty in domestic violence cases. In order to effectively work on behalf of many differently situated women, domestic violence advocates must be cognizant of and scrutinize the multiple and various factors that create any particular woman's subjectivity and affect her relationships or states of affairs (Scholz 2005a).

But intersectionality also has some flaws. Often it is associated with an identity politics that would, of course, mean that only people with the same intersections (and in more or less the same way) can articulate their oppression and strategize for liberation (Zack 2005, 2). Similarly, stacking of oppressions seems to invite a sort of hierarchy of the oppressed and may also impose certain expectations about which, how, and when oppression should be remedied. If, for instance, the oppression that black women face is judged as exponentially more damaging than that faced by lower-class men, then intersectionality might seem to indicate that working against class oppression is somehow insensitive or even wrongheaded. Competition between oppressed groups for the activist resources, it might be argued, keeps struggles for liberation in a logic of domination in contradiction to the moral strictures of solidarity.

Yet political solidarities cannot ignore the intersections of various forms of oppression as they strategize for liberation. A first step might be to dissect social movements a bit to see if there are some common goals or unifying aims. Some socialist feminists undertook such a task in response to the charge that the feminist movement had been racist and classist. They looked for ways to conceptualize all oppressions so that various struggles for liberation might see their tasks as, at root, unified. Alienation (Jaggar 1983), division of labor (Young 1980), and either/or dichotomous thinking and systems of domination (hooks 1984) were among the suggestions for a unifying concept. If various manifestations of oppression, like sexism, classism, and racism, could be found to have their roots in either/or dichotomous thinking, for instance, then theorists and activists for multiple causes might see their efforts as coordinated attempts to overcome it. Of course, as hooks points out, identifying the unifying concept is hardly sufficient for ameliorating the potential for reproducing oppressive practices within the movement for social justice. As she explains with regard to the feminist movement: "Women will know they have made a political commitment to eliminating racism when they help change the direction of feminist movement, when they work to unlearn racist socialization prior to assuming positions of leadership or shaping theory or making contact with women of color so that they will not perpetuate and maintain racial oppression or, unconsciously or consciously, abuse and hurt non-white women" (hooks 1984, 55). Part of the task of any participant in political solidarity is to examine his or her conscience and actions in an attempt to discern possible contradictions between the values one espouses in committing to solidarity and the position one takes toward others. Clearly, this may involve unlearning some deeply ingrained behaviors or thought patterns. Racism, sexism, classism, and ableism infect our lives in so many different ways. Unlearning the abusive patterns must accompany our struggles for liberation—so too participants must undergo a thorough renunciation of privilege that comes from the oppression or injustice inflicted on another. The next chapter deals with some of the moral and epistemological concerns entailed in such a renunciation, but there are also numerous positive aspects to be found when political solidarities confront, intersect, blend, or otherwise meet.

In my original articulation of a theory of political solidarity, I mentioned that individuals might make commitments to multiple causes. These varying commitments to political solidarities could result in a contradiction in the individual's social critique or activism. They might also serve as a source for richer, more nuanced understandings of social problems and more complex but more encompassing political solutions. In some sense paralleling what intersectionality and inclusivity did for theories of oppression, multiple solidary commitments shift the focus of activism and theory in order to highlight some of the connections and identify deeper social structures in need of change while once again emphasizing the importance of the individuals within solidarity. So too solidary groups might find productive avenues for building coalitions with other groups. Their values or motivations need not be identical in order for effective coalitions to change the social landscape.

As we have seen, Walzer calls for an increase in the number of associational ties claiming that by providing more opportunities for individual participation, individuals will have a "growing sense of their own effectiveness" and be "our best protection against the parochialism of the groups in which they participate. Engaged men and women tend to be widely engaged—active in many different associations both locally and nationally" (1994, 189–90). "Multiply the calls for competent people, and the people will appear. Multiply the opportunities for action-in-common, and activists will emerge to seize the opportunities" (Walzer 1994, 190). Individuals engaged in political solidarity frequently count themselves members of many different social groups and often commit to many activist causes. One person might be an environmentalist, feminist, socialist, and a supporter of civil rights for all, while another person might fight for just wages for workers, seek some social recognition of nonhuman animals, and be a vegetarian. Individuals involved in multiple groups often or even usually see their involvement as connected. That is, the commitments one accepts are rarely pursued as frivolous whims but instead form part of the web of commitments or conscious decisions that one makes, and occasionally abandons, as one makes oneself into a social being. These variations between people engaged in solidary movements lend to the fruitful conversations in social criticism within any given movement. Any one group might have members from hundreds of other groups all bringing the specificity of their other commitments to the table in strategizing and acting for social change. As individuals, the strength of their other commitments affects both their willingness to commit to a particular cause as well as their ability to share the connections between causes that they see. When women and men engaged in activism against sexist oppression began to share their commitments to other causes—like animal rights and environmentalism—they helped others see how certain actions to change one unjust social structure can simultaneously change another. Notice, however, that the connections need not be based in any sort of unifying concept (though they might be for any given individual), but instead emerge out of our collective relationships with one another in solidarity. Each individual, then, is also an irreplaceable part of the solidary group. Similarly, social movements might be connected across generations:

> By recognizing that the victorious proletarian contemporaries would be *de facto* heirs of legions of exploited slaves and workers of the past, Marx illuminates in a flash the essence of anamnestic solidarity. The unity of repressed mankind is the solidarity of the living with the dead. Marx calls for an understanding of class in terms of the continuity of exploitation across the ages. If the impending revolution goes forth without being informed by this larger historical solidarity with the dead, then it will only wipe out one injustice by replacing it with another. (Lenhardt 1975, 151)

Finally, political solidarities also run the risk of contradicting each other. A corollary of the problem of exclusion, the actions of some solidary groups might limit the ability of others to act. Similarly, when some activists employ questionable means to attain their ends, other activists might suffer retribution from society at large. In her discussion of the antinomies of action,

Simone de Beauvoir claims that the complexity of the world situation may force us into a situation where we find ourselves taking what we view to be the most urgent liberating action only to discover that it is detrimental to the cause we support. Beauvoir is particularly concerned with violence, but nonviolent liberation struggles might also meet this paradox, "that no action can be generated for man without its being immediately generated against men [sic]" (Beauvoir 1948a, 99). No easy answers to these problems present themselves, though surely one can appeal to some of what has already been said: careful social criticism, dedicated attentiveness to both the experience and the commitments of various members, and nonviolent activism that respects the dignity of others. This, of course, raises something of a conundrum: How are decisions made within political solidarity? If the group really is relatively loose and unstructured, what, if anything, can we say about collective decision-making?

Decision-Making Within Political Solidarity

There are two basic approaches to the questions of decision-making within political solidarity. Given that it is a relation that mediates between the individual and the community, it makes sense to discuss decision-making for both prongs—the individual and the collective. A great deal has already been said about how the individual commits to political solidarity and the duties entailed in that commitment. Opting to be in solidarity is opting for certain hardships, difficulties, or scorn. The temptation, perhaps, is to view the decision to join in solidarity with others as an almost heroic decision made according to conscience. Certainly some examples of individuals joining in political solidarity might merit that description. But, of course, opting in is itself a collective enterprise even if members do so from their distinct and separate places in society. Political solidarity cannot exist without others making similar commitments and at least some interest and support, if not also membership, from those subject to the oppression or injustice that political solidarity targets. In that sense, and given the notion of subjectivity discussed previously, even the personal commitment to join in political solidarity is not individualistic. Moreover, the actions of solidarity very often affect—positively and negatively—one's family, friends, coworkers, and arguably one's relations with strangers. The decision-maker of political solidarity diverges considerably from the model of an isolated decision-maker acting out of self-interest.

In addition to the original commitment, participants make daily decisions for how they carry out the solidarity in their daily lives. These decisions, as we have seen, range from how to mount the most effective protest, boycott, or other display of public disapprobation for an unjust system, to how one will let solidarity affect interpersonal relations, consumer and recreational choices, and even thought and language patterns.

Within the solidary group, individual decisions coalesce to form the collective action. Sometimes, however, opportunities for more organized collective action present themselves. This is especially true for local political solidarities, as when advocates for and of the homeless in a particular city strategize for a public protest at city hall. International solidarity movements, movements that involve people from across borders, with varying degrees of commitment, rarely have any sort of centralized decision-making, though factions within the movement likely do. This raises some interesting questions, not least of which is this: Because recent developments in democratic theory and practice arose in response to liberation struggles like political solidarity, shouldn't political solidarity be democratic in approach? Well, yes and no. Because the solidary group is somewhat amorphous, and because people join in solidarity with different levels of commitment, it is not so easy to ascribe a formal democratic procedure to political solidarity, though we can say that the mutuality and other obligations to fellow solidaristic actors requires that actions ought to be consistent with democracy or what could be democratically decided on.

Much of the recent literature on voluntary associational ties or participation in civic organizations emphasizes their importance in fostering democratic participation. Walzer discusses the benefits to the individual and the group when voluntary associational ties are formed. Although in the context of his discussion of social democracy for a multicultural society, his observations certainly have credence for political solidarity as well: "Individuals are stronger, more confident, more savvy, when they are participants in a common life, responsible to and for other people. . . . It is only in the context of associational activity that individuals learn to deliberate, argue, make decisions, and take responsibility" (Walzer 1994, 189). But, of course, these and other routes to civic engagement historically have not been open to everyone. Changes in democratic theory and practice attempted to highlight and alleviate that.

John S. Dryzek examines the roots of deliberative democracy in critical theory and focuses on politicized civil society. Although he replaces "deliberative" with "discursive," Dryzek emphasizes the fact that it arose out of a need to address oppression and seek liberation, to critique the structures or systems of power within the state. Like political solidarity, deliberative or discursive democracy, then, plays a sort of dual role: it critically identifies the systems of domination within social systems (especially the state) and it provides a voice for previously vulnerable, disadvantaged, or oppressed within those social systems. Political solidarity can be seen as one of the many varied forms of involvement in civic life and thus becomes an important tool for democratic participation in such a society. But Dryzek and other deliberative democrats assume that the voluntary associations through which individuals become involved in social and political life are themselves governed by deliberative democracy as well. Does political solidarity, with its wide degree of commitments, diverse participants, array of activities, and lack of formal organizational structure sustain a deliberative democratic framework? How might decision-making within solidarity be carried out? And is the active participation of at least some of the oppressed, vulnerable, or victims of injustice required for political solidarity?

Before we can begin to answer these questions, we need a clearer picture of what deliberative or discursive democracy entails. Although I focus on Dryzek because he emphasizes the roots of discursive democracy in challenging oppression, and because of his innovative approach to the discussions, the literature on deliberative democracy continues to burgeon. The cross-fertilization between solidarity studies and democracy studies could be quite fruitful.

Dryzek holds that those subject to a decision ought to have the opportunity to participate in it. This does not necessarily mean that they will, but it does mean that forums for discussion—and modes of discussion—must be opened. He suggests that reasoned discussion is only one possible source for communication. Other noncoercive forms that lead to greater general understanding might be found in rhetoric, storytelling, and greeting, following the lead of Iris Young on this score (1996, 120–35). A more nuanced account of deliberation, in other words, is better able to examine multiple oppressive aspects of political life. Deliberative democracy should be "attuned to plurality in subject positions and associated ways of life" (Dryzek 2000, 72). As new coercive forces propagate and new avenues for democratic deliberation emerge, political theory will be challenged to remain dynamic and attentive to the needs of the vulnerable.

Dryzek's account of discursive democracy vaguely resembles another account of decision-making within the literature on solidarity, namely, Catholic Social Teaching's principle of subsidiarity. Subsidiarity holds that actions and decisions ought to occur at the lowest possible level, that is, those closest to the decision or action with the requisite information. It is only when information is scarce or decision-making capacities are somehow limited that the decision or power to act is directed to the next level. The significant difference between discursive democracy and subsidiarity, no doubt because of its origins, is that subsidiarity still presumes some hierarchical structure whereas discursive democracy aims at ensuring equal ability to participate in the debate.

Consensus, according to Dryzek, is both undesirable and unattainable; he replaces it with "workable agreements in which participants agree on a course of action, but for different reasons" (2000, 170). To illustrate this, Dryzek suggests the workable agreement between environmental activists and a corporation in which each agree on pollution reduction but for vastly different reasons. The corporation might see the public relations benefit or be challenged by the inefficiency of waste, while the activists might employ their efforts to combat pollution for health, aesthetic, and environmental reasons (Dryzek 2000, 49). Different values do not necessarily yield different results; these two groups communicated their aims and reached a workable agreement in spite of their very different concerns—much like the coalition building suggested earlier. Dryzek ensures that deliberation occurs across boundaries, accommodating difference both nationally and internationally, attentively involving the participation of the oppressed and marginalized. He envisions an emancipated, active, plural, and transnational civil society committed to continued democratic decision-making.

As is evident from Dryzek's account, deliberative democrats believe that the practice of deliberation encourages civility, reciprocity, and further deliberation itself. In Dryzek's words, "Democratic participation can transform individuals" (2000, 21). As a voluntary association, the solidary group plays an important role in civil democracy. It helps provide and sustain a voice that previously went unrecognized and unheard. The group might be seen as a forceful entrant into the dialogue of political life. Part of this type of participation in public life through associational ties is that the groups themselves are self-determined. Political solidarity is no exception, though its process of self-determination varies tremendously from that of more formal organizations. The latter can ably employ the tools of discursive democracy, but political solidarity can adopt the ideals and aims of deliberative democracy, if not always the strictures of its practice. Certainly if factions within solidarity become more organized, then democratic decision-making would seem to be not only coherent with but mandated by the duties of solidarity. It is the informal ties and individual actions that do not easily fall into democratic decision-making.

A wide range of activities and attributes ought to be open to the individual so that she or he may practice those skills to which she or he is best suited in "satisfying and expansive" ways at any given time. This is especially important given political solidarity's reliance on the unique contributions of individuals. Civic participation of the sort that is political solidarity must ensure or protect individuals' self-respect thereby facilitating fuller participate in the self-determination of the group.

Because self-respect, which is one's "attitude toward her or his entire situation and life prospects," and the measure of self-respect depends on how an individual defines herself or himself, "how others regard them, . . . how they spend their time, . . . the amount of autonomy and decision making power they have in their activities, and so on" (Young 1990, 27), self-respect for the individual is in a sort of symbiotic relation with group self-determination. Self-respect, being the attitude one has toward one's self-identity, is also that which compels one to participate in self-determination processes. Ensuring that members of a solidary group have the potential to maximize self-respect enhances both the individual and the group. The solidary group, empowered to participate in the democratic decision-making processes of civic life, can simultaneously empower the individual self-respect and self-empowerment of its members. Sometimes that means democratic procedures, sometimes merely a coordination of efforts, sometimes a much more informal communication of individuated or small group activities, and always it means attentive listening. The next chapter raises some additional epistemological considerations for political solidarity that expand on these elements of collective participation.

Chandra Talpade Mohanty offers a revealing example of the sort of fluid decision-making that values both individual and collective deliberations and actions. She asks, "How have poor Third World women organized as workers? How do we conceptualize the question of 'common interests' based in 'common context of struggle,' such that women are agents who make choices and decisions that lead to the transformation of consciousness and of their daily lives as workers?" (Mohanty 2003, 161). She answers first by showing how women resist injustice and foster mutual aid in their daily life activities. In other words, the seemingly mundane activities of daily life of each individual in solidarity can be acts of resistance that not only transform the consciousness of the agent but also shape the decisions and actions of the solidaristic movement. Small and large actions alike, done publicly, consistently, and collectively, can radically transform unjust social structures. Participants may be so inspired by their action in common that they create formal organizations through which they interact with the civic public. Others will continue in their daily acts of resistance. All are united in the solidary group insofar as they press for the common social justice goal maintaining their obligations in relation to one another and the larger society. That is the power of political solidarity.

Conclusion

The final question in this discussion of decision-making within political solidarity is whether there is ever an obligation to coordinate activities into a collective movement. As I argued in Chapter 3, the moral relation that forms between participants in political solidarity includes a number of duties, including a coordination allowance. At times, that coordination will simply be the cumulative effects of multiple individual efforts, as when people in the United States boycott a company's products out of solidarity for people in a distant country who suffer from the effects of the unjust production or distribution of those products. But at other times, the coordination will have to be much more organized, as when a labor union organizes a strike in an effort to obtain fair working conditions or a just wage. As is clear with these two examples, the demands on any particular individual participant within the solidaristic relation will vary depending on the actions required. Participation within solidarity seems to imply that one be attentive to the needs of the group when it acts collectively and responsive in accordance with individual talents, skills, and abilities.

But can the actions of another in some way excuse one from acting? Robert Goodin addresses political activism on the part of some as relieving the responsibilities of others:

> If someone is vulnerable to the actions of several people taken together, then they all share responsibility for organizing to protect him. Although the organizational responsibility falls equally upon everyone, it will ordinarily be discharged by action by only a handful of political entrepreneurs. Once they have acted, all the rest are relieved of the responsibility, just as bystanders at a crowded beach are off the hook as soon as one of them rescues the drowning man. Until and unless someone else has made those organizational arrangements, however, doing so is a responsibility shared jointly and severally by the entire population. (Goodin 1985, 138)

Although not addressing political solidarity per se, when applied to political solidarity Goodin's position reflects what might be called a strong position, that is, that human beings have an obligation to unite in collective action to protect the vulnerable. A weak version might say that such collective action is supererogatory. For the particular issue of decision-making within political solidarity, both versions place some responsibility on individual participants to come to the aid of others through communication and action directed toward a goal. That communication takes many forms—some more organized or formal than others—but through the commitment to political solidarity, each individual agrees to act collectively or in concert with others for an end and that requires some coordination, however minimal. The strong version evident in the quotation above also assumes human solidarity as a social reality and a moral imperative. Chapter 7 examines the possibility of human solidarity and the potentiality for globalized political solidarity.

FIVE

The Paradox of the Participation of the Privileged

As we have seen, the solidary group is somewhat fluid; perhaps we might even call it disorganized. Formal decision-making structures generally do not exist, though, of course, factions within solidarity may organize and establish formal structures and procedures. The women's movement for liberation is a very useful example in this regard. The social movement is quite amorphous, but within the political solidarity of social activists opposing sexist structures, institutions, and practices, there are subgroups or organizations. While it would be difficult to attribute a particular decision-making procedure or power structure to the entire solidary group, it is possible to describe the procedures and structures of many of the subgroups.

So what, if anything, can we say about the decision-making within solidarity? Is it possible to call it, for example, a form of deliberative or practical democracy? Are there leaders? Do some people have more authority or authenticity as decision-makers than others? Does each participant contribute to the decision-making and the activity of political solidarity in the same way? In approaching these questions, it is helpful first to examine some of their constituent parts. The last chapter looked at many of the issues regarding the collective that we are calling the solidary group and ended with some discussion of decision-making. In this chapter I continue this thread by first examining the issue of equality within solidarity. As we saw in Chapter 3, solidarity requires mutuality, which presumes a sort of equality. But, as I will show, equality in political solidarity is quite different from equality within other forms of solidarity, deliberative democracy, or classical liberalism, though that does not preclude the use of deliberative democracy within solidarity's structures.

The second major question of the chapter examines the desirability of participation of non-oppressed and privileged with the oppressed in solidary groups. I raise a number of problems and highlight what Simone de Beauvoir would call the ambiguity of their participation. In particular this section cautions against the imposition of dominant modes of behavior and decision-making, thereby leaving unchallenged some oppressive practices. For example, the mere presence of an individual from a privileged or dominant social group may keep individuals from traditionally oppressed social groups from acknowledging or voicing their thoughts. The oppressive structures may run very deep. Many feminist theorists and postcolonial theorists have noted the debilitating impact of structures of language and thought, and I draw on their insights to explore the ambiguity that arises from the participation of the privileged. Often, the participation of former oppressors or of people clearly privileged by a form of oppression or injustice in the movement or movements to end that oppression takes a paradoxical form. The social movement to end oppression tries to go very deep to root out or challenge seemingly entrenched systems. Those individuals who are not subject to oppressive systems but instead benefit from them may be unaware of the myriad ways the structure of systemic oppression privileges them. They may even wish to draw on their privilege as they simultaneously recognize the need to end oppression in its other manifestations. But in order for participation to be authentic, as we shall see, it is necessary to challenge all manifestations of an oppressive structure, including the privilege that might otherwise provide power within social settings. Notice, however, that that does not necessarily mean abandoning all of the power that comes from privilege. Ultimately, I argue that it is not only desirable but, depending on the specific nature of the movement, may even be necessary for non-oppressed, former oppressors, and members of privileged groups to participate in political solidarity. Some of the power enjoyed by former oppressors or those privileged by oppression might be acknowledged and transformed effectively to aid the efforts for social change.

The third major theme of the chapter springs from this. I offer some suggestions for what is meant by authentic participation, focusing especially on the epistemological requirements that reinforce moral commitments to solidarity. I suggest a variety of commitments entailed in the initial commitment to political solidarity and a variety of strategies that may be employed to ensure authentic, non-oppressive, non-domineering participation. Throughout this last section, I draw extensively on some of the creative work done in feminist epistemology. In this body of work, one finds the most sustained confrontation of the social, political, moral, and epistemological privilege that accompanies most, if not all, forms of oppression.

This chapter, then, moves from a discussion of equality to an examination of the sometimes radical and necessary inequality within political solidarity. In the end, a more personal, more nuanced, and more epistemological notion of equality that serves the moral notion of mutuality and addresses the paradox of the privileged emerges to supplement other notions of equality that may be found in particular movements of political solidarity.

Equality and Solidarity

The issue of equality within the solidary group is somewhat troublesome, because some individual members may make a weak solidarity commitment while others opt for a strong commitment within the same movement. If this is the case, then it would seem misguided to say that all members should have equal power in the decision-making of the group, though there may be some compelling reasons to say that all members share equally the responsibility toward the cause. Similarly, the positive outcomes of the solidarity activity, whether it be the attainment of the final goal or merely advances in the conditions of the oppressed, are or ought to be equally shared by all—including those members of the oppressed group who opted not to join in the political struggle that we are here calling political solidarity.

So, what is meant by equality in political solidarity? A number of traditional understandings of equality present themselves but given that solidarity is a unique social relation mediating between the individual and the community and entailing positive duties, and that political solidarity as a species of solidarity per se is a chosen commitment, it seems at least plausible that if political solidarity is going to lay claim to equality, it will be a unique or specific form of equality.

It is worth pausing briefly here to say a word about the Philosopher of Equality himself, Jean-Jacques Rousseau. Rousseau could equally be called the Philosopher of Solidarity; indeed Mark Cladis suggests this by tracing a lineage from Rousseau to Durkheim (Cladis 2003). According to Rousseau, equality is both (1) an equal distribution of the rights and privileges under civil law, and (2) an equal participation in civil society. Each of us is both subject and sovereign so that none of us is slave. These stem from Rousseau's caution against extreme disparities between the rich and the poor, or, in other words, distributive inequality. Some arrangement conducive to at least (3) a loose equality in the distribution of resources and goods, is a precursor for civil and participatory equality.

But these three notions of equality reflect the traditional social and political understandings of equality. Solidarity may draw on these, but if the unity of solidarity is no more than some combination of traditional conceptions of equality, then there is little unique about that moral relation. Rousseau is once again instructive in ferreting out the differences between a traditional political community or organization and the group that forms under the auspices of political solidarity.

Rousseau's solidarity is probably best understood as social solidarity, but an argument may be made that it has its roots in a sort of political solidarity in opposition to unjust property relations. The community Rousseau sketches in his *Social Contract* and *Letter to D'Alembert on the Theatre* consists of like-minded, similarly tempered people. Their similarity is a mark of their social solidarity, and moral obligations arise from this commonality. Of course, one might argue that Rousseau really had a political solidarity in mind in constructing the social contract. The oppositional cause of such a political solidarity would be the injustice that arises from following the whims of public opinion and the vicissitudes of the power that accrues with the implementation of private property. The social contract aims to construct a society that enhances nature's virtues and ensures equality among all participants. In this sense, his social contract might be seen as a theoretical account of political solidarity. Certainly the French Revolutionaries and others inspired by Rousseau's writings to take action for social change support this reading. But while efforts to bring about social change may be instances of political solidarity (and remember that not every movement for social change or revolution is), the movement does not necessarily remain an instance of political solidarity. The formation of society congeals political solidarity into a social solidarity. The meaning of equality then also shifts to be much more in line with traditional political conceptions of equality.

Two additional conceptions of equality have emerged in more recent discussions within social philosophy. One is (4) equality of responsibility found in discussions of collective responsibility and the other is (5) a sort of equality in difference. Mutuality, the moral duty identified in Chapter 3 as constitutive of the duties to others within the solidary group, is crucial to unpacking the role and conception of equality for political solidarity. Recall that mutuality emphasizes the uniqueness of each participant in solidarity while affirming the interdependence and reciprocity between all. Mutuality is also mediated by the goal of the solidarity activity; individuals share a mutuality with regard to each other within the solidary group, but that mutuality need not extend beyond their collective commitment (though often it will). Mutuality presupposes some sense of equality. The task is to figure out what that sense is.

The mutuality of political solidarity cannot rely solely on a notion of equality as "equality under the law," the first notion of equality mentioned above. The loosely conjoined individuals acting in solidarity do not establish their own formal organization or system of governance and so cannot be considered equal under the law that governs the solidarity activity. The group is a part of a society but does not form a society itself, so members do not share equally in the distribution of rights and privileges meted out by the solidary group. In fact, political solidarity is not the sort of political body that distributes legal rights, though there are some reasonably expected moral and epistemological privileges that members in solidarity may expect. Very often it is a civil law or system of law that those in solidarity find oppressive or unjust. Members may be committed to the cause of ensuring that the larger society distributes rights and privileges equitably. So, *within* the solidary group, equality does not mean civil, legal, or political equality. But that is not an abandonment of this particular conception of equality. On the contrary, civil, legal, or political equality may be the motivating force of the commitment of participating individuals in political solidarity.

The second approach to equality, equality of participation or equality within decision-making procedures, would largely depend on the nature of the personal commitment an individual makes, his or her ability, and the form and extent of political solidarity. As the previous chapter suggested, relatively small social movements or groups might employ something like a deliberative structure or even seek consensus. Both models would require relative equality among participants. These measures, however, become impractical or impossible for larger solidarity movements, some of which may nonetheless have formal organizational structures in addition to or within the informal movement of political solidarity. The activity that an individual undertakes in solidarity is based on personal commitment and ability but often the activity parallels the activity of others also acting for the desired end or even in concert with others for that end. There may indeed be some opportunities to engage in formal discussions and perhaps even vote on courses of action or agendas for the social movement, but more often than not even these discussions or agendas remain fluid to allow for the contingencies that arise in social activism. Group decision-making is not always appropriate in such cases. In fact, giving too much power to the group licenses a sort of litmus test for participants by giving the group power to judge authenticity of participation. On the other hand, however, mutuality does mean that individual participants cannot merely claim to be in solidarity. There must be some sense of shared responsibility and personal transformation.

In traditional political theory, equality is also used in connection with the distribution of resources. Political solidarity may arise around the intent of obtaining a greater equality in the distribution of resources or goods, but within the solidary group other means of measuring distribution must be employed. Members of a social movement of political solidarity form only a very loose group, as we have seen, and there are no goods within the group to be distributed. On the contrary, commitment to solidarity very often requires a sacrifice of some sort—materially, physically, socially. But there is also another side to this notion of equality within solidarity. Social activism aims to alleviate injustice or end oppression. When the good or resource to be distributed is liberation, then a fairly strict notion of equality applies. This is, in fact, one of the challenges of solidarity, as oppression is often so deeply engrained in social structures that its effects are not always easily identified. The solidary group's joint commitment continues as long as individuals continue to recognize effects of injustice or oppression operative in their own lives or the lives of others. Distributional equality transforms into an ideal of mutual liberation.

Another conception of equality is equality of responsibility, which I discussed in Chapters 2 and 3 when I situated political solidarity as a form of collective responsibility and discussed the primary moral relations and their corresponding duties. Political solidarity implies that those who join the collective feel a relevantly similar sense of responsibility in attempting to alleviate injustice and agree to cooperate with others insofar as their individual powers, abilities, and exigencies allow. Certainly there will be stronger and weaker commitments to the cause, and thus each person's measure of responsibility will vary accordingly. But in making the commitment to political solidarity, one is saying, "I agree to these obligations." Of course, the obvious question is what this responsibility really amounts to. If one participant's commitment is of the weak form and another's is stronger, then how can we say that they are equally responsible? They clearly do not give equally to the cause, nor do they dedicate themselves equally. Usually "responsibility" is cast as responsible to someone or some thing or responsible for someone or some thing. In the case of political solidarity the responsibility is to one's own commitment with all its inherent duties. Equality of responsibility consists of the shared personal integrity to keep the commitment so long as one is able and to engage in the critical self-reflection necessary to see the commitment active in multiple aspects of one's life. Political solidarity's particular instantiation would determine most of the content of our equally shared responsibility.

Equality might also be conceived as the unique value of each person's abilities. In any social movement, there will be times when one person's ability to articulate the cause appears seemingly more important than another person's steadfast boycott or vice versa; at other times a smaller group within the collective may be more powerfully connected with the forces of social change than others who are nevertheless dedicated to the cause. In spite of these differences, and many others like them, within political solidarity each person brings unique perspective and contributes unique talent to the overall movement. Because of the nature of political solidarity, individuals contribute what they can, based on their personal degree of commitment. Their actions become collective insofar as they aim at a particular end or share a cause. The movement is more than an aggregate of these individuals but it would also be substantially less without each of them. As many of the examples presented in previous chapters illustrate, small actions—like electing to purchase only fair trade products or boycotting products from companies that employ unjust labor practices—can bring about tremendous social change when practiced consistently and are joined with the unique and substantial contributions of many others.

Five different forms of equality have been identified. First, there is the classical liberal notion of equality as equal distribution of civil rights and privileges or equality under the law. Stemming from this is the notion of equality as equal participation in decision-making procedures that affect one's life or the notion of equality found in deliberative democracy. The third is equality in distribution of resources. Fourth is the notion of equality modified from accounts of collective responsibility: equality of responsibility. And fifth is equality in difference whereby each person contributes uniquely to the cause or the collective according to his or her commitment and ability.

One of the distinguishing characteristics of solidarity is that it blends personal autonomy with group affiliation. Some individuals at various times might have a better understanding of the situation of injustice and might be better prepared to suggest paths of action for the group. These people might, in other words, make use of their personal power, access to knowledge, and/or social status to persuade other members of the group to adopt a course of action. All actions of political solidarity, whether part of the direct action for social change or part of the individual and communal decision-making, must be done in accordance with the other binding moral obligations discussed in Chapter 3.

Political solidarity requires a rethinking of many of our traditional conceptions within political philosophy. The relationships within the solidary group, the relation between the group and the larger society, and the particular aim or goal of solidarity activity challenge accepted notions of equality. The five conceptions discussed and transformed above compose a sketch of the role equality plays within a theoretical account of political solidarity.

Of course, by including equality within the concept of mutuality or political solidarity more generally, a troubling problem does arise. Some individuals may join in solidarity and apply their persuasive powers to lead or even co-opt the group. Others might come from the privileged or oppressor groups and may not want to relinquish a power or privilege based on their status within the wider society. Their power within the solidary group might even be based on the very social injustice that political solidarity aims to combat. We can think of this in terms of a paradox: Formerly privileged individuals have thrown off privilege in order to combat the injustice that was the source of their privilege, but their states as formerly privileged may intimidate others within the solidary group or accord them further privilege within the solidary group. Often those with the most persuasive ability, social status, or group stature might have the least experience with the situation of injustice or oppression (indeed, they may even come from the ranks of the oppressors). They may not be aware of the way their privilege becomes reinscribed in the solidary group or they may relish their new found power with a well-meaning if misplaced arrogance. Might it, then, be desirable to limit who counts as members of the group in political solidarity?

The "privilege" discussed is privilege that results from oppression of others or from injustice done to others. It is a form of social privilege, though it may not be accompanied by social status or security. Think, for instance, of southern whites during the Jim Crow era of the United States. Many did enjoy wealth and security, some of which is directly attributable to an unjust racial system. Many southern whites, however, lived in poverty or under the threat of violence but were nonetheless privileged by the racial system of the Jim Crow South. Social privilege, in other words, is a position in relation to oppression and injustice; it marks those who are not subject to the oppression and injustice and who in some way benefit from it.

Moral and epistemological privilege also results from oppression or injustice, but in an inverse fashion to social privilege. The more one experiences the hardships of oppression and injustice, the more claim one has to moral and epistemological privilege. Broadly speaking, moral privilege or moral superiority is grounded in a belief that the oppressed and those who suffer under an injustice are more entitled to set the agenda for any collective response to the particular injustice because they have more at stake. Their response may be justified on the basis of self-defense, self-preservation, rights to bodily integrity, or any number of related justifications.

Alternatively or correlatively, it might be claimed that the oppressed have an epistemological privilege or superiority because of their situation of oppression. An epistemological privilege can be interpreted in many different ways, some of which I examine below. Epistemological privilege generally holds that the experience of oppression gives the oppressed knowledge and perspective that is unavailable otherwise. Through this "insider's awareness," they are better able to assess the causes and consequences of oppression and have a better understanding of how best to respond. Both moral privilege and epistemological privilege risk conflating social solidarity with political solidarity; that is, they risk turning political solidarity into a movement open only to those who are directly affected by an oppression or injustice. There may be a number of redeeming qualities about such a movement and it is certainly possible that a local political solidarity could be a movement populated solely by those directly affected. But more expansive movements of political solidarity, national and international campaigns, require a different conception of membership, one that allows for those who have renounced at least some of their privilege—social, moral, and epistemological.

Certainly if a person experiences oppression firsthand, then that person might feel a stronger personal compulsion to respond through social activism. But does experiencing oppression grant a person moral or epistemological privilege within movements of political solidarity? I argue that the experience of oppression may give some of the oppressed more incentive to join in the struggle for liberation, but that experience alone is not necessary or sufficient to participation. An awareness of one's condition as contingent, not natural or given, is required of those who are oppressed or suffer under injustice. Individuals who do not share the experience of oppression or injustice may also be justified in their response and thus also share equivalent moral standing. They are morally justified insofar as they discerned through careful social criticism or moral deliberation that some situation is unjust and have freely chosen to respond through commitment to others and social activism. Furthermore, a diversity of perspectives on oppression as well as a diversity of experiences in society benefits a solidarity movement by allowing for much richer social criticism and much more complex utilization of skills in resistance efforts.

The Desirability and Advantages of the Privileged Joining in Solidarity

Political solidarity is a very demanding social and moral relation. It also can be quite frustrating. Efforts to bring about social change are rarely immediately embraced by the larger societies in which they operate, especially if those efforts aim to unseat important power positions or long-standing social structures. The commitment is never undertaken lightly, though it may be undertaken somewhat unwillingly initially. Given this level of commitment and the openness for personal transformation that participants in solidarity accept, it is worth asking whether any limits ought to be placed on membership. Why even consider not letting everyone who wants to participate do so? Morally, I am inclined to say that political solidarity, with its basis in an individual's commitment, could just as easily be understood as an issue for personal morality; if a person willingly accepts the sacrifices, hardships, and duties entailed in the commitment for a just cause, why even raise the specter of doubt that his or her actions might be unwelcome? But solidarity is not just an issue for personal morality. Solidarity mediates between the individual and the community, or, to be more precise, communities. One of the communities is the solidary group itself, and while it is, as we have seen, only very loosely described as a group, there are nevertheless some moral considerations regarding participation that the group must consider.

The previous section set up these considerations by noting that not every participant contributes to the collective efforts in the same way. We could state this even more strongly by saying that some efforts will in fact be more valued or valuable than others for achieving the collective end. While it is next to impossible to lay out a theory for such contributions, as we have seen, some have suggested that those who suffer from injustice or oppression themselves are not only more valuable but also contribute more authentically to the collective efforts than others. In fact, many, if not most, accounts of solidarity speak of it as a relation among the oppressed themselves.

There are ample reasons for us to be at least skeptical of an experience-based theory of political solidarity. *Oppression* is perhaps best understood through the experience of oppression itself, but *solidarity* is a distinct relation albeit interconnected with and informed by the particular experience of oppression. In solidarity, the socially privileged actually may have some insight or be able to help demystify their experience and that of other privileged people who may resist the acknowledgment that their status depends on an unjust social structure. Political solidarity skirts the insider's awareness criterion by basing participation not on experience but on commitment. If solidarity is based strictly on actually experiencing some form of oppression or injustice, then it is better identified as social solidarity rather than political solidarity. The dilemma is this: valuable knowledge about how oppression and injustice function as well as how efforts at liberation affect daily life comes from actually experiencing it. But experiencing oppression may not compel all oppressed individuals or groups to oppose it (indeed, some may not even recognize it as oppression), though it will compel many to stand up in opposition. Individuals who do not directly experience oppression but nevertheless recognize it as unjust, may lend some additional clarity to what has gone on and what needs to be done to bring about social change through their detachment. But they may also inadvertently entrench some systems or structures of oppression even within the social movement itself if they are not sufficiently aware of how oppression works.

If political solidarity is based on an initial commitment by individuals, it must allow for a much wider membership. The feasibility and desirability of including individuals from the oppressor or socially privileged castes, classes, or groups in solidarity with others more directly affected by oppressive or unjust conditions becomes one of the key questions of political solidarity. Although I focus primarily on this tougher case of social privilege, the discussion informs less problematic cases, such as others who are not counted among the oppressed but are not privileged by the oppression either. Of course, some argue that insofar as one is not a victim of oppression, one is therefore privileged in some way by the system of oppression.

Taking her cue from Simone de Beauvoir, Sonia Kruks concludes that the participation of the privileged in social movements that do not directly affect them is fraught with ambiguity. In addition to the risks already mentioned above—that those privileged by injustice or oppression will fail to renounce their privilege or usurp the power and vision within a solidaristic movement—there are risks that their participation might be counterproductive, that they might valorize the experience of oppression or assume the victims of oppression have a sort of moral superiority that extends beyond their oppressed condition. Kruks points out the risks of objectification, appropriation, and overidentification with the victims of injustice (2001, ch. 6). Clearly problems of incorporating socially privileged individuals or former oppressors abound, but there are also strong potentialities for their participation. In addition to the diversity of perspectives and blend of unique talents mentioned above, an argument in favor of more inclusive solidarity movements is that real social change, while not renouncing its oppositional politics, has to embrace, dialogue with, seek alliance with those very people who support (consciously or temporarily unconsciously) unjust or oppressive thoughts, practices, and social structures. Transforming the consciousness of only those who experience oppression and injustice is not going to bring about a thorough-enough change of social structures and practices. In addition, Kruks suggests that it may be the case that the oppressed are not in fact able to speak for themselves or be their own best advocates (2001, 173). Ultimately, she argues, the participation of privileged peoples in social movements with the oppressed or victims of injustice must be handled on a case-by-case basis. Any sort of codification risks "demobilizing" some or all parties involved. While I agree with Kruks on this point, there are some epistemological attitudes that may be discussed—though perhaps not codified—that will increase the probability that the participation of those people who do not themselves suffer from oppression or injustice does not repeat or reflect the very oppressive practices the solidaristic movement opposes.

There are also other benefits to including members of formerly privileged or former oppressors among the ranks of the oppressed in political solidarity activity if they renounce their privilege or recognize their privilege and use it to subvert the structures that give them privilege in the first place. Oppressed groups may not have all of the tools of persuasion or access to the power structures that might be necessary for effecting social change. By coming from among the group of oppressors or from among groups privileged by systemic oppression, some individuals will not only be able to suggest avenues for social change but will also have access to the social and political circles that could change policies or laws in accordance with the solidary group's aims.

In addition to the access to some of the tools and methods that might be useful for social change, individuals from non-oppressed groups or from privileged groups might assist in recognizing how the solidary group's actions affect varying interests across social strata. Movements of political solidarity may be quite concrete and focused on a single target—like obtaining adequate healthcare coverage for laborers at a particular factory—or they might be much more abstract—like ending sexist oppression. Part of the role of social criticism discussed in Chapter 3 was to ensure that the goal helped to inform the particular actions. But here we can add the additional element that the members themselves might employ a sort of social criticism to point out the way particular proposals or actions affect them or other oppressed groups. Solidarity activity ought to aim at liberation. Varying perspectives from a variety of peoples within the solidary group will help to avoid inflicting violence on other peoples or merely reversing the structure of oppression. Once again, the diversity of voices—even voices from the socially privileged or others not subject to oppression—aids in the solidarity effort to end oppression or injustice. Nancy Fraser notes, "No single oppressed group can possibly win significant structural change on its own, nor can any be trusted to look out for the interests of the others. Moreover, social transformation requires struggle in the sense of engagement with one's opponents" (1989, 13; see also Harvey 1999). Fraser's comment highlights the need not only for widely construed participation in solidarity; it also notes the importance of having some connection with those in the opposition. Individuals from the opposition who, for whatever reason, have joined in the solidarity struggle are the obvious candidates to initiate those connections.

In a contrary fashion, Sandra Bartky retains the term "solidarity" specifically for relations of outsiders with those who suffer oppression: "We do not share in the sufferings of those with whom we want to stand in solidarity. Their suffering is the intentional object to which our commiseration, a 'vicarious visualization' is directed" (2002, 81). Common parlance also frequently appeals to this use of the term, and it does have the benefit of assuming an important aspect of the point I have been arguing for in this section. Its weakness lies in the implicit structure of the solidary relation: the oppressed become object of our intentions rather than co-agents for change.

Bartky identifies another weakness inherent in solidarity relations: the "wretchedness problem." As she describes it, the problem involves the despair that could result when one realizes the extent of injustice and oppression and the seemingly endless possibilities for solidarity action: "Insofar as political activists are fully cognizant of and emotionally attuned to the wretchedness of the wretched of the earth, how can we save ourselves from despair, or from a psychological paralysis that could rob us of political effect?" (Bartky 2002, 81). The answer, according to Bartky, lies in the emotional distance that is required for action, and, I might add, such "distancing" could be accomplished not through a detached political activism but through the accumulation of multiple perspectives on the problem of oppression itself. Political solidarity requires social criticism, and that social criticism is informed by the effects of injustice on diverse peoples. Oppression does not generally just affect a single group. Men too are adversely affected by sexism even as they garner privileges from its continued practice. While we would not want to overemphasize that point, oppression itself is only one source of valuable knowledge for social criticism. At times, detachment from the experience of oppression might lend insight that otherwise would not be revealed. Solidarity action is not without emotion; it entails many interweaving sentiments. Avoiding those feelings that paralyze can be accomplished through working with multiple others for a cause.

In the end, then, political solidarity may be a response to one's own oppression or to the oppression of others. In either case, the group that forms faces many challenges as it confronts the structures of oppression that permeate their own relations as well as the relations with the wider society. Even if one does not share in the experience of the oppressed, one can still participate in solidarity with others who make a similar commitment. But these formerly privileged solidary actors will have to renounce not just their social privilege but also any epistemological privilege they might have enjoyed in the dominant culture. Only then will they be able to sustain genuine fellow feeling that would allow the experience of oppression others suffer to become more understandable. They may never know with certitude, but they can gain an understanding that serves the mutuality in the solidary group. In the next section, I explore some approaches to just such an epistemology.

Paradox of the Privileged

In the *Ethics of Ambiguity,* Simone de Beauvoir asserts that the oppressed are in some way more authentically involved in the effort to end oppression: "In any case, we can assert that the oppressed is more totally engaged in the struggle than those who, though at one with him in rejecting his servitude, do not experience it; but also that, on the other hand, every man is affected by this struggle in so essential a way that he can not fulfill himself morally without taking part in it" (Beauvoir 1948a, 88–89). But does an assumption that the oppressed will be more engaged, as Beauvoir says, indicate that their participation is more authentic than non-oppressed participants? Can non-oppressed individuals not only participate authentically but also offer something important to solidarity?

Earlier, I commented on the distinction of moral privilege, epistemological privilege of the oppressed, and social privilege. The concepts are not unrelated, but epistemological and/or moral privilege within solidarity is often granted to those who suffer oppression. Those who benefit from the unjust or oppressive social structure enjoy social privilege. In this section, I use both epistemological and social privilege. The central question is how those who enjoy social privilege can possibly share any epistemological commonality with those who actually experience oppression. Such a question assumes both that it is desirable for socially privileged people to renounce their privilege and participate in solidarity struggle and that in doing so they need some sort of knowledge or understanding of the lived-experience of oppression itself. How they get that or whether they can get that epistemological status is at issue. In the process of addressing this question, I examine some alternative models, some of which grant epistemological privilege or moral privilege to those who actually experience oppression.

What are the requirements for authentic participation of the privileged in solidarity struggles? How can we hope to resolve the paradox of privilege presented at the outset of this chapter? After examining three alternative feminist epistemological approaches to the paradox of the privileged, I use insights garnered to suggest ways the socially privileged might both renounce their status and participate in solidarity without usurping the power or goals of the solidary group for the theory of political solidarity articulated in Chapter 2. Feminist epistemology is doubly instructive here. It emerges from within a social movement and it aims at articulating solidarity among women. As we will see, the differences among the four theoretical approaches I discuss stem from what solidarity is meant to encompass: social connectedness or political aspirations or some combination of the two.

Can the Non-oppressed Authentically Participate?

Can those who do not suffer under a particular form of oppression participate authentically in solidarity action? In the present context, the focus is on the epistemological version of this question. Think, for example, of men who want to end sexism, heterosexual-identified individuals who want to end homophobia or ensure just distribution of social privileges to homosexuals, well-off individuals who advocate economic restructuring to the benefit of the poor, able-bodied persons lobbying on behalf of disabled; the list goes on and on. These participants in solidarity renounce at least some of the social and moral privilege that comes from the dominant group's position in society. Of course, it would be quite impossible to renounce one's perceived place in society entirely because other people often play a larger than expected role in maintaining one's social position. Nevertheless, the personal transformation that is entailed in one's commitment to solidarity includes an acknowledgement of the way privilege functions and possibly also a refusal of the benefits of that privilege. The epistemological question pertains to what kind of knowledge is required for authentic participation.

Given that political solidarity is based on commitment, it may seem as if the obvious answer to this problem is that one need only have adequate information about the nature and cause of an injustice in order to join in the social movement to challenge it. To some extent, this is true for social movements more generally.

But there is something special about the relationship that we call "solidarity." It presumes a form of "fellow feeling" or "feeling with" (Scheler 1970; Bartky 2002, 77) that unites the individual members of the social movement in a more complex and extensive fashion. The "fellow feeling" of political solidarity is consciously embraced as part of the commitment. Here, fellow feeling is constituted by the obligations to others in the solidary group enumerated in Chapter 3: Cooperation, communication, mutuality. The unity of solidarity, as we have seen, transforms each individual member as it simultaneously enlivens the collective effort to bring about change.

The Paradox of the Participation of the Privileged

Some have claimed that political solidarity requires an insider's awareness of the problems to be addressed by social activism. An insider's awareness comes from actually experiencing firsthand the oppression or injustice. In that case, a person who is in some way privileged (or minimally not disadvantaged) by a manifestation of oppression could not participate at all or could not participate on the same level as those who are directly affected by the oppression. For instance, one might argue that because white people lack an awareness or knowledge of the intricacies of the situation of racism within the United States, and are in many ways privileged by that racism, whites are unable to participate at the same level or intensity as blacks or those others who are directly disadvantaged by racism.

As I have argued, the solidary group of political solidarity is not equivalent to the oppressed group, though there will be some overlap. Where there is overlap—that is, where members of the oppressed do join in political solidarity—their personal commitment and not their oppression is what makes them members. Their knowledge and experience, however, probably do compel the choice and certainly serve as valuable tools for social analysis and solidarity activity.

Many of the theoretical discussions for how to accommodate the particular knowledge claims of the oppressed within the solidary group assume that the solidarity of social activism is social solidarity. That is, they assume that when speaking of solidarity it is solidarity of the oppressed. But, as I have argued, there are compelling reasons to include non-oppressed or even former oppressors among those who struggle to end the oppression. Is that simply a different kind of solidarity, or can we unite our efforts—oppressed and privileged alike—for the same cause? Clearly, I think we can, but I also agree that there is something important about the knowledge claims of the oppressed that ought to be taken into account in the identity and decision-making of the solidary group. I also argue that the specialized knowledge claims of the oppressed affect each individual's moral commitment, or, conversely, the commitment requires an active acknowledgement of the experience of the oppressed.

Three epistemological approaches to this problem in solidarity studies are the standpoint model, the dialogic model (both of which blend or conflate social and political solidarity), and the dispositional model (which expands social solidarity slightly to include others within a web of relations with the oppressed). Each model has its strength and yields useful insights for a theory of political solidarity. But each also faces a number of limitations pertaining to the participation of the non-oppressed and the nature of political involvement.

Drawing from the insights of these three alternative models for the epistemological problem of including the privileged in solidarity aids in crafting a practicable epistemology for the theory of political solidarity I articulate. Political solidarity relies on an extension of the personal commitment of each participant into the epistemological demands of solidarity. Individuals must choose not only to act in concert but also elect to attempt to understand the experience of oppression. But that understanding emerges within particular relationships characterized by openness and attentiveness. After examining the alternatives, I offer a model of epistemology for political solidarity that emphasizes and illustrates the various epistemic facets of the commitment to political solidarity.

Standpoint Theory

One of the first attempts to question the assumption of the universality of truth and the objectivity of knowledge is in Karl Marx's critique of capitalism. Marx suggested that knowledge is a product of material conditions and class relations. The owner class lays claim to objective truth, but their claim is founded on and motivated by their class position. Recognizing that knowledge is not in fact objective or truth universal is a step in throwing off the ideology that keeps the class system in place. If knowledge is a result or product of material conditions, then it follows that different social classes will have different worldviews or see different truths. That is, they will have different standpoints. Standpoint epistemology, then, developed as a nontraditional epistemology to highlight and validate the worldview of the working class within Marx's critique of capitalism.

Marx argued that only the working classes could see and understand the structures of class oppression. From their vantage point on the bottom of social structures, the working class knows not only their own situation but the structure of privilege as well. Most standpoint theory assumes a sort of two-class system—the dominant worldview and the subordinate or oppressed worldview—determined by material conditions. In the Marxist tradition, this could also be described as the owners and the workers or producers. Feminist standpoint challenges the Marxist position to recognize the gender division of labor so that standpoint takes on a slightly different character but the basic structure remains the same. From the vantage point of the working class, social and economic systems contingently give some power while others suffer. The bourgeoisie, blinded by their power within the capitalist system, see their situation and that of the workers as natural or even necessary. They thus have no incentive to question their privilege and thus fail to scrutinize the social structures that ensure it.

A standpoint is an "engaged" position. As Nancy Hartsock describes it, standpoint theory contends that some standpoints do not allow for "visibility" of real relations of humans. Social relations are conditioned by material life or class position: "If material life is structured in fundamentally opposing ways for two different groups, one can expect that the vision of each will represent an inversion of the other, and in systems of domination the vision available to the rulers will be both partial and perverse" (Hartsock 1983, 285). The dominant vision functions to structure the material relations of everyone but is necessarily incomplete. The oppressed group must struggle to achieve its vision and see beyond the surface that is structured by the dominant group. The dominant group enjoys the power and privilege of determining the social standards of truth; their consciousness becomes internalized not only among the dominant but also among the oppressed. Insofar as the dominant class successfully inscribes their worldview on society, the oppressed accept their position as natural. But, as Hartsock explains, both science and education arising out of struggle accomplish the vision of the oppressed. Both expose the oppression as a social fact rather than a natural condition. Because it is engaged, then, the vision of the oppressed exposes the reality of social life by revealing the inhumanity of the dominant or oppressive vision. The oppressed obtain an understanding that "points beyond the present, and carries a historically liberatory role" (Hartsock 1983, 285).

Standpoint holds that the different levels of social existence contradict, and out of that contradiction arises the standpoint of the oppressed and social critique of the surface structures of society. Two opposing classes characterize all social organization. While rooted in social class, standpoint theory has been extended not only to gender but also applied to other forms of oppression; it maintains, however, the dual-class system and the basis in material life by redefining the classes as men/women, white/black, able-bodied/disabled, and so forth. The challenge is to demonstrate how a subordinated group's oppression is based on class division; thus feminist standpoint theory shows how reproductive activity provides women with a unique understanding of reality.

But this approach has been criticized for excluding those women who do not engage in the praxis of reproduction but are nonetheless subject to sexism. Only those who experience oppression, the second half of the dichotomies, and experience it in a particular way, can know or explain the multiplicity of ways that it affects their lives. Those who are privileged, on the other hand, have little incentive to question their privilege. If they do throw off their privilege, perhaps because of feelings of indignation at the suffering of another human being or perhaps because they somehow recognize that their privilege structurally relies on the suffering of others, then they still will not be able to see with the eyes of those who actually experienced the oppression because they do not share in the material conditions of the oppressed or dominated. Practical activity of the worker, women, blacks, and others informs their epistemological standpoint. Exchange and production yield different epistemologies, the former is "both partial and fundamentally perverse" (Hartsock 1983, 287). The dominant group has the power to make its vision real because it has the power of defining terms for society. A standpoint challenges this position by revealing how the dominant view only represents a partial reality that itself is so skewed, "perverse," that it fails even to fully reflect the social structure crafted by the dominant group to maintain its privilege.

Twentieth-century liberation theorist Paulo Freire employs a version of standpoint theory by showing that the poor share a vision that the rich cannot similarly share. Seeing oppression from the ground up or from the eyes of the oppressed yields a more complete picture of reality, so the argument goes. According to Freire, oppressors impose their consciousness on the oppressed through prescription: "One of the basic elements of the relationship between oppressor and oppressed is *prescription*. Every prescription represents the imposition of one man's choice upon another, transforming the consciousness of the man prescribed to into one that conforms with the prescriber's consciousness. Thus, the behavior of the oppressed is a prescribed behavior, following as it does the guidelines of the oppressor" (Freire 1968, 31, emphasis in original). Although Freire posits an oppressor group that does the prescribing, prescription may result from specific societal structures that create or enforce the power of an oppressor or dominant group. The key is that the consciousness and behavior of the oppressed is determined, and the oppressed does not have the determining power. When the oppressed engage in critical reflection that reveals the influence of oppression on the formation of consciousness, liberatory praxis begins.

Sonia Kruks (2001) uses the term "epistemology of provenance" to illustrate both the potential and the limitations of grounding knowledge claims within solidarity on the lived experience of oppression or injustice. According to the epistemology of provenance, one would have to be oppressed in the same manner as others in order to understand the oppression and respond in solidarity. Those who do not share in the situation of oppression cannot engage in the same sort of social criticism or solidarity activity; indeed, they are limited from saying much about the oppression or injustice at all because the epistemology of provenance excludes the non–group member from knowledge claims.

When solidarity is presumed to arise out of the immediate experience of injustice and a desire to create social change, the social group of the oppressed is conflated with the solidary group. Freire and Marx both recognized the exigency of involving non-oppressed, usually intellectuals occupying that middle ground between oppressors and oppressed, in the struggle for liberation. But they are left with the conundrum of how to articulate the consciousness of these non-oppressed such that they can participate in social movements to end oppression without reinscribing their privilege within the movement itself.

This point is at the heart of some of the objections to standpoint theory. Standpoint arose from Marx's critique of material conditions, but as I previously hinted, not all forms of oppression are manifest through material conditions and not all those people we would count among the oppressed engage in the particular activity that defines the class (e.g., poor who do not work, women who do not reproduce). There have been some attempts to accommodate alternative forms of oppression—those that cut across material reality—but without the praxis of the subordinated group within the duality of material relations, the standpoint seems to disappear.

One way to oppose the epistemology of provenance is to realize that social groups are overlapping—as are forms of oppression. Any individual might be a member of a number of groups at any given time (for example, groups based on race, sex, or class). And oppression is rarely from a singular source. Racism, classism, sexism, ableism, ageism, and other forms of oppression intersect in multiple and varied ways. While we must be careful not to lump all oppressions together, recognizing the intersections and interconnections does help to put into perspective identity claims based on oppression. The experience of oppression is rarely monolithic—different people are differently affected by it. Group identity claims have a much more difficult time standing up once we understand that individuals experience oppression(s) differently. So too privilege and oppression are not solid categories into which people fall. One can be both privileged and oppressed. Examples are numerous. The white middle-class female who fights for just economic distribution has likely suffered under some form of sexism. The man who fights sexism may have experienced the pain of racism.

As Kruks too points out, Hartsock has modified her position to address some of these concerns and to account for differences across varying forms of oppression. Arguing that experiences differ and that we ought not to overlook those important differences, she asserts that similarities still exist: "There are a number of connections to be made and similarities to be seen in the epistemologies contained in the experience of dominated groups" (Hartsock 1998, 240–41; cited in Kruks 2001, 113). Hartsock goes on to invoke solidarity as the relation between varieties of feminists, thereby implying that liberatory activity need not be motivated by exactly the same experiential worldview or ideological position. In a similar vein, Donna Haraway develops an epistemology that challenges traditional (read: dominant) epistemologies, but she eschews some of the perceived weaknesses of standpoint epistemology by situating knowledge claims in embodied existence rather than material existence per se. This too allows for specialized knowledge claims but recognizes that those claims may come from quite varied experiences. The result is not relativism but "partial, locatable critical knowledges sustaining the possibility of webs of connections called solidarity in politics and shared conversations in epistemology" (Haraway 1991, 191; cited in Kruks 2001, 113).

Shaping the work of political solidarity does require a specialized knowledge for social critique, and standpoint theory seems to provide a good working model for how that knowledge is obtained. It is an epistemology that arises out of the context of challenge or struggle and thus seems especially relevant to political solidarity. Among the strengths of standpoint theory is that it demonstrates that there is no neutral perspective on social reality and that even the knowledge of the oppressed is limited. Traditional epistemology lost its secure hold on meaning and truth. So too the context of struggle on which standpoint relies opened the gates for exclusive knowledge claims based on varying experiences of oppression.

Care Model

One of the most important advances within moral theory in the last thirty years has been the development of care ethics. Carol Gilligan's influential book *In a Different Voice* (1982) presented the results of numerous experiments regarding moral decision-making. Gilligan found that females tended to make moral decisions differently than males. In her study, females aimed at maintaining relationships or sought alternative resolutions to dilemmas in their decision-making while males tended to base their decisions on abstract principles. While there is no end to the controversy that these findings sparked, Gilligan did provide the inspiration for some moral theorists to articulate and expound an ethics of care. Care ethics implicitly assumes an epistemology in claiming that relations inform decision-making. As I will show in this subsection, relationships do provide not only a motive for caring but also a knowledge base in how to care. In other words, a care-based epistemology draws on empathy or care for others as a source of knowledge.

There are numerous articulations of the ethics of care, and while there are important differences between them, there are also some unifying guidelines. An ethics of care is an ethics grounded on relationships rather than abstract principles. Decisions are made based on "day-to-day interactions with other persons [which] create a web of reciprocal caring" (Manning 1992, 63). These interactions oblige us to be caring persons although we remain free in our determinations of how to care appropriately. Two guidelines for an ethics of care, according to Rita Manning, are a disposition to care and an obligation to "care for" (1992, 61–62).

A disposition to care is simply the desire to work toward filling the needs of others insofar as one has the means to do so. A disposition to care indicates the contextuality of an ethics of care, "a willingness to receive others, a willingness to give the lucid attention required to appropriately fill the needs of others" (Manning 1992, 61).

Nel Noddings's (1984) account of an ethic of care also requires that moral agents "care for." An obligation to "care for" indicates the action that is required as a caring person with a place in the world. To "care for" means that we appropriately respond to persons, that is, that we provide the type and extent of care needed. Other care theorists have extended the web of care to include animals, communities, values, or even objects in need. In all these relationships and the moral situations that confront us, our response is governed by what is needed and what our ability allows us to contribute.

Although particular relationships with others put us into roles that mandate certain duties, the roles and duties are constantly recreated, reshaped, and critiqued (Manning 1992, 64). The *dynamics of the relationship,* rather than the roles themselves, are the focus in making ethical decisions. Care is also context specific—it requires active engagement with one another's concrete experience. In her book *Maternal Thinking,* Sara Ruddick developed an epistemology based on maternal practice and inspired by Hartsock's standpoint theory. She identifies maternal thinking both as a feminist standpoint and as moving beyond standpoint to a "central expression" of the rationality of care (Ruddick 1989, 46). Maternal thinking is a strategic response to the maternal practices of protection, nurturance, and training (themselves responses to the demands of preservation, growth, and social acceptability). As she develops it, maternal thinking rejects the dualistic structure of standpoint so as to give credence to the "richness and unpredictability both of the world and of the ways in which we think about it" (1989, 135). Ruddick demonstrates how epistemology emerges from the practices of mothers. As practices change, thinking must change to meet new challenges. Moreover, any criticism, according to Ruddick, "should be left to those who have engaged in these practices" (1989, 26).

Ruddick's account is instructive for our purposes because she sees the explicitly political aspects of care. Ruddick develops a feminist peace politics based on maternal practices, and she suggestively provides the grounds for application of a care-based epistemology to other social movements, like political solidarity. Early on in her account, Ruddick reclaims concrete thinking, noting the need to adjust knowledge claims and practices to accommodate shifting situations and growing children. As she explains, "The reflectiveness of concreteness must be developed through disciplined attentiveness and then expanded and tested through critical conversational challenge. In gossip and focused conversations, mothers refine their capacity for concrete ways of knowing, practicing together attentive noticing and disciplined reflectiveness about what they notice" (1989, 98). In a similar way, participants in political solidarity engage in reflective social criticism and continually refine their understanding of oppressive or unjust situations as well as the appropriateness of their concrete responses. But there is an important difference between the epistemology based on care and an epistemology for political solidarity. In political solidarity, the participants may not themselves experience oppression or even know someone who does. That is, they may not have first-hand knowledge of oppression and injustice. Based as it is in caring relations, the care-based epistemology gives little guidance for this situation.

Kruks modifies the care model slightly to propose an "affective predisposition" that might form the basis of political solidarity. As she says, "Even though common experiences of feminine embodiment do not offer a basis for 'sisterhood,' I believe they can furnish what I will call an *affective predisposition* to act on behalf of women other than and different from oneself: a predisposition toward forms of feminist solidarity" (Kruks 2001, 151). Kruks is most interested in what she refers to as the type of solidarity wherein "an injury to others does *not* directly injure oneself (or one's own group)" (2001, 154); she explores the ability and desirability of the privileged "feeling-with" those who suffer injustice. This feeling-with develops as a motive (though not the sole motive) for solidarity action among women, according to Kruks. Or, to think of it in slightly different terms, the affective bond may be a motivating force for the participation of privileged individuals in social movements that do not directly affect them. Kruks cautions that such a bond, however, does not inform political action; that is, it does not set the agenda for political activism. The solidary union of political solidarity is formed prior to the feeling-with; that is part of what distinguishes it from social solidarity.

Rita Manning's version of the ethics of care does offer an additional component that answers, or attempts to answer, at least part of this problem for applying care-based epistemology to political solidarity. She argues that the ethics of care is capable of addressing and incorporating concerns of distant peoples as well as those who are in close proximity to the moral decision-maker. Through a recognition of commonalities shared with distant people, Manning argues that care extends beyond our immediate relationships to include distant people. But, of course, not everyone who joins in solidarity will be motivated by a sense of commonality, empathy, or care. Some might be motivated by indignation at injustice, or even a rational assessment that a law, policy, or practice is unjust. There may, in fact, be no actual victims of oppression or injustice but only the recognition that a law, policy, or practice has the potential to cause suffering or harm to other people, nonhuman animals, human institutions, or things. The commitment of political solidarity includes, at some level, a conscious choice; certainly some participants will make that commitment based on the caring relationships they have or the recognition of commonalities to distant others, but some will have entirely different, non-care-based reasons.

Political solidarity based on relationships of care takes us beyond the experience-based epistemology of standpoint by including in solidarity all those who are intimately related to those who directly suffer or those who can find a caring relation based on shared commonalities with distant others. More to the point of this section, because of the reliance on relationships, is care-based epistemology able to transform understanding through the caring connections individual socially privileged people make with oppressed others? Will these loving relationships help them identify clearly the way privilege infects their consciousness as well as their relationship with others? Sympathy and empathy have long been considered possible constituents of solidarity. Friendships certainly can and do transform individuals' consciousnesses and there is little doubt that some people will be motivated to commit to solidarity activity based on their loving relations with others—both in an effort to help end their friend's suffering and in an effort to participate in like-minded activities with a friend.

But recognition of commonality or affective bonds do not provide all the epistemic resources needed to account for the varieties of peoples who will join together in political solidarity. Recognition of this sort can lead to sometimes-pernicious reductions of differences that themselves might prove to entrench the very form of oppression or injustice solidarity struggles to end, or they may introduce new modes of exclusion or domination. Although care theorists include warnings against this, care can itself be performed in a dominating form, which, of course, would be counterproductive to political solidarity.

So too, as Kruks suggested, the disposition to care and the ability to "care for" alone are insufficiently political to sustain the solidarity of social movements. This has been a common criticism of care ethics more generally. The ethics of care does not seem able to provide a strategy for achieving a liberatory ideal. That is, although an ethics of care may provide the ethics once a liberated ideal is achieved, it may not be capable of guiding a presently oppressive society to this ideal future (Bell 1993, 35–45, 267). Sarah Lucia Hoagland argues that in order for an ethics of care to be successful in overcoming the given situation of oppression, it must "provide for the possibility of ethical behavior in relation to what is foreign, it must consider analyses of oppression, it must acknowledge a self that is both *related* and *separate,* and it must have a vision, *if not a program for change*" (Hoagland 1990, 261, emphasis added). In one sense, Hoagland's point could be read as claiming that care is reactive whereas liberatory politics must be proactive. Political solidarity demands a "program for change" informed by the goal to be achieved.

In sum then, the care model expands the possible participants in political solidarity for social change and introduces some affective elements to the relationships between participants. It relies too heavily, however, on those caring relations as motive force for the solidarity bonds and is insufficiently political, in spite of the overt political applications to which Ruddick applies it. These strengths and weaknesses, like those identified for the standpoint epistemology, instruct and inform the epistemological needs of a political solidarity.

Dialogic Model

A third model for consideration comes from recent work in political philosophy on dialogue. In particular, Nancy Fraser develops a version of communicative ethics that explicitly invokes solidarity. In her "discourse ethics of solidarity," Fraser views solidarity as a means of challenging the traditionally dominant dialogue or interpretation. In order to do so, the members of the subordinated social group join together in solidarity. It is incumbent on the subordinated or excluded group to struggle "to deconstruct narrative forms and vocabularies of dominant groups and collectivities so as to show these are partial rather than genuinely shared and are incapable of giving voice to the needs and hopes of subordinated groups" (Fraser 1986, 429). Solidarity for discourse ethics and dialogic thinking, like care ethics, is context specific (Rehg 1994, 208). Like standpoint theory, discourse ethics has some grounding in shared experience of oppression. What makes the discourse model different is that the experience is shaped not by material existence but by "discourses."

Fraser tries to mediate the conflict between difference and equality or what she calls the politics of recognition and the politics of redistribution in a "postsocialist" world. Her social theory entails an ethical theory that takes its roots in Habermassian discourse ethics but moves significantly beyond Habermas's model. Fraser's discourse ethics of solidarity requires the confrontation of exclusion or injustice via dialogue within and between social groups. Such intra- and intergroup interaction challenges traditional conceptions of what is an acceptable subject of "public discourse" while also emphasizing political economy and stressing the need for social equality. Although the social groups overlap according to Fraser, there is a gap in her theory. Social groups do not appear to overlap in such a way that an individual member of a privileged or dominant social group may identify with or advocate for the cause of a corresponding subordinate social group.

Generally speaking, a discourse ethic is one that places the determination of both the content and the methodology of the ethic in a dialogue between relevant ethical participants. That is, those individuals and social groups likely to be affected by a moral decision must have a significant say in its determination. Moral decisions are thereby reliant on the particularized social-historical contexts of moral agents. There is no overarching principle that guides these decisions. Ethical decisions are made within and between social groups or dialogic communities. Political and ethical issues and the structure of the dialogue are determined by the "socio-cultural means of interpretation and communication":

> By socio-cultural means of interpretation and communication I mean things like: the officially recognized vocabularies in which one can press claims; the idioms available for interpreting and communicating one's needs; the established narrative conventions available for constructing the individual and collective histories which are constitutive of social identity; the paradigms of argumentation accepted as authoritative in adjudicating conflicting claims; the ways in which various discourses constitute their respective subject matters as specific sorts of objects; the repertory of available rhetorical devices; the bodily and gestural dimensions of speech which are associated in a given society with authority and conviction. (Fraser 1986, 425)

The two main components of the discourse ethic of solidarity, social solidarity and a reconceptualized notion of autonomy, focus on a groups' power to interpret and communicate in the discourse. The epistemology is the "standpoint of the collective concrete other," which means that knowledge claims come from within groups engaged in oppositional politics. As Fraser states it, the standpoint of the collective concrete other "would require one to relate to people as members of collectivities or social groups with specific cultures, histories, social practices, values, habits, forms of life, vocabularies of self-interpretation and narrative traditions. Here one would abstract *both* from unique individuality *and* from universal humanity to focalize the intermediate zone of group identity" (1986, 428). The collective concrete other contests the status of the dominant group or groups and its ability to determine social discourse. Fraser explains that groups come to recognize and reinterpret their needs, offering a new vocabulary, to contest the interpretations of their needs prescribed by some dominant group ("public") (1989, 171–72). The vocabularies and needs interpretations of subordinated groups challenge the hegemony of the dominant group, which heretofore set the bounds for what was considered appropriate for public debate or discussion. Many communicative ethics theorists privilege the voice of the traditionally oppressed (e.g., Benhabib 1987 and Young 1990). Fraser also prioritizes the "oppositional discourse" of subordinated groups such as the working class, welfare recipients, women, and racial and ethnic groups. She refers to such groups as acting as "subaltern counter publics." These subaltern counter publics, determined or defined according to their exclusion from the dominant means of interpretation, confront and contest the dominant public (Fraser 1996, 80–85). Solidarity requires that these subordinate groups have equal social power to participate in public discourse. In other words, solidarity requires that the dominant groups no longer have a privileged relation to the "socio-cultural means of interpretation and communication." Fraser's solidaristic groupings are multiple, overlapping, and competing (1989, 98). Radical democracy in a multicultural society requires "robust, polylogic, abnormal discourse" that allows for "contestatory interactions among competing political vocabularies" (Fraser 1989, 106).

Fraser thus has described the standpoint of the "collective concrete other" and contrasts it with Benhabib's individualized concrete other. The purpose of this contrast is to distinguish a specifically political ethic (rather than an intimate ethic) useable by a variety of traditionally subordinated social groups in their attempts to challenge and respond to the exclusion experienced when dominant social groups set the moral agenda via their favored means of dialogue and interpretation.

Fraser's goal is to blend a "critical theory of recognition" with a "social politics of equality," that is, to occupy the space between a universal ethics and group relativity (1996, 12). Within groups, agendas are determined according to procedural consideration and consequentialist considerations: "In general, procedural considerations dictate that, all other things being equal, the best need interpretations are those reached by means of communicative processes that most closely approximate ideals of democracy, equality, and fairness. . . . [C]onsequentialist considerations dictate that, all other things being equal, the best need interpretations are those that do not disadvantage some groups of people vis-à-vis others" (Fraser 1989, 182).

Fraser notes that a "non-ideal speech situation" is any situation "where the power that structures discourse is hierarchical and asymmetrical and where some persons are prevented from pressing their claims either by overt or covert force or by such structural features such as the lack of an appropriate vocabulary for interpreting their needs" (1989, 46–47). Might it be the case that in the group dialogue of the solidary group, the participation of an individual who is privileged by some social structure, but who has renounced that privilege, would result in a "non-ideal speech situation"?

Two objections to the discourse model might be made. First, reducing oppression to discourse carries some troubling implications. As Kruks (2001) has argued, when oppression is reduced to narratives and discourses, the particularity of experience is lost. Individuals do experience oppression differently, and the intricate overlapping and interweaving of forms of oppression makes impossible any attempt to easily associate with a single subordinated group.

The second objection to a discourse model is that a discourse ethics based on subordinate groups challenging dominant groups implicitly relies on an identity model. This being the case, it seems unlikely that individuals from privileged or dominant groups who throw off their privilege are welcomed into the intra-group dialogue with individuals sharing the subordinated group identity. Or if they are welcomed, then their privileged status, or rather their non-oppressed/non-subordinated group status, means that they would not be full participants. That is, the dialogue within the group functions in part to determine or identify the group. As Fraser presents it, this identity is in response to the "dominant" group and its vocabularies and interpretations. Thus, a member of the dominant group, in order to join in political solidarity with those struggling against injustice, must adopt the vocabulary and interpretation of the solidary group. The problem is that Fraser does not offer a clear source of these vocabularies and interpretations. If, for example, the structure of the dialogue does arise in direct response to the injustice, then one who does not suffer an injustice, but is instead privileged by it, cannot fully understand and thus cannot authentically enter into solidarity.

Another potential problem is that the traditionally dominant vocabularies and interpretations seem to be systematically devalued. Certainly there are instances where this devaluation would be warranted. A racist discourse should be displaced, devalued, and overthrown. But there are instances wherein the dominant discourse still holds merit even if it has been unjustly used to exclude or oppress. Some religious discourse, for example, has been used to oppress and even do violence to nonbelievers, but understanding that discourse is a crucial aspect of dialogue. In order for the intergroup dialogue to remain authentic, there must be some way to value interpretations (otherwise we run the risk of merely flipping who counts as excluded). The discourses are situated in complex histories and experiences. Unseating the dominant discourse is not always a sufficient response to unjust practices.

Commitment or Choice-Based Model

From the three models discussed thus far, a number of elements emerge. In order to accommodate the diversity of views and yet give adequate weight to the actual experience of oppression, political solidarity needs an epistemology that acknowledges multiple, overlapping, and at times contradicting knowledge claims. These will need to be negotiated in a loving way that affirms the perspective as well as the work or experience at its base. Political solidarity also requires that individuals who commit to action in solidarity do so in a non-domineering way so as to avoid reinscribing within the solidary group itself any privileged social state they may have enjoyed in the larger society.

The model of political solidarity that I have been advancing in this book views the participation of the privileged as a three-part issue. The first part asks whether in making the commitment to solidarity an individual is willing to renounce his or her privilege—epistemologically as well as socially. The second part challenges the formerly privileged to commit to *understand* the situation and experience of the oppressed. The third part involves participation in acts of resistance. Notice that the first two of these flesh out the obligations of cooperation, communication, and possibly service discussed in Chapter 3. They take a unique shape here because we are addressing the participation of peoples whose past social status makes their involvement in solidarity potentially problematic.

Examples abound of individuals renouncing their social and epistemological privilege, the first part of their participation in solidarity. Charles Mills discusses the fact that there have always been whites who eschewed the racial privilege of whiteness. These "race traitors" "betray the white polity in the name of a broader definition of the polis" (Mills 1997, 108). In an antiblack racist system, there are clear advantages not only from being white but also from maintaining the social solidarity among whites. To be a race traitor rejects both. One's very identity as white must be recognized (and in racist societies, whiteness is often taken for granted rather than recognized) and displaced. While that is likely to cause some amount of personal anxiety, it is also likely to cause social anxiety as the traitorous actions force others to similarly recognize whiteness and its privilege. In its most extreme form, white race traitors might also experience backlash from other whites who view the race traitor's actions as more than just betrayal, but as a threat to their very existence.

Alison Bailey similarly argues for a way in which whites might throw off their privilege in order to provide better social critique. Her model is useful in discussing the paradox of the privilege as it provides some of the epistemological groundwork that is required before privileged peoples are able to join with the oppressed in confronting an unjust situation. She presents models of the "privilege-evasive script" and the "privilege-cognizant script." According to the former, a white person benefits from the racist patterns in our society but fails to recognize the foundations of his or her privilege in the oppression of blacks. In contrast, the privilege-cognizant script is the race traitor script: "Traitors *choose* to try to understand the price at which privileges are gained; they are critical of the unearned privileges granted to them by white patriarchal cultures, and they take responsibility for them" (Bailey 2000, 292–93, emphasis in original). Bailey also argues that the privilege-cognizant script must be cultivated similar to Aristotelean virtue.

In spite of its potential, there are also reasons to be critical of the race traitor script. According to Linda Martín Alcoff, the race traitor script "cannot disavow whiteness"; the race traitor cannot reject all of the privileges of being white (Alcoff 2000, 273). There is also the risk that without a political movement, the race traitor's actions will be unrecognized or even counterproductive. For this reason, political solidarity requires not just a renouncing of privilege but also the positive movements toward understanding and engagement in activism. Nevertheless, the race traitor does make a conscious effort to reject the privileges conferred on him or her by a racist system. In her essay titled "What Should White People Do?" Alcoff argues that white people need to develop a "double consciousness." Borrowing from W. E. B. Du Bois's well-known concept, she explains that "for whites, double consciousness requires an ever-present acknowledgement of the historical legacy of white identity constructions in the persistent structures of inequality and exploitation, as well as a newly awakened memory of the many white traitors to white privilege who have struggled to contribute to the building of an inclusive human community" (Alcoff 2000, 281).

The race traitor script and double consciousness accompany the commitment to solidarity with the oppressed by laying aside the privilege garnered from the system of oppression. Recall that renouncing social privilege means acknowledging how it functions and, whenever possible and useful for the cause of solidarity, refusing its benefits. Similar methods can be used to recognize or acknowledge one's own privilege or complicity in other forms of oppression as well. But acknowledgement by itself does not suffice for authentic participation of the privileged in political solidarity. Adequate *understanding* of the situation of oppression or injustice and participation in resistance activity are required. As the standpoint, care, and dialogic models demonstrate, this is the crux of the authenticity question for participation of individuals who are not subject to a particular form of oppression or injustice. Drawing on some of the strength of these other models and adding some additional elements based on the meaning of the initial commitment leads to an interesting and complex epistemology for political solidarity.

From standpoint theory we should take the criticism of structure as it functions to create knowledge and reality. As Kruks explains, social change "involves more than recognizing and valorizing the *experiences* of oppression, otherness, marginalization. . . . It involves a work of critical reflection on that experience and on the *social practices* out of which it is born" (2001, 112). Kruks appeals to Sartre's notion of praxis for help in addressing the problems of standpoint theory. As she says, "It is in *doing* (rather than in seeing, or contemplating) that we come (at least initially) to generate forms of knowledge" (Kruks 2001, 119). Kruks sees praxis as opening the possibility for participation in knowledge claims by those who do not directly experience oppression:

> These sets of properties also justify the claim that our situated knowledges can encompass realities that extend beyond the scope of our own direct experience. First individual abstract praxis comes to discover that it is connected to that of others "in exteriority," through the mediations of what Sartre calls "the practical material field" or the "milieu of action." Second, individual praxis involves "interior"

qualities. It possesses a fundamental intelligibility to others because it is intentional. This is to say, no praxis takes place without a purpose, without a project to transform something existing into a future possibility. (Kruks 2001, 120)

Praxis must transform that on which it acts. The practico-inert is solidified praxis, the material creations of praxis. Social relations, however, are also affected by praxis and might be considered among the practico-inert (see Kruks 2001, 120). There is a "reciprocal comprehension of praxis" (Kruks 2001, 126) that functions better, Kruks argues, to ensure that those outside a particular situation or praxis can nonetheless understand at least some of it. The understanding may be quite minimal, such as merely recognizing that praxis is intentional, or it might be much more extensive, as occurs in cases where one's own praxis interacts with that of others more extensively. Kruks further argues that, in addition to the connections made between different epistemological standpoints using Sartre's notions of praxis and the practico-inert, we need an affective dimension to our relationships that will facilitate our ability to act as a solidary group. While she argues that our affective ties serve as a motive for our solidarity with one another, I contend that any affective tie we share with one another in political solidarity is a result of our mutually shared commitment to a cause. But that commitment entails an obligation to seek greater understanding of the experience of oppression insofar as it is necessary for appropriate action.

María Lugones offers the metaphor of "world"-traveling (Lugones 1987; Lugones and Spelman 1983). "World"-traveling requires a commitment on the part of the world traveler to be open and attentive, to lovingly and proactively attempt to understand the world through the eyes of another. Friendship is the model—when one is with a friend, one does not try to dominate or define reality for that friend but instead endeavors to join in the process of sharing views, experiences, and understandings. Ruddick uses the same notion of attentiveness in maternal thinking (1989, 119–23). Drawing on some notion of a standpoint, Lugones describes "world"-traveling by invoking the notion of "outsiders," that is, those outside the mainstream of dominant culture. An outsider acquires "flexibility in shifting from the mainstream construction of life where she is constructed as an outsider to other constructions of life where she is more or less 'at home.' This flexibility is necessary for the outsider. It is required by the logic of oppression. But it can also be exercised resistantly by the outsider or by those who are at ease in the mainstream" (Lugones 1987, 3). The key in "world"-traveling is to see the other and oneself through different eyes, through the eyes of the other rather than through one's own eyes. Lugones also notes that outsiders may occupy several worlds and knowing them, knowing their experiences, would entail knowing these other "worlds" as well (2003, 97). Given the complexity of "worlds" an oppressed person may inhabit, Lugones argues that communication must heed the effects of interlocking oppressions on representative individuals. We must be careful not to reduce the needs and sufferings of oppressed peoples to singular, easily translated meanings (Lugones 2003, 141).

Elizabeth Spelman also uses the notion of apprenticeship in *The Inessential Woman*. It denotes the relation of the advantaged to the disadvantaged; that is, the advantaged must become apprenticed to the disadvantaged. In a similar vein, Bartky discusses the demand for "a knowing that transforms the self who knows, a knowing that brings into being new sympathies, new affects as well as new cognitions and new forms of intersubjectivity" (2002, 71–72). In particular, Bartky is interested in the emotional aspects and ties for political solidarity. Bartky draws on the work of Max Scheler, who articulates four modes of fellow feeling: "true fellow-feeling" wherein the participants experience identical feeling; "emotional infection" wherein one shares in a feeling without conscious choice or knowledge of the cause of the feeling; "emotional identification," which causes the erasure of the self or the other in the intensity of the identification of feeling; and "genuine fellow-feeling." "Genuine fellow-feeling" maintains the "otherness of the Other" by holding that feelings are intentional. The object of the intention, then, is the "feeling states of others" (Bartky 2002, 77). Bartky replaces Scheler's "love" as the affective bond with "sisterhood or solidarity." She also adds "imagination" to the mix; that is, one can imaginatively enter into the experience of the other without thinking of oneself as the other. Further, Bartky turns Scheler's individual fellow feeling into collective or political fellow feeling. We can, she says, experience "fellow-feeling for an entire class of persons rather than for a single individual" or even between groups of people (Bartky 2002, 86). Like Lugones's "'world'-traveling" or Spelman's "apprenticeship," Scheler's notion of genuine fellow feeling functions to build understanding in relationships without erasing the uniqueness of either participant in the relation.

One of the strengths of the dialogic model, in spite of its reliance on identity, is that it asserts the ability to communicate across differences.

Within solidarity, that communication across differences requires additional responsibility from each individual member. Feminist epistemologists have explored the prospects for knowledge sharing across different social situations. The epistemological processes they propose counter many of the problems of simply assigning epistemological privilege to the oppressed. The diverse perspectives that participants bring to the solidary movement not only inform the rich content of political solidarity but also, because they are valued for themselves through genuine and sustained efforts, actually aid in cementing the bonds of solidarity (cf. Kahane 1999). Diverse perspectives require persistent attentiveness. The initial commitment to join in solidarity must entail a commitment to be attentive to the views of others. The work entailed in such efforts enhances relationships between unique individual members united for a cause. To be inclusive of individuals who do not suffer injustice or oppression, political solidarity must include a renunciation of privilege, a recognition of how social and material structures create or otherwise contribute to systems of oppression, an active communication across differences, and a loving/caring perception of others that has the potential to create affective bonds in addition to the solidary bonds.

Conclusion

Political solidarity is often cast as a movement of the oppressed in response to their situation. Indeed, some accounts posit a shared or collective consciousness grounded in shared experience of oppression in order to explain the solidary group. My theory of political solidarity eschews shared consciousness based on shared experience in order (1) to allow for a distinction between the solidary group and the oppressed group—after all, not all of the oppressed will join in the political struggle for liberation; (2) to acknowledge the diversity of experiences even among the oppressed; (3) to recognize the political import of commitment to action, as opposed to social solidarity's social grouping; and (4) to allow and encourage the participation of former oppressors, privileged, and other non-oppressed individuals within the movement of political solidarity.

The question of privilege requires a rethinking of the traditional explanation of solidarity and a relatively strict adherence to the distinction between social solidarity and political solidarity. Because it relies on resemblance or shared history, social solidarity would posit an identity between the oppressed group and the solidary group; it would thereby rely on insider's knowledge claims to set the agenda for action. Political solidarity, on the other hand, is based on a personal commitment, and in making that moral commitment, one also commits to an epistemological project to continually seek a variety of perspectives in attempts to understand an unjust situation. Most of the work of that understanding occurs though working with others.

Members of the solidary group reach a point of mutuality wherein they understand or even sympathize with diverse others but do not strive for or hope to attain a mutual understanding. The idea is to seek understanding in our mutuality rather than mutuality in our understanding.

SIX

The Social Justice Ends of Political Solidarity

All forms of political solidarity involve activism, but not all forms of activism constitute political solidarity. There is something special about that form of social change—even beyond the uniqueness of the relationships between members. Political solidarity is a response to injustice, oppression, or social vulnerability. That is, it is *political* in the broad sense of that term. Activists in solidarity seek not just any form of justice: they seek *social justice*. They unite their collective efforts to alleviate their own suffering or the suffering of others brought about through human action or inaction.

Patricia Hill Collins tells a story about her experience teaching in an inner-city parochial school just after she received her master's degree. She relates the multiple unexpected connections and relationships between diverse people that formed around a common cause: to save the school from closing. The groups included individuals from every social class, widely divergent educational backgrounds, multiple racial and ethnic groups, religious and lay, parents and community members. Yet they formed a "coalition" because they united their commitments to save the school. The common cause united these various people. As Hill Collins explains, "We do not all have to do the same thing in the same way. Instead, we must support each other's efforts, realizing that they are all part of the larger enterprise of bringing about social change" (Hill Collins 2004, 540).

Hill Collins' description of coalition building for a cause reflects the strength of political solidarity—a goal, end, aim, or cause has the power to unite peoples of different backgrounds and value systems, who have dissimilar motivations and desires, and who act in very different ways at times, into an effective movement for social change. Diverse individuals commit to some goal, and, through these commitments, bonds with others are formed and fostered, but surpassing even the bonds that form is the cause or goal. Political solidarities might be small local groups or widespread international coalitions. The shared social justice aim unites the group and maintains the movement. The goal of political solidarity, in other words, is central to the moral relationships and obligations that form. Moreover, as the previous two chapters showed, the commitment that individuals make extends beyond the goal itself to encompass the "support [of] each other's efforts"—epistemologically as well as morally—that Hill Collins mentions in relation to her own experience of coalition building.

A quick note about terminology might be in order here. While I use the terms "goal," "aim," "ends," "cause," and "project" interchangeably in this book, political solidarity only rarely expects a clearly defined outcome of the collective action. Instead, a more appropriate understanding allows for a certain amount of ambiguity as well as some fluid recreation of the ends as solidarity action proceeds. Each instantiation of political solidarity will seek a more or less concrete end, which we called the substantive goal, and, quite plausibly, individuals engaged in collective action will describe their project to themselves quite differently. The formative goal is easier to identify as liberation, justice, or otherwise ending the oppression or injustice. The formative goal may be more stable than the substantive goal but the two serve each other within the collective action of political solidarity. Just as a coalition to save a school works, so too a political solidarity even with a certain amount of ambiguity and fluidity in its aims, works to bring about social change and personal transformation insofar as there is some way to identify the general cause.

Both the formative and the substantive goals of political solidarity are instrumental in defining the action and collective of solidarity, but it is also important in distinguishing political solidarity from other forms of group unity. In this chapter, I collapse the two into the single goal of the solidaristic activity and only rarely separate them. Both are implicit in any discussion of the goals of political solidarity—substantive goals are informed by a desire for liberation or justice, and formative goals require the substantive social change to achieve them. I begin by examining the individual's commitment to the goal once again, this time emphasizing the goal itself rather than the commitment per se. Political solidarity as a normative ideal aims for social justice; social change is necessarily a part of that, but not all movements for social change would be political solidarity. I look at the political solidarity in response to oppression, injustice, and social vulnerabilities and contrast it with some other forms of unity for change, responses to tragedy, and natural disasters. Finally, the last section explores the problem of sustaining praxis. That is, how can we sustain interest and involvement in a movement of political solidarity, especially when the goal changes? And can solidarity continue once a goal is accomplished or otherwise ceases to be? In her early moral essays on why one should act at all, Simone de Beauvoir suggests that a goal is only a path but that the attainment of the goal is itself a new starting point (Beauvoir 2005, 99). Much the same may be said of political solidarity. I use Beauvoir's existentialist ethics as suggestive of a method for sustaining praxis, but more important, I argue that the very desire of sustaining praxis requires goals that are accomplished, transformed, overcome, and simply disappear. This fluidity of the substantive ends of political solidarity makes it difficult to offer a theory of political solidarity but ultimately serves as a crucial strength to conceptions of political solidarity by allowing social movements to alter their ends as well as their collectives.

Commitment to the Goal

Various members of the solidary group might state the purpose, aim, goal, end, cause, or project of political solidarity somewhat differently, and the individual motivations for the commitment will likely be not only diverse but perhaps even at odds. Their interests beyond the particulars of the cause not only need not overlap but may also contradict. But their unity to achieve a particular goal unites these diverse and sometimes distant individuals in political solidarity. Commitment subsumes interpersonal reciprocity in that it transforms the reciprocal other into the entire group; each individual makes the commitment to the group out of their particularity. The group does not thus take on a separate existence but exists through individual commitment. As Walzer argues, "Every man has his own revolution. Even when he joins with others in a party or movement, he does not wholly surrender his own sense of what a revolution is. Rather, he and his comrades together commit themselves to an idea they all share, and that idea must exercise some control over their future actions and obligations" (1970, 181).

Whether to an organized group or to a spontaneous cause, commitment challenges the individual to draw on his or her uniqueness and contribute to the collective project. It demands, that is, a sort of life-choice in conjunction with the project of those in solidarity. In transforming social structures or society, the individual is also transformed. One might even make the stronger claim that it is in working with others for a particular cause that one finds meaning in life. Three basic considerations govern the goal or aim but, of course, any given movement will vary considerably in how its members conceive the cause. Political solidarity is rarely a monolithic movement. Some local forms, such as a workers strike for just wages or even a citywide rally to fight homelessness, might be unified not only in their cause but in the expression of it. More expansive movements will be united by the cause but find quite divergent expressions of it. The three considerations pertinent to the aims of political solidarity are meant to be broad enough to cover both potentialities as well anything in between.

The first might be described as the oppositional clause: the aim of political solidarity is to abolish an unjust social or political order; establishing a just one is secondary or a by-product of abolishing the unjust one. The end of solidarity is the cessation of injustice or the liberation from oppression. Political solidarity employs oppositional politics—and may even be the quintessential example of oppositional politics. Members of the solidary group are defined according to their shared commitment in opposition to what they perceive to be unjust or oppressive for themselves or others. Part of the motivation for this standard is the diversity of visions for just political orders. A movement of social change may splinter along lines of the diverse paths individuals or factions within the group wish to take in order to establish their particular vision of a just society. Such a splintering is not necessarily detrimental to the movement, but unity is found in opposing the unjust. The other reason for the oppositional clause is the immediacy or urgency of calls for social justice. When real people suffer real harm from injustice or oppression, the first aim of collective action is often stopping the harm. There are, however, also often multiple ways to stop harm—including offering direct service to those who suffer. While those who act in solidarity may not always be entirely effective at providing for the needs of those who suffer or bringing about the social change to cease the harm, their opposition to the causes of that suffering unites them.

Recognizing an injustice or a situation of oppression, however, is not enough to form the commitment of political solidarity. Individuals must respond through positive efforts at social change and in many cases assistance in meeting immediate needs (what Paul Farmer [2005] calls "pragmatic solidarity"). Criticism of the injustice is a minimal first step but quickly becomes ineffectual if not accompanied by public actions that move the criticism beyond words to collective concrete action undertaken in good faith efforts, aimed at stopping the injustice or oppression through a change in social structures.

The goal or interest of solidarity may be a freeing from unjust working conditions, as in the Polish Solidarity movement of the early 1980s; liberation from political or social oppression, as the term is used in contemporary civil rights and feminist circles; or stopping other forms of injustice and oppression such as poverty, as in Latin American Liberation Theology's call for solidarity with the poor, or former Haitian President Jean Bertrand Aristide's call for all to join in solidarity to "topple the tables" where the rich sat while the poor languished underneath. At times, of course, oppression goes "deep down" and solidarity action must take a multipronged, long-term approach. I say more about the specifics of oppression, injustice, and vulnerability in the penultimate section of this chapter. Individuals who join together to struggle against oppression, injustice, vulnerability, and similar causes do so because they share an interest to abolish it, not because they wish to establish a particular political order beyond a just one.

This does not preclude participants from having opinions about what a just political order would be or from actively taking steps to establish their vision. On the contrary, the actions of political solidarity are a necessary first step. Positive proposals can also be a part of the solidarity struggle, but they are secondary to the main project of ending injustice. As Christian Lenhardt claims, "Finding out what solidarity is for socialist theory and practice, requires a teleological perspective to a much greater degree than determining, say, the shape of economic production and circulation under socialist auspices" (1975, 133). Socialist scholars in general seem more inclined to reserve the term solidarity for reformist or revolutionary movements confronting unjust systems or circumstances.

Thomas Hill addresses what counts as a justifiable goal for political solidarity in his discussion of symbolic protest. In short, "One should refuse to do, or to help others to do, what is evil." As he explains, however, this extends not just to what an individual does but also what the individual allows to happen through failure to protest: "While committing no injustice himself, a person can nevertheless associate himself with those who do by condoning their activities; and a person can disassociate himself from a corrupt group both by acting to prevent their unjust acts and also, in appropriate contexts, by protesting, denouncing what they do, and taking a symbolic stand with the victims" (Hill 1979, 90). Hill outlines two principles to guide the adjudication of appropriateness of symbolic protests: "that one should disassociate from irreparable corrupt groups" (1979, 92); and "one should refuse to associate oneself with individuals who are thoroughly corrupt," especially in cases "where silence creates a presumption of normal social relations" (1979, 93, 94). Protest should be done not to "shun" but to express lack of support or unwillingness to condone unjust action. Hill's remarks reveal the oppositional focus in protests as in political solidarity more generally.

The second consideration governing the particular goals or aims of political solidarity is the fact that the goal of the social movement tempers the means used to attain it. In Chapter 3, I argued that one of the three moral relations of political solidarity is the relation to the goal. Inherent in that relation is a system of values that govern not only the relations to other participants and nonparticipants, but also the very means used to act, as I argued was the case in the specific question of violent activism. If political solidarity forms in opposition to injustice, oppression, and vulnerability, employing unjust or oppressive methods would not only be counterproductive but also contradict the very logic of political solidarity. A movement in political solidarity to end poverty cannot advocate the impoverishment of the formerly rich; a movement to end sexist violence should not employ violent means of social transformation; and a movement to end oppression on the basis of race ought not to engage in racist politics.

Moreover, this consideration also includes the direct action on behalf of those who suffer from oppression or injustice. Social movements to end oppression or counter injustice may begin among the oppressed (though the nature of the solidary group differs from the oppressed group) who opt to respond in some forms of public, collective resistance, but they often extend to include even those who had been privileged by oppression but recognize that privilege as based on an injustice. My task has been to rescue the moral content of solidarity, and more specifically, the social justice content of political solidarity. Social justice includes two moments or elements. One is service to those in need and the other is confrontation with the system or structure that supports the injustice. One without the other is incomplete at best. Solidarity for social justice means that while we confront the systems that create, perpetuate, or legitimate that suffering, we also directly serve those who suffer. In the previous chapter, I addressed the epistemological side of that obligation. Here we own the moral side. As we discern a course of action to advance a cause, we must also use that cause to inform our direct response to those in need, regardless of whether or not they join in the struggle to change the unjust system adversely affecting them. Farmer, in particular, notes a sort of emptiness to solidarity that lacks the "goods and services that might diminish unjust hardship" (2005, 146). "Pragmatic solidarity," as I have mentioned, is Farmer's term for the side of solidarity that aims to alleviate suffering; speaking with his own work for social justice in healthcare, he describes it as "the rapid deployment of our tools and resources to improve the health and well-being of those who suffer this violence" (2005, 220). He further adds that rather than using our own models of what is needed, we must be careful to heed the needs and desires of those we serve (many of whom we stand with in solidarity to change the social structures that cause the suffering). Pragmatic solidarity, he says, "responds to the needs expressed by the people and communities who are living, and often dying, on the edge" (Farmer 2005, 230).

This standard is certainly complicated by the fact that projects change, groups factionalize, and no central or organizing body decides what sort of collective action will be undertaken. Nevertheless, individuals who commit to a goal within political solidarity set that goal as a sort of normative ideal to direct their actions and the actions of the collective. This is a slightly different ordering of Hill's dictum: "Normally one who cares for justice can show it not only by refraining from unjust acts but also by constructive efforts to reform unjust institutions, and the like" (1979, 97). In showing efforts to reform unjust institutions, one ought also to refrain from unjust acts—especially those unjust acts that resemble that which is opposed.

Third, the project of solidarity is the unifying interest; although there may be other overlapping interests among participants, there need not be. Additional interests may form throughout the process of working together, or, in the case of international solidarity movements, individuals may feel their personal choices enlightened by the project of solidarity tie them to certain other causes or peoples. The goal shapes the relations of those dedicated to solidarity.

While others have argued that interest alone does not create a bond strong enough to sustain solidarity (Feinberg 1970), I argue that shared interest does indeed create a strong bond between participants and that it has an additional potential that other bonds (of shared history or shared experience) do not allow. Having a particular project, such as ending sexist oppression or fighting global poverty, and scrutinizing the logic of that project may force some committed individuals to expand the vision of the solidary connections, to see their cause as in some way united with that of another movement of political solidarity. Solidarity members join the social movement because of a commitment to conscience. As individuals, they have discerned a problem in social arrangements or relations. And, as individuals, they respond. Similar responses from other individuals compel all to unite in a joint effort to effect change: "Solidarity must have its local and particular sites: it is built from the ground up" (Walzer 1998, 51). The social problem that is the target of collective action does not need to directly affect each participant in solidarity; there is, however, a strong likelihood that it will affect at least some. The goal may also shift with differing circumstances or conditions. In acting for a particular cause, one may simultaneously act against that same cause or another equally important cause. Conscientious social criticism will help alleviate some of that, as will the divergent voices within a movement that help to temper any single voice from becoming dominant.

A quick response to the question of what constitutes a justifiable goal for solidarity action might draw on a notion of basic rights. Henry Shue (1980), for example, argues that security rights and subsistence rights are basic rights and that every basic right entails three correlative duties. The duties are "(I) Duties to *avoid* depriving. (II) Duties to *protect* from deprivation. (III) Duties to *aid* the deprived" (Shue 1980, 52, ch. 2; see also Gewirth 1986). These might form the basis of or a motive for political solidarity. Shue further argues that obligations to basic rights, most notably the basic right to subsistence, form a primary basis for moral obligation, whereas group affiliation is at best unproven (1980, 138–39). As one might guess, the logical extension of Shue's position, which he makes explicit, is a universal application such that we all have duties to one another on the basis of the basic human rights listed above. Shue's position is compelling but somewhat different from what I have been arguing with regard to political solidarity. I will reserve the discussion of universal human solidarity until Chapter 7, but it is important to note here the difference in logic between the theory of political solidarity thus far advanced and an account of human rights like Shue's. The latter bases obligations on an assumption or understanding about human rights. We are united because we are the same in some important way—we share in humanity or simply we are human. That sameness then puts moral requirements on us—humanity as social solidarity. Political solidarity, on the other hand, bases moral relations and the obligations inherent therein on a collective cause that individuals mutually commit to. Certainly some might commit because of a belief in common humanity, but the assumption of common humanity is not a necessary premise to the moral obligations.

The aim or cause of political solidarity informs concrete activities and achievable goals that through our common interest we can agree on, however broadly construed and sometimes in spite of our differences. I have already given some indication at what political solidarity aims in this discussion of the nature of the goal. There are, of course, some similar forms of goal-oriented unities that nonetheless would not be considered forms of political solidarity. Many of these have very strong bonds, concrete moral actions, and/or guiding commitments to justice, but there is something special about political solidarity that my account hopes to elucidate. In the next section, I discuss some goals and movements for social change that do not fall under the banner of political solidarity. This is followed by a more thorough look at injustice, oppression, and vulnerability, which are the subjects of our study.

Other Unities and Their Goals

Historically, the concept of solidarity was reserved for social movements for social justice. Solidarity with the working class, solidarity with the poor, solidarity of women, solidarity with the downtrodden of every sort: these are the subjects of political solidarity. More recently, of course, the term has been used to describe just about any form of union. And, of course, we ought not forget the troubling use of the term racial solidarity, connoting both liberation from racist oppression and the insular, and sometimes violent, protectionist politics of white supremacy.

Not every group formed by individuals aiming to achieve a particular goal or purpose is said to be in solidarity generally or political solidarity specifically. In this section, I address such things as natural disasters and tragedy, some forms of unity for change that seek other forms of justice rather than social justice, and other goal-oriented unities such as sports teams. The intent is to show that the project of political solidarity has a moralizing effect on the group that forms. The next section looks at appropriate ends of solidary action, namely, oppression, social injustice, and social vulnerabilities.

Natural Disasters

Certainly there are numerous commonalities between groups that form in response to a natural disaster and groups that form in response to a real or perceived injustice. Both types of groups are goal oriented in response to an immediate need. But there are also some significant differences.

Those who respond to natural disasters may themselves be victims, as when survivors of an earthquake join together to try to rescue others from the rubble. They may also be far removed from the effects of the natural disaster, as in the summer of 1993 when individuals from all over the Midwest arrived on the banks of the Mississippi to create and place sandbags in an effort to protect towns from flooding. Doctors Without Borders routinely sends committed individuals into areas that have been devastated by a natural disaster. They also are among the first international groups to respond to human-made disasters or mass human rights violations. People from all over the United States flew or drove to Louisiana, and friends, neighbors, and strangers aided their fellow Louisianan when Hurricane Katrina devastated the Gulf Coast in August 2005. A worldwide outpouring of money and other forms of aid were sent when a tsunami in the Indian Ocean killed hundreds of thousands of people in December 2004. Like respondents to social discrimination or the violence of oppression, impassioned people respond to natural disasters often out of firmly held moral principles. They also create a coalition unified by collective efforts toward a particular goal.

Solidarity of some sort does form in the aftermath of a natural disaster. I suggest that the victims of a natural disaster experience a strong social solidarity. They become united by their shared experience or their previous unity takes on a new urgency and intimacy because of the experience of surviving a natural disaster. Of course, not everyone survives and the process of grieving and burying the dead becomes a part of the shared experience for the survivors as well. The bonds that form are infused with sympathy and perhaps even a moral courage to comfort others who share the same experience of survival. This social solidarity may even last for an extended period of time, and even with some distance from the event itself people will always feel a special connection with other survivors. In a sense, social solidarity of this sort is marked by the ease of communication that one feels when talking about the natural disaster and the process of survival with others. Knowing that the other understands from their own experience makes telling one's story personally important and socially unifying. In a similar vein, victims of other forms of tragedy or victims of similar sorts of violent crimes find some social solidarity with each other through the telling and retelling of their stories (see Brison 2002).

But survivors of natural disasters, tragedies, and violent crimes have multiple other interests and projects that will likely eventually move them beyond their experience of trauma. They will likely always feel something of a special bond with their fellow survivors, but the experience alone will eventually fade in importance and with it some of the social bonds with other survivors. (There are exceptions of course. Those individuals who, for whatever reason, are unable to move beyond the traumatic event or, alternatively, those who turn their experience into motivation for advocacy of some sort, might seek to maintain the bonds formed with other victims or survivors.)

Those who aided in the response to the natural disaster also share a social solidarity but theirs is with other responders and less with the survivors of the disaster. They share an experience and perhaps even living quarters. Many will find unity in their shared fatigue or even in the stories of successful or failed efforts. This, too, is a social solidarity because it is built on their experiences together; the relationships, or even friendships, form over a common practice or understanding. A moral compulsion to respond to the needs of others in the aftermath of a natural disaster could be motivated by employment, proximity, shared humanity, empathy, sympathy, or any number of other feelings. It could, of course, also be the result of a conscious commitment to aid those in need and in this last regard strongly resembles political solidarity.

We can describe this phenomenon as a moral response to social solidarity or, if state apparatuses are used, perhaps civic solidarity. Like political solidarity, relationships do form and those relationships mandate some moral obligations. But that others will help one in need when one is the victim of a natural disaster is expected by the bonds of social solidarity. That the state will respond, making use of a variety of mechanisms, is expected by the bonds of civic solidarity. Both the group of survivors and the group of responders are united by the goal of survival. Those affected by the natural disaster face their own survival while the responders express concern over the survival of others. There is a long history in moral theory demonstrating this moral relation. Less clear are the moral relations that form between individual survivors, between survivors and responders, and between responders.

These three relationships inform certain duties—both positive and negative. There may be obligations to aid others and there are certainly obligations not to exploit the hardships of others. Arguments could also be made that sympathy, as well as concrete effort to alleviate suffering, is part of what is owed to the victims of a natural disaster. Others have written at length on this topic, but for our purposes it is sufficient to note that the victims or survivors of a natural disaster have reason to expect that others will come to aid them in their time of need. But this expectation is in many respects grounded on common standards of basic human decency and shared feelings of vulnerability. Each of us could also be a victim of a natural disaster. That vulnerability unites us as humans in a way that motivates coming to the aid of others when one is spared the hardship.

As is clear from this discussion, the solidarity in response to a natural disaster is similar to political solidarity that aims at alleviating or ending an injustice. There are, however, some important divergences. Political solidarity is formed by the individual commitment or choice. While responders do make a choice informed by their social bonds to respond to a natural disaster, victims certainly do not. In addition, individuals and the group of political solidarity have a relationship to the larger community that mandates social criticism. Perhaps even more important, what makes political solidarity distinct from moral responses of social and civic solidarity is also the fact that the oppression or injustice that political solidarity combats is the result of human doing, whether it be through conscious intent to exploit others or through negligent system building that ignores the diverse needs of others. What makes it political is the opposition to a system with its origins in human design.

An interesting blending of social, civic, and political solidarities might be found in the collective experience of some natural disasters. Take the 2005 hurricanes that ravaged the Gulf Coast of the United States. Hurricane Katrina hit New Orleans square on but its winds inflicted only minimal damage. The volume of water it brought with it, however, caused levees to break and massive flooding that deluged as much as 80 percent of the city. Victims of the hurricane, or, as many prefer to call themselves, survivors of the floods, share an experience—life changing in its scope—that unites them. This unity may provide some solace and comfort as stories of survival are passed and shared. Implicitly, there is a bond between all residents of New Orleans and the surrounding areas at the time of the hurricane and subsequent floods. But that bond informs only minimal moral obligations to one another. Similarly, bonds between peoples who worked in relief efforts to rescue stranded people or relocate the newly homeless might aptly be called a form of social solidarity. Because of the intensity of the experience, disparate individuals find comfort with each other knowing that they share an understanding. They have endured a traumatic event and that endurance builds the bonds of a social solidarity. But it is a weak social solidarity that likely lasts only so long as individuals appeal to their shared experiences.

The aftermath of the situation in New Orleans, however, may also demonstrate a political solidarity, but with this political solidarity, what binds is not the experience of the natural disaster but the opposition to a political system that not only ignored some people on the basis of racial and social class status, but also appears to have blatantly flouted their obligation to protect fellow citizens. Numerous people in and out of New Orleans noted that the areas that flooded—the area closest to the levees—were not only among the poorest areas of the city, they were also among the poorest areas of the country. Moreover, 80 percent of the New Orleans population was African American. Could it be that an unjust social and political system allowed insecure levees—levees that they knew could not withstand a hurricane of the force that they also knew would inevitably hit the area—to exist because of an unacknowledged or unaddressed class and racial bias? Many social critics also noted a race bias in the rescue efforts. People were stranded for days in unsanitary, unsafe, and potentially violent conditions with no food or potable water. Finally, it is worth noting that many scientists noted that one of the reasons Katrina was so devastating was that the river delta had been gradually disappearing to make way for expensive Gulf Coast homes. A larger delta area would have been better able to absorb the impact of the hurricane but protecting the inland poor took a distant second to providing vacation homes for the wealthy. In a nation that prides itself on the humanitarian assistance it claims to lend to distant peoples and countries in need (a largely unwarranted pride I might add), conditions like this cannot help but raise the specter of more systematic injustice. Social critics and respondents to those systemic problems might be engaged in political solidarity.

Indeed, one might even argue that the political solidarity arises in response to failed civic solidarity. The obligation of the United States to protect its citizens through the provision of adequate infrastructure that can withstand anticipated natural occurrences was not fulfilled. It is in response to this that many people stand together in political solidarity to oppose the unjust system that allows the obligations of civic solidarity to be trampled on.

Seeking Justice Other than Social Justice

Now imagine the case of a corrupt politician and the group of citizens who rally together around the cause to unseat him. Suppose, for instance, that he is caught taking large amounts of money and gifts from a particular political lobbyist. The citizens united to unseat the corrupt politician are certainly goal oriented and political. They might circulate petitions (in person and online), protest outside the politician's office, write letters to Congress and the media, and even mount efforts for a recall vote. They are standing up for justice but we would not be inclined to call their efforts an example of political solidarity for two central reasons. First, there is no clear victimized group with which to be "in solidarity." Remember that the solidary group is ontologically distinct from the oppressed group but there still must be some people who are harmed or victimized by an injustice. General political corruption is unjust and one could argue that it adversely affects all citizens (and the rule of law itself), but there is no clear subgroup of the population that it victimizes. Second, the injustice is not social injustice. Taking bribes is a criminal offense and justice would mandate some legal action in response to the politician's actions, but social injustice is not the relevant concept in this case.

Injustice comes in many forms and activism against injustice plays a very important role in any democratic society. Social justice—which includes economic justice—is the proper realm of political solidarity according to the theory I advance. The criminal justice system, the legislature, formal political mechanisms, and to some extent even the market address other forms of injustice, though efforts to seek social justice may employ any of these mechanisms as well. Rather than strictly excluding these cases from accounts of political solidarity, the point, as I showed in Chapter 2, is that the social justice case must be proven in some way.

Suppose, however, that the lobbyist described above embezzled the money for the bribes from Native Americans with whom he worked to implement law or policy favorable to the casinos they run. (I am, of course, roughly thinking of the scandal surrounding American lobbyist Jack Abramoff, who, in 2006, pleaded guilty to fraud, tax evasion, and conspiracy to bribe public officials. He was sentenced to $9^1/_2$–11 years in prison and forced to pay millions in restitution.) A social justice issue begins to emerge in this case. Native Americans have experienced numerous other instances of exploitation, violence, cultural imperialism, and marginalization (Young 1990); the exploitative behavior by the lobbyist would be one act in a pattern of oppressive practices. (Though, as the Abramoff case also reveals, claiming status of oppressed unambiguously is rarely entirely transparent.) A political solidarity might form around attempts to redress the wrongs they have suffered, but the criminal acts of the lobbyist would be just an additional incentive rather than the primary goal of the movement. Alternatively, turning back to the politician's behavior, suppose the corruption centered not on accepting bribes but on actively working to maintain a system of law that was overtly discriminatory to women or racial minorities. There, again, a clear case of social injustice presents itself. The citizens who work to unseat the politician, drawn from among those victimized by the injustice as well as those who are not victimized but who nonetheless recognize the actions as unjust, might rightly be described as engaging in political solidarity (assuming other moral relations elucidated in Chapter 3 hold as well). Chances are good, however, that opposing the politician is just one action in solidarity rather than the aim or end of the solidarity movement per se.

One grey area in the first case of political corruption through the taking of bribes pertains to class-based social injustice. Could it be argued that the politician's actions perpetuate great harm to the lower class? Might his actions be part of a pattern of social and political policies aimed to render the lower classes voiceless within the political system? Affirmative responses to these questions might alter the earlier assessment of the case, though, like with embezzling from Native Americans, the ends of political solidarity likely would target not the actions per se, but the pattern or system of class-based injustice. The political corruption might provide an incentive for others to join the movement or a particular instance for solidary action but do not constitute the substantive ends of solidarity.

Other Goal-Oriented Unities

"Solidarity" has also been used to describe other forms of goal-oriented unities. For instance, an athletic team and its cadre of fans aim to win the game, lead the tournament, or "trounce the opponent." But the individual members on that team are not united in political solidarity with each other nor are fans united in political solidarity with the team. I would make the strong case that "solidarity" in this sense is used in its parasitical form. That is, fans may claim a solidarity with the team or the team itself may claim solidarity among its members, but that unity is incorrectly identified as solidarity. It is completely misused as political or civic solidarity and probably lacks the moral import of a social solidarity (though that is arguable). Members of a team do owe allegiance to each other, form relationships with one another around a particular goal, and share an interest in a common project. They are drawn together by this shared interest so in that sense one could say there is a resemblance to political solidarity but their project does not attempt any sort of social change oriented against injustice. One might be tempted to describe the team as a form of social solidarity insofar as they share experiences, a division of labor, and the relation mediates between the individual and the group. But it is not clear that moral obligations in the form of positive duties extend beyond the immediate aims of the team itself or, if they do, that they are any different from what would be expected of any other citizen. Certainly if a player bet against the team, compromising his integrity and providing an incentive for him to throw the game, we would say he violated his duty to the team. He owes it to his fellow teammates to perform to the best of his current ability in every game, but that seems to be the extent of his positive duties to the team (though any coach might want to foster others as well).

The role and the relationship, in other words, entail certain minimal obligations. In addition, Jean Harvey argues that there may be other obligations that arise that do not directly stem from the role or relationship but might be considered common standards of courtesy or decency. Harvey uses the example of a person waiting at a bus stop for a nonexistent bus. Common standards of decency would indicate that passersby or a clerk in the store behind where she stands inform her of her mistake rather than leave her standing frustrated waiting for a bus that will never come (Harvey 1999, 122). So too the moral duties for members of a team may at various points extend beyond merely their respective roles on the team, but these additional obligations really do not differ significantly from ordinary obligations to others and thus would not be the foundation or the effects of political solidarity (though we might describe the situation as a stronger social solidarity).

If one of the teammates is killed in a car accident and the team subsequently holds an annual fundraising tournament to provide college tuition for her children, then an even-stronger social solidarity may be used as the appropriate moral concept. The members of the team engage in positive duties beyond those necessary to their definition as an athletic team and adopt a goal beyond that of winning games. They likely bond in this mutual action to aid the family of one of their teammates, just as they likely also share a bond of shared sympathy for their loss.

Whether on or off the field, a significant moral difference exists between the goal-oriented activities of an athletic team and the goal-oriented activities of political solidarity. In the latter relation, the goal informs the positive duties that participants undertake in their commitment to one another. It is also overtly political. The team, on the other hand, has a goal and that goal guides some or even most of their experience when performing as a team during the sporting event. But the goal does not inform individual's moral actions or their relations with each other off the field.

If the athletic team's activities bring them together only once in a while in order to play a game or practice their skills, it is more appropriate to say that they are working as a team, or that they evince a high level of group cooperation or perhaps even social solidarity. Members of an athletic team do have moral obligations to one another. But in political solidarity, it is the moral commitment on the part of each of the individual members to act in such a way as to accomplish a particular task for social justice that is the motivation for forming the collective. The relations between individuals and the relation between the solidary group and the larger society are mediated by this task or goal; these moral obligations to others differ considerably from the more mundane obligations entailed in interpersonal relationships.

Social Justice as the End of Political Solidarity

Natural disasters inspire political solidarity only insofar as they reveal the injustice of a system, human in origin, that affects some people on the basis of their social-class status, race, ethnicity, gender, sexuality, or some other attribute or characteristic that marks a group. Political solidarity, in other words, combats oppression and injustice; it seeks social justice. The goal of this type of movement for social change is to challenge an unjust system, practice, or set of practices, or to overthrow and remedy an oppressive system, practice, or set of practices.

Before proceeding, it is worth pausing to address a possible objection. It might be argued that political solidarity may be used to advance social injustice as much as social justice. Of course, it would be the rare person who claims to desire injustice. Some groups might be widely recognized as pursuing unjust causes but they themselves would no doubt tout the justness of their ends. What is at issue is the question of comparative justice: How do actors within movements of political solidarity assess the justness of their cause? The discussion of social criticism addressed this to some extent, but what about those cases where the line is fine or perhaps those cases where a group claims to act in accordance with justice but is widely believed to be acting contrary to justice—the Ku Klux Klan or the Nazi regime, for instance?

One response to the issue of the fine line between justice and injustice is to note that while political solidarity is oriented toward social justice, there certainly may be times when the group is mistaken in its judgment of an appropriate substantive goal. Acting publicly and communicating openly while also engaging in careful social criticism alleviates some of the worry about mistaken aims, as these methods subject the political solidarity itself to scrutiny and social criticism. In addition, substantive goals are supposed to mediate the relations with others both in and outside the solidary group; if they fail or if the substantive goal can be shown to be in contradiction with the formative goal, then there are reasons to believe that the substantive goal ought not to be pursued at all.

In a related vein, there is a conflict between the obligations to the goal and the obligations to others insofar as violence is used, as I argued in Chapter 3. That is, an activist tool that has the potential to undermine the movement by splintering the unity of solidarity is contrary to the obligations of mutuality and cooperation. It also violates the obligations in the moral relation to those outside the movement—at times by literally cutting off potential allies for social change.

Finally, the obligations of social solidarity might themselves be instructive in determining which causes are just for political solidarity. Social solidarity, recall, is the term used to describe the cohesion of a group or society. Moral obligations are prescribed given the closeness of the group. In this case, social solidarity describes civil society or the state regulated by laws as well as social and cultural customs. Participants in political solidarity are not absolved of the obligations of social solidarity merely because they have elected to serve a particular cause. Maintaining laws and social mores are evidence of our social solidarity, and while political solidarity movements often aim at changing at least some of the laws and customs, the formative goals of justice and liberation would argue against excluding or depriving any group of such things as basic civil liberties or human rights. Hence, any group that claims justice as an end but seeks to do violence to another group or deprive that group of basic civil liberties and human rights is violating the obligations of social solidarity and thus not acting in accordance with justice; that is, it is not acting within the rubric of political solidarity.

In the rest of this section I discuss three broad categories or targets for political solidarity. There are certainly others, but the categories of injustice, oppression, and social vulnerabilities are fairly encompassing and they bring to light specific political goals. Importantly, while I discuss them as if a clear distinction may be made, often such a distinction is quite impossible. There are some injustices that do not contribute to oppression and some social vulnerabilities that do; some social vulnerabilities are unjust, and some are neither oppressive nor unjust but still unnecessary vulnerabilities that contribute to social inequality. In other words, there is significant overlap among injustice, oppression, and social vulnerabilities, but there are also areas within each that do not overlap but nonetheless are or ought to be the targets of solidary action.

Injustice

In his discussion of social or comparative justice, Joel Feinberg identifies the following as forms of injustice: "unfair discrimination, arbitrary exclusion, favoritism, inappropriate partisanship or partiality, inconsistent rule-enforcement, 'freeloading' in a cooperative undertaking, or putting one party at a relative disadvantage in a competition" (1973, 99). Feinberg's list is a non-exhaustive look at injustice for rights-based political theory. Whether formal legal rights like the right to vote, or more informal social rights like the right to enter restaurants through the front door, inequitable distribution of rights and privileges has served as the impetus for numerous movements of political solidarity. Also worth noting, Feinberg's list could demonstrate injustice in thought as well as the injustices that might be evident in both action and thought.

Injustice might take other forms as well. Iris Young defines justice in accord with an expanded notion of the political and in line with communicative theories. As she explains, "The idea of justice here shifts from a focus on distributive patterns to procedural issues of participation in deliberation and decisionmaking. For a norm to be just, everyone who follows it must in principle have an effective voice in its consideration and be able to agree to it without coercion" (1990, 34). In other words, exclusion might be from participation in public life as well as from the benefits, rights, or privileges of social and political existence. While not everyone will necessarily want to participate, prohibiting anyone from participating in public decision-making—especially those decisions that directly affect their own lives—is unjust.

Consider, for example, the first wave of the feminist movement. Some variation in how the waves or generations of feminist activism have been construed complicates this example, but, for our purposes, the first wave may be understood as the period that stretched from approximately the mid-eighteenth century to mid-twentieth century in the United States. The movement focused on obtaining civil or legal, intellectual, and economic rights for women. Lack of these rights amounts to injustice and serves as a vivid example of Feinberg's list of injustices. Moreover, not just the absence of abstract rights but also the very real exclusion of women from the public forums for decision-making (e.g., political bodies, church counsels, educational institution, and in some cases public spaces generally) extends what counts as injustice beyond distributional issues.

It is important to note that survival may also be a basis for solidarity (Mohanty 2003, 117); a scrutiny of the struggle for survival might reveal certain social obstacles that some among us confront while others of us evade. At least some of those obstacles amount to injustice. Survival here ought to be understood according to an expansive notion, that is, not just as individual survival but also the survival of a group, tribe, people, or nation.

Howard McGary argues for the strong position that a member of a group who, under certain conditions, lets an injustice occur is morally liable for the negative results of his or her failure to act. The morally liable omissions McGary discusses pertain to unjust racial practices but such moral liability is also applicable with other forms of injustice (1986). His position is useful in thinking of the solidary group and each individual member's obligation to act. He applies it to other forms of collective action as well. What is less clear, and what I take up in the next chapter, is whether humanity per se might be thought of as a group and whether, as such, each of us then has an obligation to take up the cause of political solidarity.

We could enhance these descriptions of injustice by noting that discrimination, exclusion, favoritism, partiality, and systemic obstacles to survival, when practiced against a person as a member of a group defined in opposition to or in relation to the dominant group, constitute oppressive practices. Some forms of injustice contribute to oppression, and oppression itself is unjust. I have separated them not to create an arbitrary or strict distinction but rather to concentrate on different aspects of the discussion.

Oppression

As second wave feminists argued in advancing and expanding the agendas of their first wave colleagues, oppression often extends well beyond rights distribution or even exclusion from participation in public decision-making. Accounts of oppression abound and my intent is not to add to the layers of extant analysis in that area of social philosophy but to show how oppression is one of the targets for social justice and thus one of the three main categories of goals for political solidarity. I discuss some different forms of oppression as well as some oppressive practices in an effort to illustrate how a solidary group might form around the effort to end oppression or alleviate some of its more pernicious effects.

Oppression is a human institution that systemically or systematically prescribes the life prospects and projects of some individuals. Systemic oppression arises as a by-product of attempts to construct otherwise just or morally neutral institutions. For instance, John Locke's social contract theory is a thorough attempt to articulate a just political order founded on liberty. As numerous scholars have argued, however, his theory appeals to a particular standard of rationality and property ownership such that non-propertied males, all women, and racial minorities appear to be excluded from the rights and privileges of citizenship (though they are still subject to the laws they had no say in making) (see for example Macpherson 1964, Mills 1997, Pateman 1988, Scholz 1993).

Systematic oppression is oppression that targets members of a group in a more or less regular fashion. Oppressive practices are so common, consistent, pervasive, and ubiquitous that they appear to be a natural part of the social order. The experience of inferiority, too, appears by at least some of the oppressed to be natural or at least so well entrenched as to seem intractable.

Whether systemic or systematic, oppression may be intentional or unintentional. If intentional, oppressors actively scheme to create a social system that discriminates against some people based on some attribute the framers find distasteful or based on their selfish desire to profit from the oppression of others. In other words, an oppressor group may be identified and is likely also to be privileged—or reap countless told and untold benefits—by the oppression. If unintentional, then systemic or systematic oppression is an unintended effect of some other belief or action. In this case, there is likely no oppressor or oppressor group, though there will almost certainly be a group that is privileged by the oppression of others. Notice that saying the oppression is unintentional is not equivalent to saying it is unforeseen. I am inclined to skip the moral hairsplitting, however, and put unintentional but foreseen oppression into the camp of intentional oppression. Colonization is an obvious example of intentional systemic oppression. Unintentional systemic oppression can be seen in antiquated education systems that employ gender stereotypes in designing content or pedagogy. Segregation is the obvious example of unintentional but foreseen systemic oppression that really should be called simply intentional oppression. Many of the practices of racism, sexism, heterosexism, ableism, ageism, and other forms of discrimination based on some arbitrary characteristic serve as examples of systematic oppression insofar as those practices are so consistently and pervasively employed that a member of the marked group cannot avoid them and cannot participate in many of the active and formal processes of self-determination within society. Of course, the reason for explaining these distinctions and my further explication of the nature and practices of oppression is that political solidarity is one way to respond to oppression. The goal of political solidarity will vary depending on whether there is an oppressor group (i.e., intended), whether the oppression is embedded in the structures of society and in what way (systemic, systematic, intentional, unintentional), who is privileged by the oppression, and so on.

Oppression is a group phenomenon. It is as a member of a group that an individual becomes subject to oppression. The individuals within the oppressed group share some social identity that both identifies them as a group and serves in some way as justification for their unequal position in society. John Hodge describes group oppression as that which "occurs whenever a group or class is dominated and controlled based on the characteristics which are used to define it as a group" (1975, ix).

Marilyn Frye's well-known account of oppression describes it analogous to a birdcage. Oppression involves a number of practices and beliefs that intertwine. While a single practice—say, sexist jokes—might be tolerable, oppression unites a number of practices into an intolerable whole. So too, one wire of a birdcage might not seem very confining but as a system of wires that form a cage, the combination stifles social and political freedom, personal development, self-definition, physical mobility and well-being, and any number of other elements of a person's life. As she explains, "The experience of oppressed people is that the living of one's life is confined and shaped by forces and barriers which are not accidental or occasional and hence avoidable, but are systematically related to each other in such a way as to catch one between and among them and restrict or penalize motion in any direction" (Frye 1983, 4). We have to be careful not to fall into the trap of failing to see the structure. Saying oppression is structural means it affects and constrains all the various aspects of one's existence and is embedded in the structures of social life. It is easier to just see the elements of oppression without seeing the structure as a whole. The key is to identify the ways in which oppressed peoples' lives are reduced and shaped and their mobility restricted.

Young rather famously describes what she calls the "Five Faces of Oppression" in an essay by the same name (1990). These five faces might intermix or intermingle but they could just as plausibly appear separately, consecutively, or even in isolation. They describe oppressive practices broadly construed. We might think of these as some of the wires of the birdcage, or perhaps a more appropriate analogy would be the particular metals out of which the specific wires are constructed.

The first face is exploitation, which Young describes as "oppression [that] occurs through a steady process of the transfer of the results of the labor of one social group to benefit another" (1990, 49). While exploitation is historically associated with class oppression through the Marxist critique of capitalism, Young also shows how women and racial minorities experience the unjust transfer of their power within various spheres of social existence. Exploitation takes from the work of one in order to increase the wealth of another. As Young says, challenging exploitative systems "requires reorganization of institutions and practices of decisionmaking, alteration of the division of labor, and similar measures of institutional, structural, and cultural change" (1990, 53).

Marginalization, the second form of oppression Young discusses, includes everything from exclusion from voting rights to a genocide that aims to exclude a people from existence itself. Notice how the forms of injustice coalesce in marginalization and other forms of oppression. Marginalization targets a group of people—usually based on some more or less arbitrary characteristic—and prevents them from "useful participation in social life" (Young 1990, 53). Powerlessness is in some way like marginalization and exploitation in that it affects nonprofessionals who "lack the authority, status, and sense of self that professionals tend to have" (Young 1990, 57). These deficiencies adversely affect the individual and the group and cement a social structure divided starkly along class lines. Powerlessness contributes to a lack of access to social and educational circles that would help move a person out of oppressed conditions. Generations of oppressed may see their situations grow increasingly hopeless as doors close—doors that would be and are open to others with more social status or employment clout.

Young calls the fourth form of oppression cultural imperialism: "To experience cultural imperialism means to experience how the dominant meanings of a society render the particular perspective of one's own group invisible at the same time as they stereotype one's group and mark it out as the Other" (Young 1990, 59). Language, customs, traditions, and other marks of one's unique culture might be pushed aside, ignored, or even disparaged as the dominant culture determines what the appropriate cultural expressions are. Cultural imperialism can occur within a single society but it is also evident in the global community. Some socialist scholars and postcolonialist theorists are critical of the values of consumerism and capitalism seemingly imposed by globalization; they note the imperializing effects of importing American businesses or cultural and business models. Others might cite the "spread of democracy" as a rhetorical trope to hide culturally imperialistic practices, including religious practices.

Violence is the final form of oppression Young discusses. Instances of violence that plague oppressed groups might be no different than other random acts of violence against individuals if it were not for the systematic nature of targeting on the basis of group affiliation. Young further comments on violence that is systemic:

> What makes violence a phenomenon of social injustice, and not merely an individual moral wrong, is its systemic character, its existence as a social practice.... The oppression of violence consists not only in direct victimization, but in the daily knowledge shared by all members of oppressed groups that they are *liable* to violation, solely on account of their group identity. Just living under such a threat of attack on oneself or family or friends deprives the oppressed of freedom and dignity, and needlessly expends their energy. (Young 1990, 62)

These forms of oppression can, of course, intermix or compound. But they offer some concreteness to the concept of oppression by identifying oppressive practices and their effects on those subject to them. Efforts to advance social justice will have to examine the myriad manifestations of these faces of oppression as well as their impact on not only the oppressed group but also on individuals within that group and on society as a whole.

One of the most prominent effects of oppressive practices on individuals is the way identity is socially constructed rather than personally crafted. Kate Lindemann describes the dehumanizing element of socially constructed identity that an individual is subject to as a member of an oppressed group. Importantly, she also notes that even those privileged by socially constructed identity suffer some aspect of dehumanization. Socially constructed identities place arbitrary requirements on citizenship or even full humanity and often fail to recognize unique characteristics of minority groups. Lindemann explains, "Social institutions that severely confuse being human with qualities of age, gender, race, rank, talent, or the possession of property are dehumanizing because they encourage false consciousness in those who participate in them" (1992, 5). Charles Taylor also notes that "withholding recognition can be a form of oppression" (1992, 36). Almost every oppressed group has gone through or will have to go through a process of laying claim to human status, personhood status, or rights of citizenship. Some oppressed groups will find their status stripped away, as when campaigns of ethnic cleansing redefine cultural codes and intensify processes of dehumanization.

The social construction of identity occurs through any number of different patterns, processes, and policies. At times, it arises as a result of other oppressive practices and sets the groundwork for still further oppression. Paulo Freire, in *Pedagogy of the Oppressed,* uses "prescription" to indicate the way a person's consciousness is shaped by another and offers the following description: "One of the basic elements of the relationship between oppressor and oppressed is *prescription.* Every prescription represents the imposition of one man's choice upon another, transforming the consciousness of the man prescribed to into one that conforms with the prescriber's consciousness. Thus, the behavior of the oppressed is a prescribed behavior, following as it does the guidelines of the oppressor" (Freire 1968, 31). Crucial in this description is the way a limitation of choices, lack of access to all life's options, and even a lack of ability to see life's options shapes consciousness for the oppressed. The oppressed come to accept their condition as natural or inevitable because their consciousness has been shaped by prescription: "[D]ominant groups tend to entrench their hegemony by inculcating an image of inferiority in the subjugated. The struggle for freedom and equality must therefore pass through a revision of these images" (Taylor 1992, 66). The oppressor too has a consciousness shaped by the oppression and, according to Freire, it too must be overcome in order for social justice to be achieved.

Although Freire posits the existence of an oppressor group that does the prescribing, prescription may result from specific societal structures rather than any particular social group labeled "oppressor." The key is that the consciousness and behavior of the oppressed is determined and the oppressed does not have the determining power. If the oppression is structural rather than there existing a particular oppressor group, then the "prescriber's consciousness" *just is* the structure. Accordingly, one must look at the structure itself to evaluate its role in legitimating or perpetuating the oppression of a social group. Regardless of its source, prescribed consciousness contributes to socially constructed identity. (The two are not equivalent, as one can be well aware of the socially constructed identity and not internalize it oneself; that is, others might identify an individual according to oppressive stereotypes of the group while the individual need not self-identify with this oppressive identity. So too oppressed consciousness often prohibits one from being able to see the non-oppressed alternatives or the social construction—as opposed to perceived naturalness—of identity.)

An individual's identity formation through group association in oppressive systems, rather than the individual's own behaviors, principles, and values, is described by Michele M. Moody-Adams in "Race, Class, and the Social Construction of Self-Respect." Moody-Adams convincingly argues that an individual's self-respect is affected by the identity of the group as established by nonmembers of the group to which she or he has been assigned. That is, the measure of how others regard a person and how that person regards him- or herself is in relation to the person's oppressive social group identity rather than or prior to personal attempts at identity formation (Moody-Adams 1992, 259). Taylor notes that "the projection of an inferior or demeaning image on another can actually distort and oppress, to the extent that the image is internalized."

A person's identity, in other words, is shaped by how she or he sees the world and herself or himself, as well as how the world (social structures) identifies him or her. Identity, in this case, is socially constructed, and if the social organization constructs the group based on stereotypes grounded on how a group differs from some arbitrary norm, that identity is oppressive. To say that an identity is oppressive is to say that those who are so identified have no part in the identity formation, which, it should be noted, is not to say that they have no part in its perpetuation (nor is it necessarily an encompassing identity—oppressed identity is likely just part of an individual's overall identity). To the extent that a social group adopts the externally prescribed identity, they are said to be complicit in the oppressive nature of that identity. Indeed, members of a social group may perpetuate the prescribed identity (behavior, concerns, "essence"). For example, Moody-Adams describes students who, according to their externally prescribed group membership, are not expected to excel in a certain academic subject. Those members of the group who do excel are then accused of trying to be what they are not. In this instance, certain members of the group have internalized those attributes that originally set their "conceptual space" as a group (Moody-Adams 1992, 259). This internalization of the prescribed social reality then affects oneself as a member of the group (what Lindemann calls "false consciousness" following the existentialists Sartre and Beauvoir) or one may, as Moody-Adams and Freire describe, keep other members of the social group in their oppressive identities (Moody-Adams 1992, 262).

Oppression marks, constrains, stereotypes, and violates a group of people such that individuals are identified as members of the group; unique individual identity and personal relationships are shaped by external prescriptions of oppressed group status. Oppression prevents members of the oppressed group from all the tools for self-determination and social interaction. They are not as free to shape their own identities and relationships nor do they have access to the ability to establish or challenge the prescribed group identity. For example, a person's gender may elicit a prescribed identity that entails activities of what has traditionally been called the private sphere. An instance of this is seen when individuals, because they are women, are stereotyped as good at or only capable of activities associated with the maintenance of a home or family. Such individuals are thereby limited in their access to participation in activities outside the domestic realm.

It is important to note that if the oppressed group identity is determined, then qua oppressed group, they have little access to the tools of self-determination that are required for participation in a democratic society. This was, as we saw, one reason for making a distinction between the oppressed group and the solidary group, though, of course, there may be as much as a one-to-one overlap between the members. The key, described in Chapter 4, is that the nature of the group differs. Oppression keeps individuals from having access to the social institutions and from processes that would challenge the entrenched structure of oppression. That is why individuals must overcome at least some of their oppressed identity in order to participate in solidary action—or indeed any form of resistant activity.

At least one group benefits or is privileged in some way due to the oppression of another group. In intentional oppression (systemic or systematic), the oppressor group benefits and may also be held morally blameworthy for the oppression. If the nature of the oppression is systemic, or rooted in the structure of society, rather than there being a specific oppressor group, no social group is held morally blameworthy for the oppression of another social group, but there will still be some who are privileged by the oppression. The privileged status of the group or individuals benefiting from the oppression of another social group (or individual members of oppressed social groups) seemingly legitimates oppression in that the privileged have no incentive to alter the system. In other words, the oppression and/or exclusion may not be recognized, especially by those who benefit from it. If oppression is systemic or systematic and intentional, then an oppressor group does exist and the solidary group has not only a goal but also a clear opponent.

If the oppression is unintentional, there will not be an oppressor group but there will be a privileged group. Solidary action would be aimed at changing that structure. Some of those privileged by oppression may oppose efforts to change a system by which they benefit but where there is no clear oppressor group. There is no incentive on the part of the privileged group to change the social conditions that result in the systemic oppression of some. Doing so would remove their privileged status.

It is also important to note that individuals may be oppressed by a multiplicity of forces, agents, and forms of oppression. Any individual member of a group may be both oppressed and oppressor. That is, one may be oppressed as a member of a certain class (e.g., working class) and simultaneously be oppressor as a member of another social group (e.g., men). Or, to use another example, a feminist may be conscious of her oppression as a woman and not recognize her role in the perpetuation of the oppression of other women because of differences in other women's situations or contexts that her feminist theory fails to take into account. Solidary activity needs to address and will likely confront these overlapping oppressions/privileges (which is another reason why theorizing solidarity is a complicated task).

Social Vulnerability

Social vulnerability is the final category of social ills serving as appropriate targets for solidary action. There are numerous forms of vulnerability—many of which we are all equally subject to; some may be based on geographic location, others are human conditions, and still others may be unforeseen happenstances. For instance, anyone living in the Midwest United States is vulnerable to severe weather involving tornadoes, and southeastern coastal states are vulnerable to hurricanes. All of us are vulnerable to a severe strain of the flu (though, as Rousseau pointed out, our living so close to one another might be at some fault there); and fire, wind, rain, ice, meteors, and shifts in the plates on which we live are fairly indiscriminate in whom they target. *Social* vulnerabilities are those vulnerabilities that are created through human means and are either outside the universal distribution of vulnerabilities (i.e., they do not apply to all people equally) or are exacerbated by insensitive or unjust social situations. Such social vulnerabilities include economic hardship, disabilities, and age discrimination, among others.

When thinking of vulnerability, it might be helpful to juxtapose it with a concept of trust. We are often thrown into situations where we must trust that someone else will act in our own best interest. At times we can choose who we will trust but at other times no choice presents itself or the only choice is between equally undesirable options. In all three cases we are vulnerable to those with power over us, but in the latter two (when we do not choose or we are forced to choose between undesirables) our vulnerability is heightened even more. Childhood, for instance, is among the most vulnerable periods of our lives. We do not choose our parents or other adults who will supervise this important period of development or growth. Children also lack a voice in public decision-making so they must rely on others to speak and act on their behalf. Very young children compound the social vulnerability with a natural vulnerability because they are not yet able to provide the means of survival for themselves. Social vulnerability allows others in positions of power to take advantage of the vulnerable. In the case of children, this might take the form of neglect or abuse (physical, sexual, or emotional), exploitation or trafficking, discrimination and exclusion from avenues that might provide some representation or outlet for the views of children. Children are at the mercy of the specific adults charged with their care as well as the society that structures power relations—especially those over children such as education and childcare facilities but extending to political representation bodies.

All of us are vulnerable when we are sick or injured and in need of a doctor, but those are natural vulnerabilities. Many of us are able to choose what doctor we see and many of us also have both the resources to get the service we want and the self-confidence or training to know what questions to ask and how to work the medical system. While not all of these characteristics are tied to social class, many of them are. Economic conditions radically differentiate experience in healthcare and have a tremendous impact on relative levels of vulnerability within the social system. The *New York Times* published a revealing comparison among three people, from three different income brackets, who had similar heart attacks within days of each other (Scott 2005, 27–50). The wealthiest among them was taken to a university hospital with a well-trained cardiologist licensed to perform angioplasty. Within three hours of his heart attack he was recovering with a stent to keep his artery open. He subsequently joined a health club and his prospects for future health were extremely good. The woman at the lowest end of the income ladder delayed going to the hospital out of fear of the cost of the ambulance ride. When she finally did go in, it was after significant damage to the heart had occurred, to a city hospital with a busy emergency room and not licensed to perform angioplasty. She never got the procedures ordered by her doctor and had a difficult time making any lifestyle changes that would improve her future prognosis. Her recover was further hampered because she had to return to work as a housekeeper relatively soon after her heart attack. As this example shows, social inequities limit or prohibit choice of doctor thereby increasing social vulnerability. The woman had to trust a doctor she did not choose and a hospital with less than sufficient facilities for the kind of care she needed. As the author of the article suggested, they all "faced a single common threat" but "social class—that elusive combination of income, education, occupation, and wealth—played a powerful role in [their] . . . struggles to recover" (Scott 2005, 28).

Another case of vulnerability compounded by lack of choice of those in whom one must trust and/or who have power over one is the case of prisoners—both state prisoners and prisoners of war. This is a particularly interesting case because where the child's innocence contributes to his or her social vulnerability, the prisoner's lack of innocence puts him or her at the mercy of others. Prisoners must trust powerful strangers with everything from their personal hygiene to healthcare to legal rights. Prisoners of war are often held by military personnel who do not speak their language and who have a deeply ingrained and heightened feeling of enmity toward them.

Notable about these cases of social vulnerability—childhood, healthcare, and prisoners—is the potentially temporary nature of the vulnerability itself. Childhood inevitably ends; there is some, albeit limited, social mobility that might change one's experience in the healthcare system; and prisoners of war or prisoners of the state might be freed, exonerated, or transferred. Political solidarity with the vulnerable takes up some part of their cause in an effort to protect them from abuse of their vulnerable status. Political solidarity actively resists measures that would exacerbate existing natural vulnerabilities and seeks protection against abusive powers that might take advantage of the socially vulnerable.

Robert Goodin argues that "one is always vulnerable to particular agents with respect to particular sorts of threats" (1985, 112). His account of vulnerability illustrates the potential for multiple forms of vulnerability coalescing in the lives of individuals. Some of these vulnerabilities are part of oppressive structures but some are natural vulnerabilities sharpened by unjust social systems: "Dependencies and vulnerabilities are all largely created or exacerbated by existing social arrangements. By altering those arrangements, we could mitigate if not necessarily eliminate those conditions" (Goodin 1985, 192).

Goodin examines our obligations to distant people through the lens of vulnerability: "We do have a responsibility to aid distant peoples in distress but . . . it is a collective rather than an individual responsibility. While people in the Third World may not be vulnerable to us in the First World as individuals, they are enormously vulnerable to us as a collectivity" (1985, 163). He defines the vulnerability here broadly, claiming that "protecting the vulnerable is primarily a matter of forestalling threatened harms" (Goodin 1985, 110). Goodin's argument ultimately supports a strong system of civic solidarity insofar as he uses vulnerability as a justification for a universal moral obligation. We have, he argues, a moral obligation to protect the vulnerable. Chapter 7 explores various conceptions of human solidarity for moral theory and whether a universal moral obligation to solidarity is possible. Those who commit to political solidarity take on something beyond what might be assumed or expected of common humanity. They make a personal commitment—not reliant on their state—to act, to be part of the effort for social change.

Political solidarity might also arise in response to or to protect some against political vulnerability. This could range from protecting refugees fleeing a state engaging in genocidal violence to guarding against congressional redistricting that would effectively silence a minority group within national politics. This is differentiated slightly from social vulnerabilities because in the case of political vulnerability, participants in solidarity must necessarily work with states or state mechanisms.

Summary

I have grouped the ends of political solidarity according to responses to injustice, oppression, and social vulnerabilities for ease of discussion. No doubt there are other classes of social ills currently, or perhaps there will be some in the future, that would call us to respond through solidaristic activity. With any discussion of the ends of solidarity, however, we ought to keep in mind the requisite victims with whom one can be in solidarity. Political solidarity would surely have no role to play in social theory and practice if there were no victims. In addition, political solidarity is a human unity. One might feel compassion and be compelled to act on behalf of nonhuman animals or trees but one cannot be united in solidarity with them. Mutuality, inherent in the moral relations of solidarity, mandates that requirement. In solidarity, each individual mutually forms a reciprocal relation with the group. That is not to say, however, that political solidarity is unconcerned with the environment or nonhuman animals. Political solidarity might form in response to the social justice issues that are entailed in factory farming chickens, clear cutting forests, mountaintop mining, or river delta preservation, to name just a few. Solidarity would not be with the chickens, forests, mountains, or river but rather with the people whose lives and livelihoods are adversely affected by these practices. When environmental hazards affect an already marginalized group, then social justice efforts may opt to fight not just the marginalization but also the environmental problem. Importantly, I am not here claiming that political solidarity ignores the environment or nonhuman animals, or that activist are not also interested in those issues. I am merely highlighting the political aspect of the moral relation of political solidarity as one among many forms of activist responses to injustice.

One possible objection to the discussions in this and the previous section is that I have engaged in a certain amount of philosophical hairsplitting that has little impact on how we actually act in the types of relationships developed and the array of goals sought. I do not doubt that there is some truth to this objection. The actions and relations between victims of and responders to natural disasters and victims of and responders to injustice, to take just one comparison, are certainly similar. But in a recovery of the moral import of the concept of solidarity, some philosophical hairsplitting is necessary in order to reveal the unique moral relationships and obligations of solidarity generally and political solidarity more specifically. Moreover, the discussions and comparisons in these sections also reveal the directionality or logic of moral obligations and social bonds dedicated to bringing about social justice through solidary action. Social solidarity emphasizes the bond between members as ontologically prior to moral obligations but political solidarity underscores the importance of a moral commitment to a goal as the creation of and driving force for any bonds that form between participants.

Sustaining Praxis

There certainly is no guarantee that solidarity movements will achieve their ends. Nor is there any guarantee that those ends are the best possible outcome, the truest path to justice or good. Nonetheless, like symbolic protest (Hill 1979), even if the long-term effects of solidarity action prove minimal, there are still reasons why solidarity activity is better than antipathy.

Because each individual comes to the movement by way of a commitment, each establishes a relation to the goal or cause of solidarity. The extent of this relation may vary for each person but, in order for one to claim solidarity, the obligation must have some transforming effect on the self, on personal relations, and on one's actions and decisions. Such a personal transformation has potentially lifelong and life-changing effects. But the substantive end or goal in solidarity is not always as long-standing as the individual transformations or the desire for the solidarity. Think, for example, of a localized movement to obtain adequate second-stage housing for residents of a domestic violence shelter, that is, affordable, safe housing after a shelter stay. Out of financial necessity, most shelters must have a maximum time limit for residency, and women must move to some alternative location. But women who have been victimized by domestic violence often come to shelter without any money, identification, bank records, birth certificates for themselves or their children, or even basic necessities like clothing and personal hygiene items. Once in the shelter, she faces discrimination from landlords who fear that any woman who has stayed in a shelter is a poor bet for a tenant; severe economic hardship because landlords want rent for the first and last months, security deposits, and other incidentals; social stigmas from neighbors, family, friends; and if she has children, an additional layer of vulnerability to social services, schools, financial institutions, employment prospects, and so forth. All this while she must also live with the realization that her batterer may hunt her down in her new residence, inflict violence on her or her children, and she may be forced to seek shelter or new housing again. Individuals from diverse walks of life may recognize the injustice of the variety of social conditions that converge to make women victimized by domestic violence multiply vulnerable. Individuals uniting in a movement might involve victims and former victims—or survivors—of domestic violence, advocates and social workers, academics and other intellectuals committed to the cause, local community members and politicians, and any number of other people willing to commit to collective effort. They may be motivated by self-interest, employment requirements, honest conviction, or even public relations notoriety. The bonds may intensify or wane throughout the movement as membership changes. For many within the movement, the struggle and the relationships that form within it become consuming activities that give greater meaning to one's existence. How do we ensure that the spirit within the group stays alive until the ends have been achieved? And what happens once the goal is accomplished? When they achieve their aim of quality second-stage housing, what happens to the group? What happens to the individuals who were so dedicated in their efforts? Once the aim of their collective actions ceases to exist, for whatever reason, does the group itself cease to exist? They might experience some extended moments of self and mutual congratulations; they might ask, "What's next?" and find another sustaining project to unify them; or the group might simply fade away.

Perhaps because of the urgency of the cause or because of the length of commitment required to address it, political solidarity can sustain or foster rather intense relationships among the members. Of course, some participants in less localized movements might not be intensely affected by the group but will nonetheless be affected in their own lives by the goal and the group action. At times, the group may waver between a group united by their commitment to a cause and a group united in social solidarity based on shared experience. For instance, students spending their summer living and working with the poor of Nicaragua to effect social change (i.e., living and working in political solidarity) might also share a social solidarity or community bond that descriptively unites them on the basis of their situation. The shared experience, however, is not the experience of oppression or injustice but the experience of working together to accomplish a project. I do not wish to deny that such a confluence of solidarities occurs; in fact, numerous examples used throughout this project acknowledge such a convergence. My aim is to show what is morally distinct about political solidarity even if or when it is seen together with social or civic solidarity. In political solidarity, individuals see their action as part of something bigger than themselves. Struggling for social justice, they see their collective action having an effect that is often first recognized in the personal transformation of each of the individual members.

For some, once a goal has been accomplished, died away, or otherwise ceases to unite the group, they consider their commitment complete and redirect their energies elsewhere. But for others, there remains nevertheless a desire to maintain the group, to adopt a new cause that members might rally around to sustain the energy of their collective action. In other words, group members might wish to sustain their praxis. Praxis here just means collective action, but, because it is within a discussion of solidarity, it carries with it the connotation of "reflective action" also found in some theological uses of the term.

Sustaining praxis is not always possible. Quite effective groups that become united around a cause might quickly disperse or linger a bit to contemplate their successes and failures. Individuals who have made only a weak commitment will likely be the first to leave while those who embraced a cause through multiple aspects of their personal as well as their political lives might have additional, individualized incentive to find or create some reason for the group to stay united in action. Alternatively, once one substantive goal has been overcome—for whatever reason—it is also possible for those individuals who made only a weak commitment to the initial cause to make a much stronger commitment to a subsequent endeavor and the group to reshape itself. So too individuals who shared a strong commitment to the initial project might disagree, be burned out, or be uninterested in pursuing any subsequent project by the same, albeit fluid, solidary group.

Elsewhere I have argued that Simone de Beauvoir's confrontation with this problem of sustaining solidarity relies on the solidary group composed of individuals transcending the goal of political solidarity (Scholz 2005b). In other words, given that each individual makes a commitment to the collective cause, each individual has to see the goal passing away in order for a new goal to emerge. Beauvoir's discussion of workers in "Moral Idealism and Political Realism" explores the motivations for group struggle; Beauvoir sees the aim of political action as not just the particularity of the situation but the opening up of future possibilities. The project should always turn back on freedom and open up the future (Beauvoir 1948a, 1948b; see also Arp 2001, 34). Each cause, rather than being an end in-itself, ought always to be an end toward freedom, according to Beauvoir. Concomitant with this fact, no cause ought to take on a life of its own over and against the group or against the constituent participants. Transcending one project (through accomplishment, defeat, or obsolescence) means a new project has to replace it. Often, rather than a single transition, projects seem more or less to naturally flow into each other because of the similarity of their aims. In such an instance, sustaining praxis involves maintaining the energy of the overlapping solidary groups in different contexts.

In order for the transcendence or any similar replacement of one substantive project with another, individuals must commit anew. Many will make a smooth transition from one project to the next and many will be already involved in a new or alternative project long before one project ceases. Some, of course, will abandon their former comrades—moving on to different projects perhaps unrelated to social change for justice. In other words, sustaining praxis must be an individual as much as a group project.

With the transformation of the substantive ends, aim, goal, or project of political solidarity comes the transformation of the constituent moral relations. A new project or cause informs different obligations to it and to fellow actors in a new collective. In short, sustaining praxis might best be understood as a personal recommitment to communal action. In solidarity, then, I *choose* to be part of a collective movement engaged in praxis. Choice, or more accurately, commitment, holds the key to the question of sustaining praxis. Like the commitment that creates a reciprocal relation between an individual and a group thereby establishing political solidarity, it is commitment that will maintain the solidary relation or a new one after that initial cause has passed away.

A new cause or aim informs a new praxis that might resemble the old but also moves the group beyond the old and thus redefines the group. Sonia Kruks explains that it is through praxis that the very identity of the group exists. Our collective *doing*, as opposed to our collective *being*, identifies the group and simultaneously transforms participants who themselves have transformed the group. Praxis "constitutes and reconstitutes social identities" (Kruks 2001,

119). Politics becomes a living reality when individual commitment transforms not just social structures but the life of the revolutionary as well. Active, committed solidarity entails a group structure that necessarily acknowledges individual freedom while also mediating that freedom through projects limited by and interconnected with the projects of others.

Culture of Protest

There is a small risk that political solidarity will devolve into something like a "culture of protest." A culture of protest is protest for protest's sake. When the ends become the protest itself rather than whatever inspired the collective action—even if it is still somewhere in the background—protest becomes a way of life rather than an active choice. This danger is especially relevant for political solidarity because political solidarity does require an integrated response from the individual that involves multiple facets of personal decisions as well as multiple aspects of various relationships. Protest would, in other words, easily slip into becoming a lifestyle for the individual and a culture for the group rather than a means of resistance to social injustice or an avenue to social change.

Some protestors even turn protesting into a career. Paid protestors, like mercenaries, may have some connection to a cause and are not necessarily acting contrary to their conscience, but no doubt there will be some who are solely "in it for the money." I should be clear here that by "paid protestor" I do not mean to include those people who work in advocacy and related social justice careers who also receive a wage or salary when they are engaging in protest. The paid protestor is someone who views the protest primarily as a means to make a wage. The protest (or the wage), rather than a social justice cause, becomes the end.

As is clear with the case of the paid protestor, a culture of protest contradicts political solidarity in principle. As Chapter 3 illustrates, political solidarity entails three primary moral relations—the relation to the goal, the relation to others in solidarity, and the relation to the larger society. A culture of protest violates at least two of these relations and perhaps all three. Protest for protest's sake violates the relation to the goal because the goal no longer informs collective action. Collective action takes on a life of its own that could easily slip into mob action if it lacks the principled commitment of its constituent members. The relation to the larger society is also debased by a culture of protest. Recall that one of the obligations of political solidarity was to negotiate in good faith. Protest that has taken on a life of its own aims only at itself, not at negotiation or even at social change. Protestors protest in order to be seen as protestors or to be part of the protest, but in political solidarity protest ought always to be informed by the cause or aim and with the sincere hope that it will somehow contribute to social change. Arguably, the culture of protest also violates the relations between fellow participants insofar as it fails to exert social criticism on the movement itself or to use a principled end to mediate their relations.

Another hazard of a culture of protest is that the cause or culture could overshadow or even subsume the individual. Here again it is useful to examine Beauvoir's insights regarding the appeal of an absolute, that is, an entity that takes on a godlike status insofar as it rules and orders one's life. Beauvoir's ethics presents a number of attitudes that individuals adopt once they confront the fact that they are free. These attitudes might also be described as relations to an absolute (as Mussett 2005 does). That is, in an effort to avoid freedom, human beings might posit an absolute in which they might abdicate their freedom. In other words, just as the cause risks subsuming the individual, the culture of protest risks subsuming the cause as well as the individual.

Moral Sentiments Revisited

As a final note in this chapter, I would like to revisit some of the moral sentiments that may motivate some individuals to take up a cause and join in political solidarity. Related to the culture of protest in some way, some dedicated privileged people might be tempted through intense feelings of indignation or pity to experience the victimization, oppression, injustice, and vulnerability of the oppressed. As I argued in Chapter 5, however, solidarity does not ask formerly privileged to experience the victimization or oppression of others; it does ask committed individuals to stand alongside of these others, who similarly commit, to bring about social change. Standing alongside those victimized by oppression does entail potentially great sacrifice; Sandra Bartky highlights this point saying, "To stand in solidarity with others is to work actively to eliminate their misery, not to arrange one's life so as to share it" (2002, 74). The point is to challenge the unjust system, overthrow the oppressive practices, or protect the vulnerable, not to increase the population of victims of injustice, oppression, or social vulnerabilities.

Political solidarity will unite people who make both strong and weak commitments to a cause based on one's own situation, needs, and abilities. But a weak commitment is still a commitment. Consider, for instance, an example I used earlier in this book: a person in the United States commits to a movement to fight unjust wages for workers in the Global South. She acts on this commitment by seeking fair trade products whenever possible. At times, of course, fair trade products are not available. Does that mean that she is no longer acting in solidarity when she purchases a non–fairly traded product? It might but it does not necessarily signal that. The commitment to political solidarity is a commitment to a moral relation. While she may not always be able to act on that relation, it does not necessarily mean that she has renounced it. The personalism of her commitment to the cause is outwardly manifest in her actions but inwardly manifest in her conscience. The blending of her actions with similar acts by others makes the communal response of political solidarity. She might give up on her commitment and feel no qualms about doing so. But sometimes exigency may require her to act contrary to her commitment in spite of still strongly maintaining it.

Passion or indignation will not be enough to sustain the solidary activity. Although he extends his analysis to include other forms of solidarity, Michael Walzer makes this point when he says, "Solidarity can be dangerous when it is only a feeling, an emotional substitute for, rather than a reflection of, actual, on-the-ground, day-by-day cooperation. The sense of closeness with other people has to be earned—by fighting together or working together for a cause; responding together to difficulty, crisis, natural disaster; studying a common history and literature; celebrating the holidays, enacting the rituals of common life" (1998, 50). Notice the emphasis on collective action for a cause that ought to transform feelings into action. Feelings may inspire someone to join a cause but part of the unique beauty of all forms of solidarity is that it, unlike other forms of unity, mediates between the individual and the community. An overreliance on sentiment risks paralyzing the individual from being able to take positive steps for collective action. But when feelings are measured through the lens of the cause for social justice, they might be put to good use to motivate even more people to join the cause. Consider what Henry Shue has to say on this topic:

> Sentiments, both in others and in ourselves, can be judged critically. The expression in action of some sentiments is to be welcomed, the expression of others is to be discouraged. For assessing sentiments

one needs principles. Principles, on the other hand, will be adopted only if they evoke the support of some felt sentiment. Action in accord with a principle needs to be motivated. . . . the principle must somehow appeal to motivational springs of action that preexist the appeal. (Shue 1980, 146)

Shue appears to make a stricter distinction between sentiments or feelings and principled action than I wish to make, but his point is very similar to what I have been arguing here. The cause or goal of political solidarity mediates the relations with others and can also be useful in mediating some of our relations with ourselves. But it would be a mistake to claim that sentiments do not play a role in political solidarity or even that they play a secondary role. Feelings, like principles, can motivate someone to act. But feelings, like principles, also need to be balanced and in political solidarity, the ends do a fair bit of the balancing.

Perhaps even more important, sentiments and feelings may help to sustain praxis before a goal is accomplished. The spirit of the solidary group may weaken or intensify in turns; the struggle against oppression and injustice often requires stamina. The more passionate participants in political solidarity might find effective means of inspiring perseverance by sharing their passion. In his book on the civil rights movement in one small town in North Carolina, Timothy Tyson also wryly notes the positive effects of intimidation and peer pressure on sustaining economic boycotts and related solidary praxis (2004). Friends who see weakening resolve in their colleagues in the struggle for liberation can bolster the conviction for social justice with a well-placed comment or look. Feelings are contagious—infusing others with hope for success, joy at small successes, anger at injustice, and belief in personal power has tremendous effect in sustaining the praxis of a collective movement. Not to be too rosy eyed about it, however, as Walzer, Shue, and Kruks illustrate, it is the *doing* of collective action and the principles coupled with the feelings that sustain the movement.

Conclusion

One obvious question throughout all this discussion of what constitutes the ends of political solidarity or what counts as social justice is whether we have an obligation to solidarity. That is, given that injustice, oppression, and vulnerability are so pervasive, does every human person have an obligation to struggle for social justice through political solidarity?

This question rapidly gives way to many more, but perhaps the most important is whether our common humanity, if there is such a thing, does not in fact require us to respond to the suffering of others. In the next chapter I examine these questions and what assumptions they entail not just for political solidarity but for social and civic solidarity as well.

SEVEN

On Human Solidarity and the Challenge of Global Solidarity

Article 2 of the 1948 United Nations Convention on the Prevention and Punishment of the Crime of Genocide understands "genocide" as

> any of the following acts committed with intent to destroy, in whole or in part, a national, ethnical, racial or religious group, as such:
> (a) Killing members of the group;
> (b) Causing serious bodily or mental harm to members of the group;
> (c) Deliberately inflicting on the group conditions of life calculated to bring about its physical destruction in whole or in part;
> (d) Imposing measures intended to prevent births within the group;
> (e) Forcibly transferring children of the group to another group. (UN Convention on the Prevention and Punishment of the Crime of Genocide)

Although genocide was not an entirely new phenomenon, in the wake of World War II the international community believed that it was imperative to ensure that genocide be named, identified, and, when possible, halted. In spite of this effort, genocidal campaigns continue.

Bangladesh, Cambodia, Yugoslavia, Rwanda, and the Darfur region of Sudan serve as poignant and horrifying examples that genocide continues to mar the world. The intent of genocide is to destroy a people. Among the means used are murder, indiscriminate bombing, starvation, displacement, rape, and forced pregnancy (so children will have a different ethnicity than their mothers).

In March 1971, Bangladesh declared independence and shortly thereafter the Pakistanis began a nine-month campaign of murder and mass rape, killing an estimated three million Bangladeshis and raping 200,000 to 400,000 women, 25,000 of whom became pregnant (Brownmiller 1975, 80, 84). In the early 1990s, Serbs in the former Yugoslavia killed an estimated 200,000, targeting primarily Muslims in Bosnia. The international community was well aware of the "ethnic cleansing" but largely sat on its hands until 1993 when the genocide escalated. Estimates for the Rwanda genocide, when the Hutus raged against the Tutsis between April and July 1994, range from half a million to one million (including women and children).

What, if anything, does a theory of political solidarity have to contribute to our understanding of and responses to such gross humanitarian crises as genocidal campaigns? Can a theory of solidarity work with a theory of human rights to help prevent or respond to genocide and other inhumanities? Some response is required. Numerous social and political theorists have assumed, asserted, or argued that human solidarity is not only possible but that it exists. The basic premise is that we are united by our very humanity. Genocidal campaigns—as well as a number of other more frequent instances of humanity's inhumanity—make it difficult to accept this premise however.

Regardless of whether the solidarity of humanity is seen as a realistic goal or an idealistic dream, the possibility of solidarity across national differences raises some interesting theoretical questions. What sort of solidarity would it be? Is human solidarity its own distinct form of solidarity? Can social solidarity be extended to encompass all humanity? What about civic and political solidarity? What sort of human-authored injustice or oppression would force all of humanity to unite under the banner of political solidarity? Or is such a globalized notion of political solidarity inherently contradictory?

In this chapter, I argue that human solidarity may be a subcategory of either social solidarity or civic solidarity. In the course of this argument, I present and examine some different theories of human solidarity. I contrast human solidarity as a subcategory of social solidarity with human solidarity as a subcategory of civic solidarity. At times, categorization of these theories is not always entirely clear-cut but examining the array of approaches to human togetherness offered enlightens an overall account of solidarity. I then present global solidarity and revisit international solidarity, which I argue are the most expansive forms of political solidarity. Genocide, and more specifically, mass rape campaigns within genocide, serves as a sort of case study through which to examine the varying challenges to human and global solidarity.

Human Solidarity as Social Solidarity

Social solidarity assesses or appraises the coherence of a group of people. The tightness of the social bonds, descriptively determined, then informs the moral obligations members have to one another. Often, social solidarity is presented as the degree of mutual identification between members of the group. Perhaps they share a history, consciousness, location, or experience. The nature of the social bonds, according to social solidarity, establishes what members owe to one another. The tighter the group, the more that is expected. The obligations might be expressed in explicit rules or laws, or they might be implicitly assumed in the relations or roles within the society. Some policing in order to hold individual community members accountable might be necessary. Moreover, the various obligations of social solidarity arise out of the day-to-day interactions. Each of us is a member of numerous communities or social groups that display varying levels of social solidarity. The normative side of our group affiliations minimally upholds the stated or unstated rules of those social groups. An obvious question for social solidarity is whether the group of human beings displays any social solidarity, and if so, what the normative obligations are.

There are probably countless different approaches to or justifications of a unity of all humanity. Many make essentialist claims about what it means to be a human person; others make antiessentialist arguments (some vehemently so) about the human situation, condition, or potential. These arguments for the social solidarity of all humanity are not merely descriptive—they also make normative claims about our obligations and responsibilities to one another. Atrocities, like genocide, and even everyday sorts of evils like deliberate insensitivity or prejudice, are then explained as moral failures, as people violating the requirements of social solidarity.

In this section, I present some of the various arguments for human solidarity. Because the social solidarity of all humanity rests on some common feature or shared experience, I begin with essentialist accounts and then move on to discuss accounts that rest on division of labor (Durkheim), extension of empathy (Konstantin Kolenda's "incremental solidarity"), and unity in difference (Richard Rorty and Alain Locke). Although the presentation of these accounts is brief, they share in common the aim of articulating some means of achieving the unity of all of humanity. The normative side of human solidarity conceived through social solidarity might be a minimal account of human rights that could be useful in evaluating breaches of human solidarity. The section ends by addressing some of the criticisms of human solidarity.

Human solidarity as a manifestation of social solidarity assumes that there is a distinct group, called "humans," membership within which is determined by status as human. There are two ways of discussing human solidarity of this sort: descriptively and normatively. Descriptively, we are simply concerned with what binds humans together, what constitutes our humanity. Normatively, we would try to articulate how best we might approximate an ideal of human solidarity. One prominent method is by looking at the rights and obligations that accompany human status.

Numerous theorists argue that the nature of human rights entails universal obligations to one another (Gewirth 1986, 342; Shue 1980) and thereby ensures social solidarity. Some accounts of the unity of humans describe membership in this group according to a particular characteristic (like rationality, intelligence, self-awareness, or egoism) while others consider it a sort of "all-or-nothing" proposition (Nino 1991, 35). (Notice that we talk of "humans" rather than "moral persons" or simply "persons." These latter categories need not and generally do not include the entire class of humans and thus would not be applicable to this sort of discussion for human solidarity.)

Emile Durkheim addressed the question of social solidarity of all humanity. Given that social solidarity is based on the division of labor, he held that human solidarity or "the ideal of human fraternity" could only be realized "in proportion to the progress of the division of labor" (Durkheim 1973, 143). In other words, human solidarity is simply the result of an ever-expanding society that eventually encompasses all humanity. Durkheim argues that "we must choose: either to renounce our dream, if we refuse further to circumscribe our activity, or else to push forward its accomplishment under the condition we have just set forth" (1973, 143). We might be inclined to see globalization as one form of the progress of the division of labor. Raw materials from one location might be shipped to another for rudimentary assembly, forwarded to another to be combined with parts from raw materials and production in still other locations. These might then be shipped to still more locations for final assembly, branding, marketing, and sale. Companies may have their headquarters in one part of the world, their warehouses and manufacturing facilities in another, and their customer service in a third location. Although oversimplified, surely such interdependence in global business and commerce at least approximates what Durkheim might have envisioned for a globalized division of labor. An obvious objection to this, however, is that even if we do accept globalization in business as a form, model, or manifestation of a global division of labor, it is not at all clear that we can affirm, with Durkheim, the presence of increased solidary bonds with more substantial moral obligations among participant members (be they individuals, corporations, or nations). Many have noted, in fact, an opposite sort of phenomenon. Globalization, at times at least, appears to resemble cultural imperialism more than human solidarity. Contra Durkheim, there is no guarantee that the division of labor will be accompanied by the sort of moral ties he envisions for organic solidarity. The key, as Kevin Doran explains, is that "a proper appreciation of the function of each organ of society is only possible where there is a sense of belonging to the whole" (1996, 16). In other words, the global community must be seen as a whole (and each part must see itself in relation to that whole) in order for division of labor to foster normative universal human solidarity.

Another approach is to gradually extend the reach of social solidarity. That is, a well-established social solidarity can grow to encompass more people. As it grows, the ties that bind and the moral structures that maintain those ties grow with it. Consider what Konstantin Kolenda calls "incremental solidarity." As he explains, "To follow it is to take into account both our limitations and the desire which gave birth to the humanistic ideal of fostering good will toward *all* human beings. That desire is fulfilled when we manage to extend somewhat the reach of our interest and concern. To include among *us* at least some of *them*" (Kolenda 1989, 43). Incremental solidarity calls on us to respond to a "person or persons toward whom we have been indifferent because of blindness, prejudice, or inertia" (Kolenda 1989, 43). The challenge is to see people as part of our circle when we initially consider them outside it. The "actual contingencies of our situation" elicit these responses. "Even a modest extension of interest, attention, empathy, and sympathy is likely to make us feel a bit better about ourselves" (Kolenda 1989, 43). Kolenda is certainly correct that extending sympathy and interest incrementally will likely lead to greater understanding of our differences and perhaps as well a more genuine communal feeling. In some ways, Kolenda has suggested for solidarity what Rita Manning and others have done for the ethics of care.

Manning (1992) suggests a gradual widening of our circle of care (or think of expanding concentric circles) to eventually include distant others can justify moral responses to those distant others. Incremental solidarity, like Durkheim's organic solidarity, holds human solidarity as a goal to be realized. The incentives for both are based on the reciprocal benefits to be had when one expands the circle of social solidarity.

A different sort of incremental solidarity comes out of the pragmatist tradition. Alain Leroy Locke, instrumental in the Harlem Renaissance, wrote about cultural pluralism that was aimed at achieving "unity in diversity" and world solidarity. He turned to cultural customs, traditions, and artistic expressions, more or less abandoning political means, to locate cultural diversity and in turn to hold the promise for world solidarity (Scholz 1998b). Locke's world solidarity is also an idealized goal that he thinks could help guide our moral behaviors.

Locke claims that customs, traditions, artistic expressions, language, differences in experiences and history, all distinguish one culture from another. Commonality of physical attributes or segregated social life do not serve to support cultural particularity primarily because, according to Locke, nothing about them lends to group solidarity (Washington 1994, 15). The uniqueness of culture is also about cultural conflict, which Locke believed was a natural part of different cultures interacting. This conflict, however, should not be mistaken for incompatibility or a support for rivalry cultural separatism (Locke and Stern 1946, 5; Washington also makes this point, 1994, 98). Cultural interactions might be positive, as when diverse cultures recognize the functional parity between seemingly divergent practices. Another component of Locke's conception of cultural particularity is that cultures are composites; cultures are dynamic and their vicissitudes are affected in part by contact with other cultures: "In modern times and under modern conditions, as mechanisms of intercommunication are multiplied and group contacts inevitably increase, cultures tend to become increasingly hybrid and composite" (Locke and Stern 1946, 7). This aspect of cultural particularity reminds us that "each culture ... incorporat[es] aspects of other cultures with which it comes into contact" (Locke and Stern 1946, 6). As composites, cultures borrow from one another in a dynamic progression toward world solidarity (Locke 1989, 206).

In other words, a culture's positive identity of itself is a necessary component to its empowerment in interactions with other cultures. To this end, cultures should continuously pursue their particularity while also acknowledging parity with other cultures and engaging in cultural reciprocity and composition. Locke envisions a union of the diverse cultures brought about by the artists—this is what he calls world solidarity. By gaining knowledge of other cultures we gain an understanding also of our own. Cultural exchanges reveal our diversity as well as the fallacy of assuming one's own culture is superior or otherwise the norm for value judgment (see also Washington 1986, 72). According to Locke, the elite from diverse cultural groups within the United States begin the process of coming together and gradually extend solidarity to the hemisphere and the world. The political meaning of solidarity is replaced by the aesthetic: "The solidarity they [the artists] can and will achieve is not to be a doctrinal one of common interests and universalized traditions, but an integrating psychology of reciprocal exchange and mutual esteem" (Locke 1925, 75).

Locke's theory of world solidarity, although focused on cultural or artistic connections rather than mutual reliance or incremental feelings of association, is like Durkheim and Kolenda's insofar as it offers an ideal to attain. All three understand the benefits of an expansive human solidarity as including some forms of mutual respect or protection that would cancel out the conditions that give rise to gross violations of human solidarity like genocide. Many of the genocidal campaigns of the last few decades were, for instance, based in long-standing cultural or ethnic conflicts. Locke offers the first step in cultural tolerance: "disestablishing the use of one's own culture as a contrast norm for other cultures, [thereby leading] through the appreciation of the functional significance of other values in their respective cultures to the eventual discovery and recognition of certain functional common denominators" (Locke 1989, 77; see also 15, 98; and Locke and Stern 1946, 93). Thus human solidarity or world solidarity is a gradual process carried out by the artists, according to Locke, who seek not a unifying sameness but a unity in diversity that allows for greater appreciation of other cultures and recognition of similarity or parity of cultural practices. This, in turn, invites people to see themselves in the diverse practices of another. The other theories of human solidarity also seek to posit some justification for each person and each society to develop mutuality with all others.

Richard Rorty uses a pragmatist method similar to Alain Locke's, though, unlike Locke, he focuses on similarity in pain rather than artistic accomplishments. Rorty denies that there is some "human essence" or human nature that all of us have and that forms the basis of human solidarity. That is, he denies the premise that by recognizing the "humanness" of others we come to their aid in times of need. Instead, Rorty argues that "a belief can still regulate action, can still be thought worth dying for, among people who are quite aware that this belief is caused by nothing deeper than contingent historical circumstance" (1989, 189). Drawing on the pragmatist tradition, Rorty argues that differences ought to be minimized "one difference at a time—the difference between Christians and Muslims in a particular village in Bosnia, the difference between blacks and whites in a particular town in Alabama, the difference between gays and straights in a particular Catholic congregation in Quebec. The hope is to sew such groups together with a thousand little stitches" rather than posit a common human essence (Rorty, unpublished manuscript, cited in Kuipers 1997, 73). The image of the "polychrome quilt" that Rorty here invokes provides a vision of human solidarity that is created when the vast array of differences meet at differing points.

After citing a number of examples, he notes "that our sense of solidarity is strongest when those with whom solidarity is expressed are thought of as 'one of us,' where 'us' means something smaller and more local than the human race" (Rorty 1989, 191). His idea is that with human progress, we extend the notion of the "us" such that human solidarity "is thought of as the ability to see more and more traditional differences (or tribe, religion, race, customs, and the like) as unimportant when compared with similarities with respect to pain and humiliation" (Rorty 1989, 192). Novels and ethnographic descriptions of pain and humiliation can aid us as we approach human solidarity. For example, humans all feel the pain of humiliation when their language and belief structures are stripped. Rorty uses Orwell's *1984* to illustrate the unmaking of a person's world and the pain that this destruction reaps (1989, 177). He argues that feeling a sense of solidarity with all other human beings is a moral obligation but is not built on shared human essence: "[H]e does not deny that attempts to exhort global solidarity are valuable. He argues merely that we should see these as 'urging us to create a more expansive sense of solidarity than we presently have,' not as appealing to the moral significance of some common human essence" (Mason 2000, 175, citing Rorty 1989, 196).

Another central tenet of Rorty's argument is the distinction between public and private. As he describes it in the last chapter of *Contingency, Irony, and Solidarity,* "Our responsibilities to others constitute *only* the public side of our lives, a side which competes with our private affections and our private attempts at self-creation, and which has no *automatic* priority over such private motives.... Moral obligation is, in this view, to be thrown in with a lot of other considerations, rather than automatically trump them" (Rorty 1989, 194). He uses this to argue for human solidarity. Pain falls into the public/moral realm while traditional assertions about the essence, nature, or purpose of human life fall into the private/nonmoral realm. Similarities of our experiences of pain bind us together. Many other personal experiences will fall into the natural realm, thereby affecting how oppression is conceived. Oppression becomes linguistically determined—the public side about which we can make moral claims.

Rorty holds a radical constructivist position that would make solidary action merely struggles for new social constructs. If we can change the linguistic practices, he argues, we change the phenomenon. Applied to a particular movement on behalf of women or workers, for instance, Rorty's position has been read to indicate that oppressed conditions are one way of describing things. Its existence depends on being articulated. A new description yields a new social construct. As Sonia Kruks points out, however, "The costs of reducing women's experience to feminist linguistic creation *alone* are high. For personhood then becomes an attribute of linguistic competence and is denied to the silent or silenced" (2001, 134). Rorty does have a response insofar as he notes that linguistically powerful persons can aid the silenced and speak on their behalf. Clearly, this runs into the problems identified in Chapter 5. The situation of the oppressed may not be described accurately (of course Rorty would question the very notion of accuracy as it implies that the description corresponds to some reality rather than creates the reality).

These differing approaches to human solidarity might signal the possibility of rich theoretical debates on how human solidarity is justified and what morally it entails. But through those debates sounds a question asked at the beginning of this chapter. How does solidarity, and in this case human solidarity as a form of social solidarity, help us to understand and respond to atrocities like genocide? Interestingly, the word "genocide" was coined only relatively recently. Rapheal Lemkin coined the word in 1944 in his *Axis Rule in Occupied Europe*. Lemkin combined the Greek word for people, race, or tribe with a word derived from Latin meaning "to kill." The international community, through the documents of the United Nations, adopted a standard definition of genocide, presented at the outset of this chapter. But in creating the word, Lemkin was not creating the phenomenon. Genocide was not new, just the term. Certainly having a name for murderous brutality on a mass scale may have assisted organized responses to it but there were organized responses to the atrocity before the term as well. In other words, this was not a new social reality. As we theorize human solidarity based on a shared trait ("humanity"), a division of labor, incremental recognition of similarities, cultural reciprocity and composition, or overlapping commonality, we ought to also notice the many ways that humans act to block human solidarity.

Bayertz (1999a) points out that universal human solidarity is hindered by external factors such as conflict, animosity, and egoism. The genocide and ethnic cleansing of the past three decades are just the extreme examples of these external factors. More moderate and everyday biases, prejudices, and hostilities bar human solidarity worldwide and, in some cases, even within national borders. In addition, there is the problem of cultural conceptions of humanity. Women are still not considered full moral persons or even fully human in some traditions and are often seen as little more than property. Other examples of social practices that stand in the way of human solidarity because they fail to see someone as human include the treatment of children, who are routinely subject to domination by adults; and the elderly, who in some cultures are patronized or socially discarded. The risk with human solidarity is that in the very attempt to include and foster the moral dignity of all humans, some will be excluded—whether it be women or some other minority or oppressed group whose socially constructed identity marks them as somehow failing to meet the criteria for human status. One could argue that the ability to perpetrate atrocities such as those found in genocidal campaigns demonstrates either a lack of ability to feel empathy toward a fellow human or a failure to see as human the victims they target. Human solidarity is seriously compromised when some group is excluded because of some attribute or externally prescribed identity. International racism, a phenomenon discussed by Charles Mills (1997), structurally inhibits human solidarity, as does the global class system, nuclear arms, and any number of other structures that divide peoples. Larry May also notes that most people identify with race, class, religion, or gender over humanness. These accentuate our differences rather than our commonalities as human. Individualism, which is the hallmark of many Western democracies, may stand as an ideological barrier to human solidarity. Individuals and peoples may have well-entrenched social systems that do not value cross-border alliances; some may not even value a notion of universal humanity. Even recent developments within philosophy not only deny that there is some universal human identity but also make it ideologically or theoretically impossible to posit one for the sake of moral acting. Internal barriers based on reason or sentiment also can and do impede the practical potential for human solidarity. Sympathy and empathy, for instance, simply may not extend universally (Bayertz 1999a, 7–8; Gould 2007; May 1996). Nor is it clear that being able to train oneself to feel real empathy for all human persons individually is always a positive attribute to moral acting.

There is certainly some potential for incremental solidarity or expansive circles of care, but, as we have seen, while one might be able to expand one's horizons enough to share in the interests of distant others, it is not clear that individual moral agents can extend their moral circle to care or share interest with all humanity. More plausible might be a sort of overlapping of circles with degrees of separation.

Consider the Hutus of Rwanda for instance. They suffered years of oppression under colonial rule merely because their physical features were less like their colonizers than the Tutsis. Extending our empathy aids us in understanding their history and may even lead to a greater understanding of their violent actions (without, of course, justifying them). Incremental solidarity would extend also to those they killed, and, of course, if we were to view it as a universal normative idea, incremental solidarity ought to have extended from the Hutus to the Tutsis and somehow halted their actions before they began. My point is that empathy is a fickle thing and may also be culturally bound. Somehow, there also needs to be some principles that keep us from acting inhumanely to each other. Human rights are an obvious candidate. Perhaps an incremental solidarity with a strong notion of international human rights might be coupled for a workable approach to human solidarity that would also meet at least some of the challenges posed by genocidal campaigns.

As I mentioned in Chapter 1, claims about human solidarity are often grounded on some sort of agenda. Human solidarity as a manifestation of social solidarity attempts either to describe the unity of all humanity or set that unity as a normative ideal. Moral obligations consist of those actions or inactions that sustain this human community. Human solidarity, in other words, would require each of us to respond morally to the suffering of other humans. Descriptively, it is safe to say we have not yet attained human solidarity of this sort. Prescriptively or normatively, some version of human rights, universal empathy, shared condition, or mutual potentialities might at least approximate the ideal, though there are serious doubts about whether that ideal is ever attainable.

Human Solidarity as Civic Solidarity

Civic solidarity, with its focus on strengthening civic society and ensuring the well-being of members of a civil community, attempts to maintain a system of social protections. As we saw in Chapter 1, it generally refers to the relationship between the state apparatus and the citizens. In particular, each citizen forms a relation to the whole state and vice versa; this relationship entails certain obligations of protection against vulnerabilities that would inhibit full civic participation, such as lack of adequate healthcare, inadequate income to provide for oneself and one's family, and insufficient protection against dangerous products or environmental hazards. Civic solidarity holds that the state ought to utilize social policy to decrease individuals' vulnerabilities and justifies this position based on the rights of individuals and the social good. Civic solidarity presumes that when individuals lack the basic necessities, society as a whole suffers. As I discussed in Chapter 1, the civic whole carries the bulk of the responsibility, but individuals are in a reciprocal relation with the whole.

Human solidarity as civic solidarity might turn on the role and responsibility of the international community and the obligations of the international community to protect and provide for the most vulnerable among us. The vulnerable and powerful alike would be identified through national, geographic, or political groupings. Because we reside in nations, states, and are part of the international community, our location rather than our nature (as in social solidarity) constitutes the basis for the solidary relation. Poverty and development, global healthcare, and war crimes and crimes against humanity are all pressing topics to which international civic solidarity can contribute.

In his discussion of the welfare state, Albert Weale uses the term "social solidarity," which he calls politically embodied, to indicate the ties that bind the social whole and a sort of unity based on membership in a state offering protection. In spite of the difference in terminology—I would call Weale's politically embodied social solidarity "civic solidarity"—he offers a model of human solidarity appealing to formal structures to protect against vulnerabilities, which fits our need for a theory of human solidarity as a subcategory of civic solidarity: "Social solidarity has a political embodiment when the state is prepared to take on the responsibility of insuring its citizens against a range of common misfortunes or contingencies, including sickness, interrupted earnings, and old age" (Weale 1990, 477). According to Weale, social solidarity need not be an example of equality although it may have some connection to equality. Weale suggests that people seek security against "human frailties" and adds that the "treatment of people in respect to these frailties should be in terms of their common humanity rather than their differences of status" (1990, 478). Notice that Weale starts from a shared human condition of risk or harm and embeds the response in a civic solidarity in order to posit a common humanity or social solidarity.

It could be argued that Weale blends social and civic solidarity to some extent in his argument. The common denominator or minimal provision of state insurance against "a range of common contingencies" (e.g., illness, unemployment, poverty) but "leaving open the possibility that the coverage may be of widely differing value" (Weale 1990, 477) is the moral obligation of civic solidarity. The social solidarity comes out with his appeal to common humanity in the treatment of frailties; as he says, "The implication is that inequality of provisions marks a lack of social solidarity" (Weale 1990, 477). Notice that with either conception, solidarity entails a notion of "common risks." By extending this to "human frailties against which some security is sought," Weale suggests that "treatment of people in respect to these frailties should be in terms of their common humanity rather than their differences of status" (1990, 478). Weale juxtaposes the equality of resources with the equality of life chances, arguing that "in principle the idea of social solidarity could be given an egalitarian interpretation in the form of equality of provision, so that the practice of social solidarity in this egalitarian form leads to greater equality of life-chances" (1990, 479).

On a global scale, Weale's position calls for a relatively robust international community ensuring "equality of provision" and "greater equality of life-chances." Such an international civic solidarity asks more developed countries to aid in the development of lesser-developed countries in order to protect them from the vulnerabilities associated with poverty and underdevelopment. There are human rights documents pertinent to this task, but it is also worth pointing out the mission of the World Bank. Established in 1944 to aid in postwar reconstruction, the World Bank now views as its mandate to alleviate worldwide poverty. While there are likely to be controversial practices and policies of the World Bank, it nevertheless stands as an example of an institution of the international community that works, at least in principle, to alleviate poverty and protect some of the world's most vulnerable people. Other multinational development banks, international humanitarian associations, and worldwide organizations that respond to human rights, sociopolitical, and economic crises demonstrate at some level human solidarity conceived as civic solidarity. This is particularly evident in the mission of the International Federation of Red Cross and Red Crescent Societies, founded in 1919 and professing 185 members. Their mission reads in part: "The Federation's mission is *to improve the lives of vulnerable people by mobilizing the power of humanity*. Vulnerable people are those who are at greatest risk from situations that threaten their survival, or their capacity to live with an acceptable level of social and economic security and human dignity. Often, these are victims of natural disasters, poverty brought about by socio-economic crises, refugees, and victims of health emergencies" (IFRC, emphasis in original).

Catholic Social Teaching, which dates back to 1891 with the publication of *Rerum Novarum* by Pope Leo XIII, is one of the few sustained discussions of solidarity as a moral value and duty. Pope John Paul II developed the concept most thoroughly—applying it to the global issues of development—and is even credited with inspiring the Polish Solidarity movement during his visit in 1979. Kevin Doran (1996) offers an interesting and complete history of "solidarity" within Catholic Social Teaching, so I will not rehearse that here. Instead, I will concentrate on the single document where Pope John Paul II explains and applies the duty of solidarity to the global issue of development, *Sollicitudo Rei Socialis (On Social Concern)*, published on the twentieth anniversary of Pope Paul VI's *Populorum Progressio (On the Development of Peoples)*. It is enough for our purposes in this chapter to note that Doran describes Catholic Social Teaching on solidarity up until 1978 when Pope John Paul II took office as "the social bond which exists within and between societies and nations, through the awareness of a common human nature and of mutual human necessity" (Doran 1996, 90). Pope John Paul II shifts that emphasis a bit from the social solidarity of humanity to emphasize the moral obligations of nations. He charges nations, especially wealthy nations, to respond to the needs of peoples in the developing world in his concept of solidarity. Although not issuing from an international community per se, this concept of solidarity qualifies as a form of civic solidarity. It is grounded in a human community that the pope describes as "interdependent."

Interdependence, according to Pope John Paul II's encyclical, is a global experience—it is the recognition that we are tied to one another in a situation we all share. This interdependence is not merely economic. He describes interdependence as also cultural, intellectual, technological, ecological, political, and simply human. Our decisions and actions—both personally and nationally—have an effect on other peoples regardless of whether these other people are considered in the decision-making process. This relation is evident, for example, in the values displayed in television programs produced in the United States and how they affect the cultures in which the programs are shown. So too the resources used and/or abused in one nation or region affect another nation or region's access to and the value of those resources. The empirical fact of interdependence among peoples, Pope John Paul II argues, demands an ethics of solidarity wherein nations and international organizations protect the most vulnerable and create the conditions that would allow all people to flourish. Interdependence challenges nations to reexamine decision-making so as to consciously incorporate the real or potential impact of a decision on other people or peoples. When the fact of global interdependence is separated from its moral requirements the results are detrimental not only to the poorest or weakest countries/regions. Indeed, interdependence is such that the strong also suffer from the underdevelopment of some. The duty of solidarity in Catholic Social Teaching requires the recognition of full personhood of *all* human beings in solidarity. As Doran explains, "Membership and participation in a particular social community is but a limited expression of membership in the community of all humanity" (1996, 153). Thus, solidarity entails the recognition that insofar as some are oppressed no one can truly flourish. The underdevelopment of some countries or regions also adversely affects the capacity for authentic development of all the nations (including the strongest):

> It [that men and women feel personally affected by injustices and human rights violations in distant countries] is above all a question of *interdependence*, sensed as a *system determining* relationship in the contemporary world, in its economic, cultural, political and religious elements, and accepted as a *moral category*. When interdependence becomes recognized in this way, the correlative response as a moral and social attitude, as a "virtue," is *solidarity*. This then is not a feeling of vague compassion or shallow distress at the misfortunes of so many people, both near and far. On the contrary, it is a *firm and persevering determination* to commit oneself to the *common good;*

that is to say to the good of all and of each individual, because we are *all* really responsible *for all*. (*Sollicitudo Rei Socialis*, §38, emphasis in original)

As this quotation mentions, true development includes social and cultural development of the entire person, not just economic development. The emphasis is on *being more* rather than *having more* (*Sollicitudo Rei Socialis*, §28; see also Yoder 1991, 265–66; Dorr 1992, 324). Programs of economic development must, then, take these various facets of the human person and national/international relations into account in the content as well as the strategies of development. Doran shows that solidarity inspires "authentic human development" and is the responsibility of nations and peoples, including the peoples of the developing world (1996, 200–202). "Solidarity helps us to see the 'other'—whether a *person, people or nation*—not just as some kind of instrument, with a work capacity and physical strength to be exploited at low cost and then discarded when no longer useful, but as our 'neighbor,' a 'helper' (c. Gen 2:18–20), to be made a sharer, on a par with ourselves, in the banquet of life to which all are equally invited by God" (*Sollicitudo Rei Socialis*, §39).

The international civic solidarity articulated in Catholic Social Teaching emphasizes the obligation to anticipate and respond to the needs of the poor, oppressed, and most vulnerable using personal, national, and international means. Additionally, Catholic Social Teaching places the primary emphasis on "duties" rather than "rights." This too is a way to shift the focus from the self to the community, or from what is good for the individual to what best promotes the common good. Indeed the very term "social justice" in Catholic Social Teaching "was born in reaction to excessively individualistic notions of justice and out of a desire to demand the participation of all, especially the poor, in the economic well-being of the whole community" (Paulhus 1987, 274). Notice that the good of the individual or individual rights is affirmed through the acknowledgement that it is interdependent on the common good (*Sollicitudo Rei Socialis*, §10).

In earlier writings, Cardinal Karol Wojtyła described solidarity as an attitude. In *On Social Concern* he uses the stronger language of "obligation" in addition to "attitude" (Wojtyła 1981, 47; Doran 1996). Whether as moral attitude or obligation, human solidarity conceived of in this way as an expansive form of civic solidarity, recognizes the reciprocal relation between individuals and states, and between states and the international community. Mutuality in this relation of civic solidarity upholds the dignity of all participants in solidarity; it emphasizes that the authentic human dignity of all is contingent on autonomy or, for nations, sovereignty and self-determination (see also Anderson 1991, 112). "An essential condition for global *solidarity* is autonomy and free self-determination, also within associations such as those indicated. But at the same time solidarity demands a readiness to accept the sacrifices necessary for the good of the whole world community" (*Sollicitudo Rei Socialis*, §45). Self-determination must be present not only between countries, regions, or social groupings but also within social groupings.

Catholic Social Teaching has contributed a great deal to theological and philosophical conceptions of solidarity. It is limited insofar as appeals to a particular conception of God and a particular religious tradition, but it nevertheless may be read as providing something of a model for how human solidarity conceived through the lens of civic solidarity might be theorized (see also Scholz 1997 for a fuller discussion of solidarity in Catholic Social Teaching).

Genocide poses some interesting problems for human solidarity as civic solidarity. If we accept at least some of the tenets of the version of human solidarity as civic solidarity articulated in Catholic Social Teaching, for example, the duties that emerge from global interdependence, then active genocidal campaigns affect all of us and demand a response—preferably a concerted response from the international community. Genocide not only affects the targeted group but also adversely affects the entire global community. Human solidarity as expansive civic solidarity also illustrates that there are important tools that the international community might employ to prevent future genocides.

Catholic morality has a long tradition of just war theory, which is taken up in at least some of the documents of Catholic Social Teaching. Opposing a genocide would arguably fulfill the *jus ad bellum* principles for a just war, but solidarity seems to oppose even a just war. Doran argues, for instance, that while "struggles are necessary, . . . war is an inhuman struggle because it is against the other person. As such it places the civil co-existence at risk. War sows the seeds of division, and this in itself is enough to make it clear that war can never be compatible with true solidarity" (1996, 230). Earlier, I argued that violence was contrary to the principles of political solidarity. Doran takes it a step further to show that the violence of war is contrary to solidarity per se: "Solidarity is a duty imposed by fidelity to the memory of those who have been and remain the victims of conflict. The establishment of solidarity, however, requires a struggle against the logic of war" (1996, 230). If just war is not an option against genocide, what does human solidarity conceived as civic solidarity require of us? The international community has to respond in such a way that seeks justice for both the victims of the genocide and the perpetrators. In the rest of this section, I examine the United Nations documents and actions in response to genocide with particular focus on mass rape campaigns.

The United Nations Universal Declaration of Human Rights serves as a primary document on human rights for the international community. The first article reads, "All human beings are born free and equal in dignity and rights. They are endowed with reason and conscience and should act towards one another in a spirit of brotherhood" (UN Universal Declaration of Human Rights). One interpretation of this is that the document assumes that membership in the human community grants each person rights to protection by that community. If the document were written today, given our acknowledgement of the oppressive role of sexist language, I have little doubt that "brotherhood" would be replaced by "solidarity."

In spite of the purported "universality" of the rights articulated in the UN Declaration, it has been widely criticized as failing to account for cultural differences. The UN's account of human rights, it is argued, suffers from a Western bias. Many of the rights articulated there are not, in fact, universally agreed on and some are even seen as contrary or contradictory to deeply held cultural values for some people. So too women and issues distinct to gender were ignored in the original document. Women do not yet share an equal social, political, or economic status with men in most parts of the world. "Human rights" have not generally been extended to women; Catharine MacKinnon argues that violations of women have long been excluded from the catalog of human rights violations: "Atrocities committed against women are either too human to fit the notion of female or too female to fit the notion of human" (1994, 6). Violations against women often disappear from human rights talk because such violations are seen as "gender issues" (MacKinnon 1994, 5–16). Subsequent UN documents and covenants aim to remedy that gap and recognize the human rights of women and address the problem of violence against women. The United Nations has worked to gain recognition for human rights in international law not only through the UN Declaration of

Human Rights (1948) but also through the International Covenant on Civil and Political Rights and the International Covenant on Economic, Social and Cultural Rights (both adopted in 1966, and entered into force in 1976). The UN Declaration on the Elimination of Violence Against Women (1993) explicitly aims at extending the rights enumerated in the UN Universal Declaration of Human Rights to women. (The irony of that last sentence should not be overlooked.)

Mass rape campaigns, however, pose additional challenges to the rights approach. Mass rape constitutes a violation of human rights on an extreme scale and was categorized in 1993 as a crime against humanity and genocide. But that hardly scratches the surface of the harms of rape on such scale used by states. Mass rape forced the international community to confront directly the lack of acknowledgement of women as human rights bearers, but it also forced us to see the gendered dimensions of war and the incalculable harms of rape. Women's bodies were and are being used as the field of battle. Rape is done strategically to destroy the morale of enemy troops as well as the morale of civilian communities. Women are directly targeted and their bodies used as instruments of war to destroy a culture. A rights approach alone pays "insufficient attention to the bodily nature of rape during war," often lacks appropriate means for reporting of violations within lines of state (and because many of the recent genocidal campaigns have been within states, this becomes quite a serious problem), and fails to "address the cultural prescriptions that prohibit (for lack of a better word) reparation to survivors such that they can resume their place in community" (Scholz 2006b, 283).

Although the United Nations Declaration of Human Rights (1948) does not explicitly mention rape, Articles 3–5 may be read as including the prohibition against rape:

> Article 3 Everyone has the right to life, liberty and the security of person;
> Article 4 No one shall be held in slavery or servitude; slavery and the slave trade shall be prohibited in all their forms;
> Article 5 No one shall be subjected to torture or to cruel, inhuman or degrading treatment or punishment.

Article 2 also indicates that the entire declaration applies to all people regardless of sex. In addition, because rape is considered an "honor crime," we might appeal to Article 12 (in spite of its sexist language), which includes a prohibition against attacks on a person's honor:

> Article 12 No one shall be subjected to arbitrary interference with his privacy, family, home or correspondence, nor to attacks upon his honor and reputation. Everyone has the right to the protection of the law against such interference or attacks.

Though, of course, calling rape an honor crime is not without controversy, especially given its history as the father's or husband's honor that was violated.

In spite of its weaknesses, the UN Universal Declaration of Human Rights is probably the best tool currently in existence to advocate for human solidarity as civic solidarity. It issues from an international community, articulates a list of social protections, and holds nations to some standard of justice. Although it is not fully accepted and nations are often reluctant to appeal to it because of the high standards it sets, it gives some structure to a human solidarity as civic solidarity.

International war crimes conventions also contribute to a more robust structure for civic solidarity of all humanity. Principle VI of the Principles of the Nuremberg Tribunal (1950), for instance, establishes what constitutes war crimes and crimes against humanity in international law:

> *War crimes:*
> Violations of the laws or customs of war which include, but are not limited to, murder, ill-treatment or deportation to slave-labor or for any other purpose of civilian population of or in occupied territory, murder or ill-treatment of prisoners of war, of persons on the seas, killing of hostages, plunder of public or private property, wanton destruction of cities, towns, or villages, or devastation not justified by military necessity.
>
> *Crimes against humanity:*
> Murder, extermination, enslavement, deportation and other inhuman acts done against any civilian population, or persecutions on political, racial or religious grounds, when such acts are done or such persecutions are carried on in execution of or in connection with any

crime against peace or any war crime. (Principle of the Nuremberg Tribunal 1950, Principle vi)

At least some of the supporting documents are in place for a concerted effort at civic solidarity. Moreover, these documents, if adopted and embraced by peoples, nations, and states, could serve as preventatives to mass rape and genocide.

Criticisms of human solidarity as civic solidarity range from problems with interfering with the sovereignty of nations to problems in *not* interfering in the sovereignty of nations. As Andrew Mason argues, "Since political communities in the ordinary sense may be oppressive or fail to protect some of their citizens, leaving them alone to run their own affairs can stand in the way of promoting global community, for global community in the moralized sense requires the absence of systematic injustice between individuals" (2000, 226). A robust international community capable of protecting all people worldwide from social vulnerabilities would require states to agree and contribute at a much higher level. The International Criminal Court is one case in point. An effective and strong International Criminal Court (ICC) is clearly needed, but there are multiple practical and political reasons hampering its potential, not least of which is the United States' reluctance to sign on. The United States refuses in part because they view the ICC as potentially infringing on state sovereignty, yet if civic solidarity is a realistic ideal for humanity, then future and already-established mechanisms to prevent and punish violators must be empowered and meaningful. This has tremendous effects on justice seeking in the aftermath of mass rape: "One reason for the dearth of prosecutions is that in the absence of any international penal tribunal with jurisdiction over such crimes, the only alternative is to rely on national courts. Unfortunately, such courts are often under the control or influence of the governments or military forces responsible for precisely the kinds of offenses that should be prosecuted" (Wippman 2000, 91).

In many ways, the international community both recognizes the need for and appears to be working to achieve a civic solidarity expanded to include all humanity. With the United Nations and other international cooperative efforts, a robust international community with the social structures in place to alleviate poverty and foster development, respond to and prevent humanitarian crises, and generally protect the most vulnerable among the world's peoples begins to look like a real possibility. Of course, there are numerous practical obstacles that may prevent it from ever coming to fruition. I have already discussed some of the most entrenched—the failure to see some as human and thereby worthy of human rights protections. Catholic Social Teaching raises another important issue. Insofar as states maintain a posture of dominance or superiority, human solidarity as a form of civic solidarity is not possible. Civic solidarity requires something like an attitude of humility that accepts our global interdependence, mutuality, and reciprocity.

Global Solidarity (Political Solidarity)

Each of the forms of human solidarity previously discussed in this chapter demonstrates different ways of enacting individual and collective solidaristic activities across borders and around the globe. With the increased interest in other cultures, the heightened interdependence of global economic markets, and the ever-present growing disparity between the privileged and the vulnerable peoples of the world, human solidarity and global solidarity assume more meaning and urgency. As we have seen, a social solidarity that extends to all humanity looks for ways to establish and strengthen bonds between peoples. A civic solidarity encompassing humanity looks to the structures and policies of an international body charged with protecting the most vulnerable and destitute among humanity. A global political solidarity, in contrast, is a worldwide collective response to injustice that involves international and global efforts at social critique and social transformation. Part of the challenge of global solidarity, however, is to recognize not just unified global movements but diverse movements that draw participants from the worldwide population.

A *true* global political solidarity would unite all people in a collective effort against an injustice, oppression, or social vulnerability. The true global solidarity would unite everyone in struggle against a common threat. Yet what is the source of the threat? Who is to blame? Such a unified global effort might arise in response to our collective injustice or neglect. For instance, we may find it necessary to join together in political solidarity in response to pollution, environmental degradation, global warming, or other human-in-origin threats that endanger all human beings. To take one of these examples, global warming endangers all of us in one way or another, though in fairly different ways depending on where we live and what resources are available to us. But it is a bit more difficult to imagine the practical instantiation of a unified global political solidarity effort. Would not some individuals decide not to contribute—perhaps seeing the benefits to be had if they do not make the personal sacrifices that the rest of the globe commits to making? Or might entire countries choose to flout global treaties in an attempt to preserve their pollution-producing lifestyles?

Christian Lenhardt points out that solidarity arises in opposition—a truly universal global solidarity would not have an opposition party: "[A] state of human solidarity to whose realization collective energies, be they reformist or revolutionary, might be devoted defies conception. Affirmative thought is anathema because consistent dreams are impossible, quite apart from the sorry fact that, if they were possible, they would be 'mere' dreams. The mankind of the future with its inherited memories of the past cannot even begin to think about what it means to correct historical injustice" (1975, 139). Lenhardt argues for a different sort of "universal brotherhood" compatible with Marx's thought (Lenhardt 1975, 134). Intergenerational loyalties (i.e., anamnestic solidarity) mediates the unity of the species, he argues (Lenhardt 1975, 151). One could read this as a unity in our history—that we have histories of oppression, or histories of domination, unites us in some way.

> By recognizing that the victorious proletarian contemporaries would be *de facto* heirs of legions of exploited slaves and workers of the past, Marx illuminates in a flash the essence of anamnestic solidarity. The unity of repressed mankind is the solidarity of the living with the dead. Marx calls for an understanding of class in terms of the continuity of exploitation across the ages. If the impending revolution goes forth without being informed by this larger historical solidarity with the dead, then it will only wipe out one injustice by replacing it with another. (Lenhardt 1975, 151)

Lenhardt's anamnestic solidarity is useful in thinking about expansive political solidarity for a number of reasons. It challenges political solidarity to maintain an aspect of the duty of social criticism, namely, to check solidary actions against the past and the future—that is, to see oneself acting not just in response to an immediate present injustice but to learn from efforts for social change in the past and anticipate liberation struggles in the future. But more important, it suggests that global political solidarity be thought of not as universal or *true* but rather as a form of political solidarity that stretches across national borders and unites different people in a collective effort to bring about international and global social change. I look at such a movement on behalf of women everywhere focusing especially on the changes that activism in political solidarity on an international or global scale has brought to the prosecution of perpetrators of mass rape.

Before leaving it entirely behind, it is worth noting that universal global solidarity does help to raise the question of whether there is an obligation *to* political solidarity. Do we have an obligation to join in a struggle to end oppression or injustice regardless of whether it affects us? Global political solidarity—that is, a political solidarity that extends universally across the globe—practically may amount to little more than modifications on the common humanity theme of human solidarity. The moral structure between the two is different; that is, in global political solidarity there is a more or less conscious commitment to the cause that forms the bonds uniting humanity. In human solidarity (an extended social solidarity), the social bonds are based on common humanity and the moral obligations issue forth from that. Practically, the two will look very much alike.

Political solidarity is a unique commitment that issues forth in multiple moral relations and sometimes quite demanding positive duties. There is no inherent duty to join in political solidarity itself, though the commitment one makes to solidarity does bind one in some ways. That being said, there may nevertheless be moral obligations to respond to injustice, oppression, or the suffering and vulnerability of others. I am not claiming that we do not have some obligations both not to oppress others and not to knowingly perpetrate injustice; I think we do and one could even suggest that that is the very purpose of all moral theory. Nor am I claiming that we do not necessarily have some positive obligations to aid those who do suffer (in whatever way). Arguing for a universal obligation to aid the poor and oppressed is a common feature of moral theory (see, for instance, Shue 1980). But solidarity is a relationship—in fact, it demarcates multiple relationships, as I argued in Chapter 3. There is no justification for mandating that someone form a relation that carries potentially heavy obligations and even sacrifices with a nonfamilial person. Of course, a person may decide for him- or herself that it is imperative he or she respond, and that person may feel morally blameworthy if he or she does not respond: "A person may very well, having perceived the moral necessity for revolution, feel himself to be morally responsible for his own lack of revolutionary activity" (Bates 1971, 346). We could go a bit farther to say that if a person publicly espouses certain principles or values, it very well may be the case that not joining in a political solidarity movement may be seen as contrary to those values but that still would not oblige the person to join in an activist movement for social change.

David Hollinger discusses global solidarity in the context of his argument for a "postethnic" America. Hollinger claims that "a postethnic perspective is alert for opportunities to construct global solidarities capable of addressing ecological and other dilemmas that are global in their impact" (1995, 12–13). The crucial aspect of global solidarity that emerges is that it arises in response to conditions shared among peoples across the globe. This is in sharp contrast to a human solidarity that is based on some notion of "common humanity." Rather than a common feature, shared humanity, or basis of human dignity, global solidarities link various nations, cultures, individuals, states, and so forth, insofar as a those nations, cultures, individuals, or states share a response to a common plight. While there is some slippage in his account that seems to put the basis of solidarity back on a notion of shared identity as a step toward global solidarity—for example, solidarity of Americans (Hollinger 1995, 158) or "fraternal solidarity with the species" (Hollinger 1995, 142)—we might be able to explain that by invoking his argument in favor of "affiliation" rather than "identity" as the basis for postethnic groupings. As he presents it, "Postethnicity prefers voluntary to prescribed affiliations, appreciates multiple identities, pushes for communities of wide scope, recognizes the constructed character of ethno-racial groups, and accepts the formation of new groups as a part of the normal life of a democratic society" (Hollinger 1995, 116).

As is evident, Hollinger argues against both universalism and particularism. The postethnic perspective offers a way to balance the tension between "the one and the many": "A postethnic perspective tries to bring to issues of affiliation a consciousness of the increasing interdependence of the world's peoples, and of the global arena in which many of the forces that affect the lives of individuals and groups in our society, as well as in others, are generated and played out" (Hollinger 1995, 109–10). Among other things, we can think of this as suggesting a worldwide coalition between movements of political solidarity. Of course, there will still be the problem of outliers or free riders. Not everyone will embrace collective action in voluntary associations or engage in the sort of epistemological openness that is required for a global coalition. (I raised a similar problem regarding language barriers in Scholz 1998b.)

Kurt Bayertz, recall, suggested that solidarity aimed at revolutionary action for a just cause, or what I have termed political solidarity, may be a "sample of what human beings are capable of when social obstacles hampering the development of their moral strengths are removed" (1999a, 20). In Chapter 1, I read this as an indication that political solidarity brings out an already existing social solidarity among humans by virtue of their shared humanity. The struggle for a just cause effectively taps into the solidarity that humans as humans are capable of expressing in noncrisis situations. Bayertz explains that solidarity is both archaeological and anticipative. It is archaeological insofar as it "uncovers dispositions towards cooperation, mutual aid, common feeling," and it is anticipative insofar as it "draws a picture of the future human being who will ultimately be free to develop its cooperative and common strengths unhindered" (Bayertz 1999a, 20). The latter, which Bayertz identifies as utopian, indicates the prospects of human potential. Solidarity for a just cause, he thinks, brings that potential to light for brief but intense and inspiring moments.

I have argued for a slightly more nuanced reading of the distinctions in solidarities. Relationships or connections between forms of solidarity are contingent on the particular instantiations, and political solidarity is therefore a collective response to a perceived injustice or situation of oppression motivated by any number of factors for each individual participant. Nevertheless, I agree that some social solidarities will issue forth a political solidarity and vice versa. But, as we have seen, there are important obstacles that continue to hamper any possibility of a full human solidarity. Bayertz thinks human solidarity is probably a utopian dream; but political solidarities that unite diverse peoples at sometimes-great distances hold some promise even if the unity of all humanity is not the intended aim.

Global and international political solidarity does not aim to extend to encompass all of humanity, nor does it presume any sort of agreed-on or presupposed conception of human dignity. Rather, it is an extension of political solidarity beyond national borders. International political solidarity, as I suggested in Chapter 2, can be conceived in three different ways. These three ways are not necessarily distinct forms of international solidarity, though they could be that as well.

First, international political solidarity could be an individual's commitment to the cause that spans national borders. The struggle to raise awareness and combat violence against women seems to be just such a cause. Violence against women is not confined to a particular culture or national tradition. This is a cause that unites men and women from all over the world and transcends national affiliations. Another way to conceive international political solidarity is through individual commitment to combat oppression, injustice, or vulnerability that is itself located at a distance. Through protests, boycotts, lifestyle changes, and direct questioning of international development policy, among other things, people in the United States join in solidarity to fight against poverty and AIDS in Africa. In either case, international solidarity might involve individuals from all over the globe. Carol Gould offers the antiapartheid movement as an example of international solidarity that would fit this conception (2004, 66; see also Gould 2007). (Gould adds, "Solidarity may also involve the performance of an action that expresses a sympathetic understanding at a distance of the situation of oppressed others." While I disagree with her on aspects of her characterization of solidarity, it does show the relation with distant others in solidarity that is the second conception of international solidarity.) The third conception of international solidarity involves nations committing to a social justice cause and forming bonds of collective action through their commitments. Economic sanctions in protest of human rights violations serve as a pertinent example. It is worth mentioning that this last form of solidarity differs from civic solidarity of humanity because it demonstrates a unity of nations committed to a particular cause. Such international coalition building in political solidarity is likely to be ad hoc and responsive; the civic solidarity of all humanity presumes a unity of all nations that obliges them to provide and protect the most vulnerable.

International political solidarity has global impact. By looking at some of the recent efforts by various branches of the women's movement, we can see this impact and take note of the potentiality for international political solidarity movements. In the rest of this section I look at the effect international efforts to combat violence against women, especially sexual violence during conflict situations, has had on men and women worldwide, the international community, and the social structure for addressing women's issues.

In solidarity with victims of mass rape, individual feminists and women's groups have drawn international attention to the problem of rape during war by arguing that all sexual violence against women during war violates human rights (see, for example, Scholz 2006a and 2006b; Card 2002; Barstow 2000). This is an important step to attaining human rights protections for women during conflict situations. The notable absence of rape or persecution based on sex or gender in the original human rights and war crimes documents has made gaining recognition of unlawful violence against women during war difficult. As many radical feminists argue, women were not always included in the "humanity" of a "crime against humanity," and a crime against women was not as seriously prosecuted. But through ongoing collective action, we have already seen some significant social change. Many of the international human rights structures have been forced to address the problems in their social and organizational structures and in the documents they issue.

In June 1993, the United Nations held a Conference on Human Rights in Vienna. Two days before the conference began, the Tribunal for Women's Human Rights, one of the nongovernmental organization (NGO) working groups, heard testimony from women all over the world who had been victimized by sexual violence during conflict situations: "What emerged from all the testimony was that women's bodies are used as the site of combat, both figuratively and actually" (Barstow 2000, 237). The testimony brought diverse experience and knowledge together to illustrate the systemic nature of rape. Many activists argued, sometimes at great risk to their personal safety, that states often supported sexual violence against women or looked the other way when it happened. Moreover, the knowledge sharing and political organizing around this issue made clear that violence against women often had the intent to forcibly impregnate, disintegrate communities, and devastate morale. Through this meeting of people who suffered injustice and willingly shared their experience together with scholars, policy makers, and other activists, the Tribunal for Women's Human Rights effectively set the agenda for the Vienna meetings. In other words, their political solidarity directly affected the UN meetings and brought about global change. As Anne Llewellyn Barstow reports,

> The final Vienna Declaration included major gains for women: statements that women's rights are human rights, that they must be taken into account in all parts of the United Nations' work, that UN personnel must be trained to recognize violence against women, and that systematic rape, forced pregnancy, and genocide must be condemned. The declaration however left much undone: the legal definition of rape in wartime (systematic rape) was not exact, and no court was set up to deal with gender-related crimes. (Barstow 2000, 237)

Similarly, in 1995, the United Nations Fourth World Conference on Women in Beijing concentrated efforts on violence against women and created the Beijing Platform for Action. Participants came from around the world to detail the numerous ways women are affected by violence during war, specifically highlighting rape. Like in Vienna, and like countless other global and international political solidarity movements, this meeting brought together activists with varying experiences and cultural and ideological differences. They were united in their commitment to a cause—to bring awareness of the causes and effects of violence against women and seek internationally recognized protections, especially in conflict situations. The Platform explicitly named rape as a violation of women's human rights, saying, "Grave violations of the human rights of women occur, particularly in times of armed conflict, and include murder, torture, systematic rape, forced pregnancy and forced abortion, in particular under policies of ethnic cleansing" (Platform for Action, §11). The Platform for Action spelled out the relation between "human rights of women" and "the fundamental principles of international human rights," saying, "Violations of the human rights of women in situations of armed conflict are violations of the fundamental principles of international human rights and humanitarian law. Massive violations of human rights, especially in the form of genocide, ethnic cleansing as a strategy of war and its consequences, and rape, including systematic rape of women in war situations, creating a mass exodus of refugees and displaced persons, are abhorrent practices that are strongly condemned and must be stopped immediately, while perpetrators of such crimes must be punished" (Platform for Action, §131). The Beijing conference thus directly confronted an issue that had the potential to obscure the connection between violations of women and violations of human rights. By strongly stating that rape is a violation of the "fundamental principles of international human rights," the Platform for Action asserted that women have human rights, that rape violates those human rights, and that rape is still also a gender issue. This claim stresses the importance of including gender analysis in human rights work. The writers of the Platform further argued that national and international tribunals "address gender issues properly by providing appropriate training to prosecutors, judges and other officials in handling cases involving rape, forced pregnancy in situations of armed conflict, indecent assault and other forms of violence against women in armed conflicts, including terrorism, and integrate a gender perspective into their work" (Strategic objective E.1). It offered a number of strategies to prevent violence against women during armed combat, to address it should it occur, and to punish the perpetrators (individuals and states). The coalitions of women's groups and individual women who came to Vienna and Beijing, as well as all those solidaristic supporters working from their own locals and contributing in accordance with their individualized abilities and needs, demonstrate the powerful and empowering potentialities of political solidarity.

Moreover, collective action in political solidarity with victims of war rape has challenged the military's callous attitude about rape, especially rape during conflict situations. Efforts to obtain punishment for war crimes of soldiers regardless of what side of the battle they were on continue. Online petitions, letters to Congress, public forums, and other forms of protest oppose the injustice of a military system that fails to punish rapists or that allows sexist domination to go unchecked. Victims are speaking out against the culture that seems to protect criminals rather than prosecute them. Concerted efforts to change military culture, demand prosecution and accountability, and study the causes and effects of rape in the military or during war combine in political solidarity. Anne Llewellyn Barstow states that "(1) women's groups must continue to press for changes in law so that at every level of justice crimes against women are recognized and (2) women's groups must continue to press for changes in procedures so that women believe that the courts will give them a fair hearing" (2000, 245). Claudia Card suggests that one strategy of resistance, "as a more long-range goal building on the short-term goals, [is that] both domestic and international protection rackets might be dismantled, thereby creating the potential to alter the symbolic meaning of rape" (2002, 130). Engaging in thorough social criticism is one concrete way that the protection rackets are dismantled. Exposing the structures of dominance as well as the effects is crucial to creating lasting social change. Card's proposal aims at changing how sexist dominance is played out in culture, especially military culture. She explains, "The basic goal is to combat rape's symbolism of dominance by removing the instrument of power as a consequence of its abuse. The hope would be to eliminate reliance on rape as a weapon at the level of strategic planning. Were the symbolic meaning of rape changed, there would be less to fear about being female" (Card 2002, 134). The symbol of dominance associated with rape can only be removed by altering its place in our social and international relations. In other words, social criticism that looks at the ideological structures that support or maintain unjust systems aids our efforts to dismantle those systems.

The further element to political solidarity in this issue is the "pragmatic solidarity," to use Paul Farmer's term, that attempts to meet the needs of the victims while also advocating for social change. Activists in solidarity with victims of mass rape campaigns have argued that positive steps must be taken to protect women who come forward to name their rapists. Robin May Schott discusses the various forms of trauma suffered by rape victims during war (1999, 173). Trauma has multiple and varied effects on the body that range from pain and disfigurement to physiological memories recurring at the slightest stimulant. But even beyond these effects on the body are the social perceptions of the body both before and after rape. Cultural accounts of purity, as Schott argues, may affect how a victim of rape is received by her community or how she responds to forced pregnancy (1999, 178). Often, a person victimized by war rape is ostracized from her community, and should she become pregnant because of the rape, her child may be abandoned by her, her community, or both. Rehabilitation for the victim means that attentiveness to these factors must enter into pragmatic solidarity. Todd Salzman cautions against some well-meaning attempts to raise awareness of the war crime of rape. For instance, once the extent of the Serbian crimes had become widely known, many groups—feminist and other humanitarian activists—flew to the former Yugoslavia to interview victims. Without providing proper physical and psychological care, such measures could simply add an additional layer of exploitation onto the victims. While research into current and past atrocities is crucial to prevent future ones, Salzman argues that researchers need to be sensitized "to the delicate nature of the situation and the need for prolonged support and care in the psychological and emotional recuperation of the traumatized victims" (2000, 87). Barstow similarly chronicles the potentially traumatizing experiences of war crimes tribunals (2000, 242). Adequate care must be taken to, as best as possible, restore a victim's (and/or a victim's family's and community's) sense of empowerment and integrity. Moreover, advocates argue that adequate means be provided to care for and educate any children that resulted from the rapes, physical and mental healthcare for the individual victims of the rapes, rehabilitative services for victims and victims' families, and compensation/reparation for land and housing destroyed in the mass rape campaigns. Further, Rhonda Copelon suggests that in meeting the needs of the victims, personnel (human rights personnel, war crimes tribunals, other humanitarian aid agencies) need to be trained for gender sensitivity, and females ought to be adequately represented in the courts. This training should include detailed information about the relevant cultural ideologies and practices. Copelon also suggests that "female investigators [be] trained to get information in a way that respects the woman's privacy and feelings" (cited in Barstow 2000, 241). Notice how these strategies are attentive to all three of the moral relations of political solidarity discussed in Chapter 3.

International women's groups have worked diligently to get recognition for rape in war, compensation for the victims of rape, and punishment for the perpetrators. Activists draw on the energy of political solidarity among feminists, peace activists, women's groups, and others. International efforts in political solidarity address the risks that women and women's rights are separated from and inferior to humans and human rights, that victims fail to receive justice, that systematic cultural and political causes go unquestioned, that violence against women continues, and they begin to lay the groundwork for international social change.

In her 2000 essay "Feminism, Women's Human Rights, and Cultural Difference," Susan Moller Okin describes the connection (and frequent divide) between, for instance, academic feminism/feminists and the activists for women's human rights over the last few decades. As she points out, at just the time that academic feminists were chastising each other for adopting real or perceived essentialist claims about women or women's experience of oppression, women's activists the world over were noting the commonalities between and among the experiences of women. Okin sees an important role for the recognition of similar experiences and problems "across cultural, class, and ethnic lines" (2000, 37) and criticizes those academic feminist theorists who themselves criticize such efforts at recognizing commonality. She concludes, saying that one of the needs of women struggling for women's human rights is "the kind of intellectual and political support from Western feminists, and from the international community, that does not assault other cultures, but takes care to acknowledge their many valuable or neutral aspects while it criticizes those aspects that are harmful to women and girls" (Okin 2000, 42).

Okin's point, it seems to me, is that the exercise in building bridges between groups resisting violence and oppression need not rest on essentialist claims about the experience of women per se (though she is not afraid of that). On the contrary, her point is to highlight the possibilities for feminist politics when ideological divides are set aside. Others have similarly presented arguments for a transnational solidarity or international feminist politics (Gould

2007; Hawkesworth 2006; May 2007). Okin's example of women's activists working for human rights for women and feminist academics might actually be misleading. The activists and the scholars might actually see themselves as united in the relation of political solidarity. At least some of the debates and ideological divides would likely fall under her criticism of futility, but some might actually be aimed at that solidaristic relation insofar as they engage social criticism or, to use Card's words, challenge symbolic meanings, in a collective effort of feminist politics. Rather than working in isolation, political solidarity both locally and globally invites us to commit to collective action that, although potentially fraught with sacrifice, might also empower oneself and others. As Alison Jaggar reports, "Many Third World feminists argue that women's community organizing promotes the political as well as the economic empowerment of women in the global South" (Jaggar 2005, 94). This is at least part of the aim of a feminist global or international political solidarity.

Conclusion

In her book *Visions of Solidarity,* Clare Weber offers an interesting sociological account of political solidarity. Weber recounts her experience working with Witness for Peace in Nicaragua. Her story chronicles the transformation of the Nicaraguan antiwar activist movement to women's activism and ultimately to antiglobalization activism. Although Weber does not herself discuss the moral relations of political solidarity that formed, she does present a number of examples of how those relations become enacted both in local movements and in international coalitions. She describes how different and evolving issues shaped the movements and how different participants crafted their involvement or used their skill to bring about social change. "Women's Empowerment Project," for instance, "engaged in a grassroots strategy of participatory and democratic decision making, with efforts at learning from the situated and lived realities of Nicaraguan activist women. They were clear," she says, "that they wanted an exchange of information and as equal a relationship as possible" (Weber 2006, 86). The women in Nicaragua and the women in the United States had very little that might unite them except their commitment to challenge the social systems that they perceived to be unjust. Weber's story shows how important it was for all participants to learn the cultural codes of their fellow solidaristic actors and, for the U.S. participants, to challenge one's own social position, perhaps at the cost of putting one at odds with one's own government. Weber also highlights the irony of the U.S. participants recognizing that the very structure that gave them their social privilege was both what they targeted and what they could effectively use to protect and work with their Nicaraguan counterparts.

Weber's is one among many stories. Solidarity has a tremendous potential for modeling political and social participation in the twenty-first century. It blends group identity with personal choice in a way that no other social theory does. As a voluntary organization, political solidarity is one of the many avenues for enhancing civil society through citizen participation. More important, it demonstrates multiple ties that bind each person who courageously commits with others for a common cause.

Kurt Bayertz argues that "the concept of solidarity is . . . indispensable for a philosophy of morality and politics, if this is to pay justice to the true complexity of the moral conscience" (1999a, 26). Solidarities abound and there is a clear relation between them, but they are not equal and we do a disservice to the history and potential of the concept when we fail to acknowledge that. One of the unstated aims of this book has been to appreciate the tremendous efforts and sometimes-heroic sacrifices of individuals who join in political solidarity against injustice, oppression, vulnerability, and tyranny. A collective movement that simultaneously serves those in need while it challenges the social structure that created that need, challenges traditional moral and political theory almost as much as it challenges social and political practice. The theory I have sketched here is, I hope, just an intermediary point to a burgeoning dialogue on the richly complex moral relation of solidarity.

References

Alcoff, Linda Martín. 2000. "What Should White People Do?" In *Decentering the Center,* edited by Uma Narayan and Sandra Harding, 262–82. Bloomington: Indiana University Press.
Anderson, Ana Flora. 1991. "Catholic Social Doctrine: Brazil, 1891–1991." In *Rerum Novarum: A Symposium Celebrating 100 Years of Catholic Social Thought,* edited by Ronald Duska, 109–22. Lewiston, N.Y.: Edwin Mellen Press.
Appiah, K. Anthony. 1996. "Race, Culture, Identity: Misunderstood Connections." In *Color Conscious: The Political Morality of Race,* edited by K. Anthony Appiah and Amy Gutmann, 30–105. Princeton: Princeton University Press.
Arp, Kristana. 2001. *The Bonds of Freedom.* Chicago: Open Court Press.
Bailey, Alison. 2000. "Locating Traitorous Identities: Toward a View of Privilege-Cognizant White Character." In *Decentering the Center,* edited by Uma Narayan and Sandra Harding, 283–98. Bloomington: Indiana University Press.
Barstow, Anne Llewellyn. 2000. "The United Nations' Role in Defining War Crimes Against Women." In *War's Dirty Secret,* edited by Anne Llewellyn Barstow, 234–43. Cleveland: Pilgrim Press.
Bartky, Sandra. 1990. *Femininity and Domination: Phenomenology of Oppression.* New York: Routledge.
———. 2002. *Sympathy and Solidarity and Other Essays.* Lanham, Md.: Rowman and Littlefield.
Bates, Stanley. 1971. "The Responsibility of 'Random Collections.'" *Ethics* 81 (4): 343–49.
Bayertz, Kurt. 1998. "Solidarity and the Welfare State: Some Introductory Considerations." *Ethical Theory and Moral Practice* 1:293–96.
———. 1999a. "Four Uses of 'Solidarity.'" In *Solidarity,* edited by Kurt Bayertz, 3–28. Dordrecht: Kluwer.
———, ed. 1999b. *Solidarity.* Dordrecht: Kluwer.
Beauvoir, Simone de. 1944. *Pyrrhus et Cinéas.* Paris: Gallimard.

———. 1948a. *The Ethics of Ambiguity*. Translated by Bernard Frechtman. Secaucus, N.J.: Citadel Press.

———. 1948b. "Idéalisme moral et réalisme politique." In *L'Existentialisme et la Sagesse des Nations*, 49–88. Paris: Nagel.

———. 2005. *Philosophical Writings*. Edited by Margaret Simons. Champaign: University of Illinois Press.

Bell, Linda. 1993. *Rethinking Ethics in the Midst of Violence: A Feminist Approach to Freedom*. Lanham, Md.: Rowman and Littlefield.

Benhabib, Seyla. 1987. "The Generalized and the Concrete Other: The Kohlberg-Gilligan Controversy and Moral Theory." In *Women and Moral Theory*, edited by Eva Feder Kittay and Diana T. Meyers, 154–77. Lanham, Md.: Rowman and Littlefield.

Bernstein, Richard. 1989. "Interpretation and Solidarity—An Interview with Richard Bernstein." Interview by Dunja Melčić. *Praxis International* 9 (3): 201–19.

Blum, Lawrence. 2007. "Three Kinds of Race-Related Solidarity." *Journal of Social Philosophy* 38 (1): 53–72.

Boshammer, Susanne, and Matthias Kayb. 1998. "Review Essay: The Philosopher's Guide to the Galaxy of Welfare Theory." *Ethical Theory and Moral Practice* 1:375–85.

Brison, Susan. 2002. *Aftermath: Violence and the Remaking of a Self*. Princeton: Princeton University Press.

Brownmiller, Susan. 1975. *Against Our Will*. New York: Simon and Schuster.

Brunkhorst, Hauke. 2007. "Globalizing Solidarity: The Destiny of Democratic Solidarity in the Times of Global Capitalism, Global Religion, and the Global Public." *Journal of Social Philosophy* 38 (1): 93–111.

Capaldi, Nicholas. 1999. "What's Wrong with Solidarity?" In *Solidarity*, edited by Kurt Bayertz, 39–56. Dordrecht: Kluwer.

Card, Claudia. 2002. *The Atrocity Paradigm: A Theory of Evil*. New York: Oxford University Press.

Cladis, Mark. 2003. *Public Vision, Private Lives: Rousseau, Religion, and 21st-Century Democracy*. Oxford: Oxford University Press.

Crenshaw, Kimberlé. 1997. "Intersectionality and Identity Politics." In *Reconstructing Political Theory*, edited by Mary Lyndon Shanley and Uma Narayan, 178–93. University Park: Pennsylvania State University Press.

Crocker, Lawrence. 1977. "Equality, Solidarity, and Rawls' Maximin." *Philosophy and Public Affairs* 6 (3): 262–66.

Dean, Jodi. 1996. *The Solidarity of Strangers: Feminism After Identity Politics*. Berkeley and Los Angeles: University of California Press.

Doran, Kevin P. 1996. *Solidarity: A Synthesis of Personalism and Communalism in the Thought of Karol Wojtyla/Pope John Paul II*. New York: Peter Lang.

Dorr, Donal. 1992. *Option for the Poor: A Hundred Years of Catholic Social Teaching*. Maryknoll, N.Y.: Orbis Books.

Dryzek, John S. 2000. *Deliberative Democracy and Beyond: Liberals, Critics, Contestations*. Oxford: Oxford University Press.

Durkheim, Emile. 1973. *On Morality and Society*. Edited by Robert N. Bellah. Chicago: University of Chicago Press.

Dussel, Enrique. 2007. "From Fraternity to Solidarity: Toward a *Politics of Liberation*." *Journal of Social Philosophy* 38 (1): 73–92.
Egonsson, Dan. 1999. "Local Solidarity." *Ethical Theory and Moral Practice* 2:149–63.
EUROPA. 2000. "The Charter of Fundamental Rights of the European Union." Available: http://Europa.eu.int/scadplus/leg/en/lvb/133501.htm. Accessed May 2005.
Fanon, Frantz. 1952. *Black Faces, White Masks*. New York: Grove Press.
———. 1963. *The Wretched of the Earth*. New York: Grove Weidenfeld.
Farmer, Paul. 2005. *Pathologies of Power*. Berkeley and Los Angeles: University of California Press.
Feinberg, Joel. 1970. *Doing and Deserving: Essays in the Theory of Responsibility*. Princeton: Princeton University Press.
———. 1973. *Social Philosophy*. Englewood Cliffs, N.J.: Prentice Hall.
Ferguson, Ann. 2005. "Can Development Create Empowerment and Women's Liberation?" *APA* Newsletter on Feminism and Philosophy 5 (2): 9–15.
Fraser, Nancy. 1986. "Toward a Discourse Ethic of Solidarity." *Praxis International* 5 (4): 425–29.
———. 1989. *Unruly Practices: Power, Discourse, and Gender in Contemporary Social Theory*. Minneapolis: University of Minnesota Press.
———. 1996. *Justice Interruptus*. New York: Routledge.
Freire, Paulo. 1968. *Pedagogy of the Oppressed*. Translated by Myra Bergman Ramos. New York: Herder and Herder.
French, Peter, ed. 1972. *Individual and Collective Responsibility: Massacre at My Lai*. Cambridge, Mass.: Schenkman.
———. 1992. *Responsibility Matters*. Lawrence: University Press of Kansas.
Friedman, Marilyn. 1992. "Feminism and Modern Friendship: Dislocating the Community." In *Explorations in Feminist Ethics: Theory and Practice*, edited by Eve Browning Cole and Susan Coultrap McQuin, 89–100. Indianapolis: Indiana University Press.
Frye, Marilyn. 1983. *The Politics of Reality*. Freedom, Calif.: The Crossing Press.
Gewirth, Alan. 1986. "Why Rights Are Indispensable." *Mind* 95:329–44.
Gilligan, Carol. 1982. *In a Different Voice*. Cambridge, Mass.: Harvard University Press.
Golubović, Zagorka. 1982. "Historical Lessons of the Social Movement in Poland." *Praxis International* 2 (October): 229–40.
Goodin, Robert. 1985. *Protecting the Vulnerable: A Reanalysis of Our Social Responsibilities*. Chicago: University of Chicago Press.
Goodwyn, Lawrence. 1991. *Breaking the Barrier: The Rise of Solidarity in Poland*. New York: Oxford University Press.
Gould, Carol. 2004. *Globalizing Democracy and Human Rights*. Cambridge: Cambridge University Press.
———. 2007. "Transnational Solidarities." *Journal of Social Philosophy* 38 (1): 148–64.
Gundersen, Adolf. 2000. *The Socratic Citizen: A Theory of Deliberative Democracy*. New York: Lexington Books.
Habermas, Jürgen. 1990. "Justice and Solidarity: On the Discussion Concerning Stage 6." In *Hermeneutics and Critical Theory in Ethics and Politics*, edited by Michael Kelly, 132–52. Cambridge, Mass.: MIT Press.

Halldenius, Lena. 1998. "Non-domination and Egalitarian Welfare Politics." *Ethical Theory and Moral Practice* 1:335–53.
Haraway, Donna. 1991. *Simians, Cyborgs, and Women: The Reinvention of Nature.* New York: Routledge.
Hart, H. L. A. 1955. "Are There Any Natural Rights?" *Philosophical Review* 64 (2 April): 175–91.
Hartsock, Nancy. 1983. "The Feminist Standpoint: Developing the Ground for a Specifically Feminist Historical Materialism." In *Discovering Reality: Feminist Perspectives on Epistemology, Metaphysics, Methodology, and Philosophy of Science,* edited by Sandra Harding and Merrill B. Hintikka, 283–310. Boston: D. Reidel.
———. 1998. *Feminist Standpoint Revisited and Other Essays.* Boulder, Colo.: Westview Press.
Harvey, Jean. 1999. *Civilized Oppression.* Lanham, Md.: Rowman and Littlefield.
———. 2007. "Moral Solidarity and Empathetic Understanding: The Moral Value and Scope of the Relationship." *Journal of Social Philosophy* 38 (1): 22–38.
Hawkesworth, Mary. 2006. *Globalization and Feminist Activism.* Lanham, Md.: Rowman and Littlefield.
Hechter, Michael. 1987. *Principles of Group Solidarity.* Berkeley and Los Angeles: University of California Press.
Held, Virginia. 1970. "Can a Random Collection of Individuals Be Morally Responsible?" *Journal of Philosophy* 67 (14): 471–81.
Heyd, David. 2007. "Justice and Solidarity: The Contractarian Case Against Global Justice." *Journal of Social Philosophy* 38 (1): 112–30.
Hill, Thomas J. 1979. "Symbolic Protest and Calculated Silence." *Philosophy and Public Affairs* 9 (1): 83–102.
Hill Collins, Patricia. 2004. "Toward a New Vision: Race, Class, and Gender as Categories of Analysis and Connection." In *Oppression, Privilege, and Resistance: Theoretical Perspectives on Racism, Sexism, and Heterosexism,* edited by Lisa Heldke and Margaret O'Connor, 529–43. New York: McGraw-Hill.
Hirschmann, Nancy J. 1997. "The Theory and Practice of Freedom." In *Reconstructing Political Theory,* edited by Mary Lyndon Shanley and Uma Narayan, 194–210. University Park: Pennsylvania State University Press.
Hoagland, Sarah Lucia. 1990. "Some Thoughts About 'Caring.'" In *Feminist Ethics,* edited by Claudia Card, 246–64. Lawrence: University Press of Kansas.
Hobbes, Thomas. 1982. *Leviathan.* Introduced by C. B. Macpherson. New York: Penguin Classics.
Hodge, John. 1975. *Cultural Bases of Racism and Group Oppression.* Berkeley, Calif.: Two Riders Press.
Hollinger, David A. 1995. *Postethnic America: Beyond Multiculturalism.* New York: Basic Books.
hooks, bell. 1984. *Feminist Theory: From Margin to Center.* Boston: South End Press.
Huntington, Patricia. 1997. "Fragmentation, Race, and Gender: Building Solidarity in the Postmodern Era." In *Existence in Black,* edited by Lewis Gordon, 185–202. New York: Routledge.

References

Ibana, Rainer R. A. 1989. "The Essential Elements for the Possibility and Necessity of the Principle of Solidarity According to Max Scheler." *Philosophy Today* 33 (1): 42–55.

IFRC. "International Federation of Red Cross and Red Crescent Societies." Available: http://www.ifrc.org/who/index.asp?navid=03_01. Accessed June 14, 2006.

Isasi-Diaz, Ada Maria. 1990. "Solidarity: Love of Neighbor in the 1980s." In *Lift Every Voice: Constructing Christian Theologies from the Underside*, edited by Susan Brooks Thistlewaite and Mary Potter Engel, 30–39. San Francisco: Harper.

Jaggar, Alison. 1983. *Feminist Politics and Human Nature*. Totowa, N.J.: Rowman and Allanheld.

———. 2000. "Globalizing Feminist Ethics." In *Decentering the Center*, edited by Uma Narayan and Sandra Harding, 1–25. Bloomington: Indiana University Press.

———. 2005. "Arenas of Citizenship: Civil Society, the State, and the Global Order." In *Women and Citizenship*, edited by Marilyn Friedman, 91–110. New York: Oxford University Press.

Kahane, David. 1999. "Diversity and Civic Solidarity: Diversity, Solidarity, and Civic Friendship." *Journal of Political Philosophy* 7 (3): 267–86.

King, Martin Luther, Jr. 1969. "Letter from the Birmingham City Jail." In *Civil Disobedience: Theory and Practice*, edited by Hugo Adam Bedau, 72–89. Indianapolis: Pegasus.

Kolenda, Konstantin. 1989. "Incremental Solidarity." *The Humanist* 49 (September–October): 43.

Kruks, Sonia. 2001. *Retrieving Experience: Subjectivity and Recognition in Feminist Politics*. Ithaca, N.Y.: Cornell University Press.

Kuipers, Ronald Alexander. 1997. *Solidarity and the Stranger: Themes in the Social Philosophy of Richard Rorty*. New York: University Press of America.

Ladd, John. 1998. "The Idea of Community, an Ethical Exploration, Part I: The Search for an Elusive Concept." *Journal of Value Inquiry* 32:5–24.

Lenhardt, Christian. 1975. "Anamnestic Solidarity: The Proletariat and Its *Manes*." *Telos* 25 (Fall): 133–54.

Libiszowska-Żółtkowska, Maria. 1991. "The Relevance of Catholic Social Teaching in Poland, Especially During the Socialist Period and in the Rise of the Solidarity Movement." In *Rerum Novarum: One Hundred Years of Catholic Social Teaching*, edited by John Coleman and Gregory Baum, 96–104. Philadelphia: Trinity Press International.

Lindemann, Kate. 1992. "Philosophy of Liberation in the North American Context." *Contemporary Philosophy* 14 (4): 5–9.

Locke, Alain. 1925. "Internationalism: Friend or Foe of Art?" *The World Tomorrow* 8 (1 March): 75.

———. 1946. Editorial section introductions in *When Peoples Meet: A Study in Race and Culture Contacts*, edited by Alain Locke and Bernhard Stern. New York: Hinds, Hayden, and Eldredge.

———. 1989. *The Philosophy of Alain Locke: Harlem Renaissance and Beyond*. Edited by Leonard Harris. Philadelphia: Temple University Press.

Locke, Alain, and Bernhard Stern, eds. 1946. *When Peoples Meet: A Study in Race and Culture Contacts.* New York: Hinds, Hayden, and Eldredge.

Lugones, María. 1987. "Playfulness, 'World'-Traveling, and Loving Perception." *Hypatia* 2 (2): 3–19.

———. 2003. *Pilgrimages/Peregrinajes: Theorizing Coalition Against Multiple Oppressions.* Lanham, Md.: Rowman and Littlefield.

Lugones, María, and Elizabeth Spelman. 1983. "Have We Got a Theory for You: Feminist Theory, Cultural Imperialism, and the Demand for 'The Woman's Voice.'" *Hypatia* WSIF 1:573–81.

MacKinnon, Catharine. 1994. "Rape, Genocide, and Women's Human Rights." *Harvard Women's Law Journal* 17:5–16.

Macpherson, C. B. 1964. *The Political Theory of Possessive Individualism: Hobbes to Locke.* Oxford: Oxford University Press.

Manning, Rita. 1992. *Speaking from the Heart.* Lanham, Md.: Rowman and Littlefield.

Mason, Andrew. 2000. *Community, Solidarity, and Belonging.* New York: Cambridge University Press.

May, Larry. 1992. "Insensitivity and Moral Responsibility." *The Journal of Value Inquiry* 26 (1): 7–22.

———. 1996. *The Socially Responsive Self: Social Theory and Professional Ethics.* Chicago: University of Chicago Press.

———. 2007. "The International Community, Solidarity, and the Duty to Aid." *Journal of Social Philosophy* 38 (1): 185–203.

McGary, Howard. 1986. "Morality and Collective Liability." *The Journal of Value Inquiry* 20:157–65.

Metz, Karl. 1999. "Solidarity and History: Institutions and Social Concepts of Solidarity in 19th Century Western Europe." In *Solidarity,* edited by Kurt Bayertz, 191–208. Dordrecht: Kluwer.

Mills, Charles. 1997. *The Racial Contract.* Ithaca, N.Y.: Cornell University Press.

Min, Anselm Kyongsuk. 1989. *Dialectic of Salvation: Issues in Theology of Liberation.* Albany: State University of New York Press.

Mohanty, Chandra Talpade. 2002. "'Under Western Eyes' Revisited: Feminist Solidarity Through Anticapitalist Struggles." *Signs: Journal of Women in Culture and Society* 28 (2): 499–535.

———. 2003. *Feminism Without Borders: Decolonizing Theory, Practicing Solidarity.* Durham, N.C.: Duke University Press.

Moody-Adams, Michele M. 1992. "Race, Class, and the Social Construction of Self-Respect." *The Philosophical Forum* 24 (1–3): 251–66.

Mueller, Franz H. 1952. "Rejecting Right and Left: Heinrich Pesch and Solidarism." *Thought: Fordham University Quarterly* 26 (103): 485–500.

Mussett, Shannon M. 2005. "Personal Choice and the Seduction of the Absolute in *The Mandarins.*" In *The Contradictions of Freedom,* edited by Sally J. Scholz and Shannon M. Mussett, 135–56. Albany: State University of New York Press.

Narayan, Uma. 1995. "Male-Order Brides." *Hypatia* 10 (1): 104–19.

Neuffer, Elizabeth. 2001. *The Key to My Neighbor's House: Seeking Justice in Bosnia and Rwanda.* New York: Picador.

Nino, Carlos Santiago. 1991. *The Ethics of Human Rights*. Oxford: Clarendon Press.
Noddings, Nel. 1984. *Caring: A Feminine Approach to Ethics and Moral Education*. Berkeley and Los Angeles: University of California Press.
Okin, Susan Moller. 2000. "Feminism, Women's Human Rights, and Cultural Difference." In *Decentering the Center*, edited by Uma Narayan and Sandra Harding, 26–46. Bloomington: Indiana University Press.
Pateman, Carole. 1988. *The Sexual Contract*. Palo Alto, Calif.: Stanford University Press.
Paulhus, Normand. 1987. "Uses and Misuses of the Term 'Social Justice' in the Roman Catholic Tradition." *Journal of Religious Ethics* 15 (2): 261–82.
Pesch, Heinrich. 2003. *Ethics and the National Economy*. Translated and introduced by Rupert Ederer. Norfolk, Va.: IHS Press.
"Principles of the Nuremberg Tribunal." 1950. Available: http://deoxy.org/wc/wc-nurem.htm. Accessed September 13, 2004.
Raz, Joseph. 1994. "Multiculturalism: A Liberal Perspective." *Dissent* (Winter): 67–79.
Rehg, William. 1994. *Insight and Solidarity: A Study in the Discourse Ethics of Jürgen Habermas*. Berkeley and Los Angeles: University of California Press.
———. 2007. "Solidarity and the Common Good: An Analytic Framework." *Journal of Social Philosophy* 38 (1): 7–22.
Rich, Adrienne. 1986. *Of Woman Born: Motherhood as Experience and Institution*. New York: Norton.
Rippe, Klaus Peter. 1998. "Diminishing Solidarity." *Ethical Theory and Practice* 1:355–74.
Rorty, Richard. 1984. "Solidarity or Objectivity?" In *Post-Analytic Philosophy*, edited by John Rajchman and Cornel West, 3–19. New York: Columbia University Press.
———. 1989. *Contingency, Irony, and Solidarity*. New York: Cambridge University Press.
Rousseau, Jean-Jacques. 1967 [1755]. *Discourse on the Origin and Foundation of Inequality Among Mankind*. In *The Social Contract and Discourse on the Origin of Inequality*, edited and translated by Lester G. Crocker, 149–258. New York: Washington Square Press.
Ruddick, Sara. 1989. *Maternal Thinking: Toward a Politics of Peace*. Boston: Beacon Press.
Salzman, Todd. 2000. "'Rape Camps,' Forced Impregnation, and Ethnic Cleansing: Religious, Cultural, and Ethical Responses to Rape Victims in the Former Yugoslavia." In *War's Dirty Secret*, edited by Anne Llewellyn Barstow, 63–92. Cleveland: Pilgrim Press.
Sandel, Michael. 1996. *Democracy's Discontent: America in Search of a Public Philosophy*. Cambridge, Mass.: Belknap Press of Harvard University Press.
Sartre, Jean-Paul. 1991 [1960]. *Critique of Dialectical Reason*. Translated by Alan Sheridan-Smith. New York: Verso.
Sass, Hans-Martin. 2001. "Introduction: European Bioethics on a Rocky Road." *Journal of Medicine and Philosophy* 26 (3): 215–24.
Scheler, Max. 1970. *The Nature of Sympathy*. Hamden, Conn.: Archon Books.

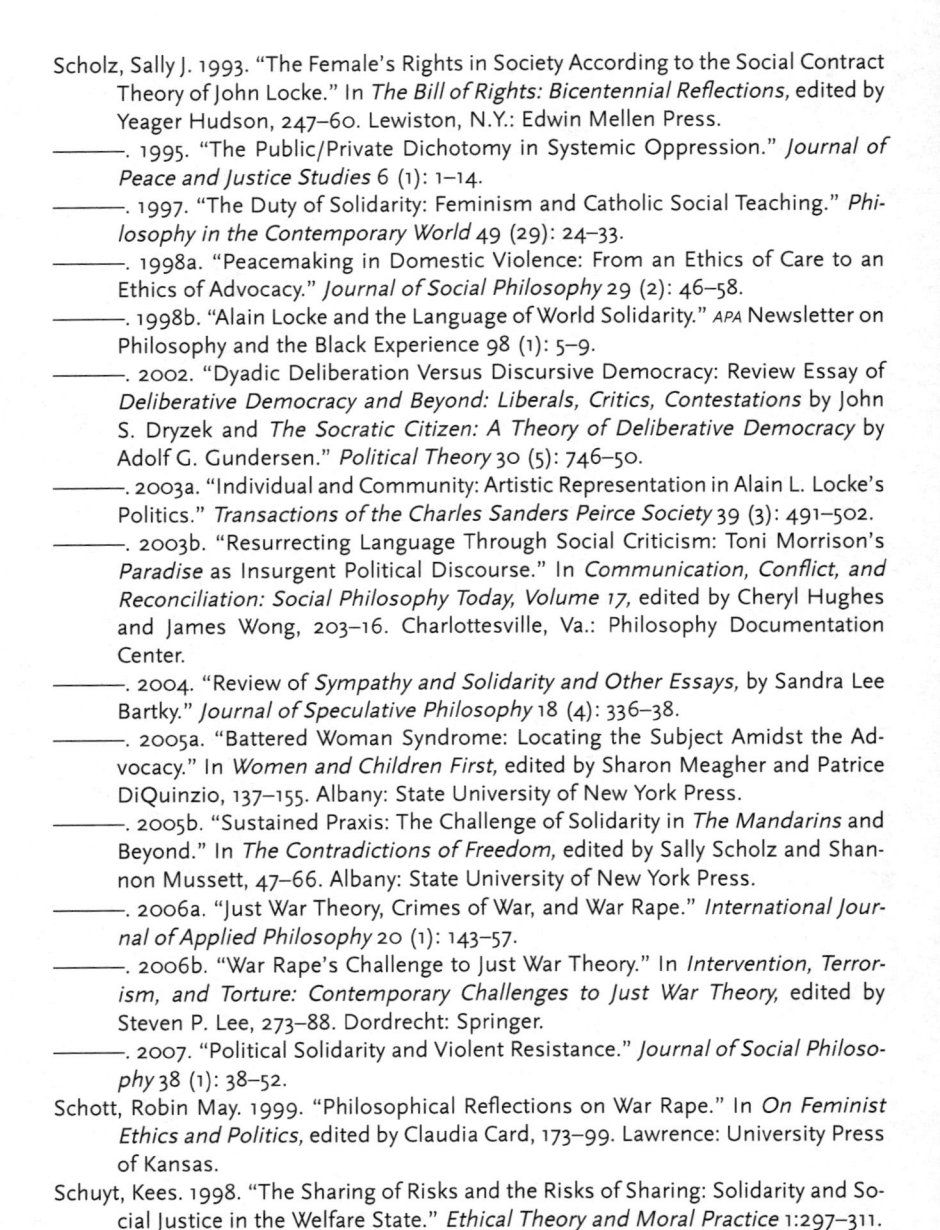

Scholz, Sally J. 1993. "The Female's Rights in Society According to the Social Contract Theory of John Locke." In *The Bill of Rights: Bicentennial Reflections*, edited by Yeager Hudson, 247–60. Lewiston, N.Y.: Edwin Mellen Press.
———. 1995. "The Public/Private Dichotomy in Systemic Oppression." *Journal of Peace and Justice Studies* 6 (1): 1–14.
———. 1997. "The Duty of Solidarity: Feminism and Catholic Social Teaching." *Philosophy in the Contemporary World* 49 (29): 24–33.
———. 1998a. "Peacemaking in Domestic Violence: From an Ethics of Care to an Ethics of Advocacy." *Journal of Social Philosophy* 29 (2): 46–58.
———. 1998b. "Alain Locke and the Language of World Solidarity." APA Newsletter on Philosophy and the Black Experience 98 (1): 5–9.
———. 2002. "Dyadic Deliberation Versus Discursive Democracy: Review Essay of *Deliberative Democracy and Beyond: Liberals, Critics, Contestations* by John S. Dryzek and *The Socratic Citizen: A Theory of Deliberative Democracy* by Adolf G. Gundersen." *Political Theory* 30 (5): 746–50.
———. 2003a. "Individual and Community: Artistic Representation in Alain L. Locke's Politics." *Transactions of the Charles Sanders Peirce Society* 39 (3): 491–502.
———. 2003b. "Resurrecting Language Through Social Criticism: Toni Morrison's *Paradise* as Insurgent Political Discourse." In *Communication, Conflict, and Reconciliation: Social Philosophy Today, Volume 17*, edited by Cheryl Hughes and James Wong, 203–16. Charlottesville, Va.: Philosophy Documentation Center.
———. 2004. "Review of *Sympathy and Solidarity and Other Essays*, by Sandra Lee Bartky." *Journal of Speculative Philosophy* 18 (4): 336–38.
———. 2005a. "Battered Woman Syndrome: Locating the Subject Amidst the Advocacy." In *Women and Children First*, edited by Sharon Meagher and Patrice DiQuinzio, 137–155. Albany: State University of New York Press.
———. 2005b. "Sustained Praxis: The Challenge of Solidarity in *The Mandarins* and Beyond." In *The Contradictions of Freedom*, edited by Sally Scholz and Shannon Mussett, 47–66. Albany: State University of New York Press.
———. 2006a. "Just War Theory, Crimes of War, and War Rape." *International Journal of Applied Philosophy* 20 (1): 143–57.
———. 2006b. "War Rape's Challenge to Just War Theory." In *Intervention, Terrorism, and Torture: Contemporary Challenges to Just War Theory*, edited by Steven P. Lee, 273–88. Dordrecht: Springer.
———. 2007. "Political Solidarity and Violent Resistance." *Journal of Social Philosophy* 38 (1): 38–52.
Schott, Robin May. 1999. "Philosophical Reflections on War Rape." In *On Feminist Ethics and Politics*, edited by Claudia Card, 173–99. Lawrence: University Press of Kansas.
Schuyt, Kees. 1998. "The Sharing of Risks and the Risks of Sharing: Solidarity and Social Justice in the Welfare State." *Ethical Theory and Moral Practice* 1:297–311.
Scott, Janny. 2005. "Life at the Top in America Isn't Just Better, It's Longer." In *Class Matters*, edited by Bill Keller, 27–50. New York: Times Books.
Shelby, Tommie. 2005. *We Who Are Dark: The Philosophical Foundations of Black Solidarity.* Cambridge, Mass.: Belknap Press of Harvard University Press.

Shue, Henry. 1980. *Basic Rights: Subsistence, Affluence, and U.S. Foreign Policy.* Princeton: Princeton University Press.
Singer, Peter. 1972. "Famine, Affluence, and Morality." *Philosophy and Public Affairs* 1 (3): 229–43.
Steger, Manfred. 1994. "A Perspective on Solidarity in a 'Post-Socialist' World." *History of European Ideas* 19 (1–3): 325–31.
Steinvorth, Ulrich. 1999. "The Concept and Possibilities of Solidarity." In *Solidarity*, edited by Kurt Bayertz, 29–38. Dordrecht: Kluwer.
Stout, Jeffrey. 2003. *Democracy and Tradition.* Princeton: Princeton University Press.
Stubblefield, Anna. 2001. "Races as Families." *Journal of Social Philosophy* 32 (1): 99–112.
Sunstein, Cass R., and Edna Ullmann-Margalit. 2001. "Solidarity Goods." *The Journal of Political Philosophy* 9 (2): 129–49.
Taylor, Charles. 1992. *Multiculturalism and "The Politics of Recognition."* Edited by Amy Gutmann, with commentary by Steven Rockefeller, Michael Walzer, and Susan Wolf. Princeton: Princeton University Press.
Thome, Helmut. 1999. "Solidarity: Theoretical Perspectives for Empirical Research." In *Solidarity*, edited by Kurt Bayertz, 101–32. Dordrecht: Kluwer.
Toton, Suzanne. 2006. *Justice Education: From Service to Solidarity.* Milwaukee, Wis.: Marquette University Press.
Tyson, Timothy. 2004. *Blood Done Sign My Name.* New York: Three Rivers Press.
United Nations Fourth World Conference on Women. "Beijing Platform for Action." Available: http://www.un.org/womenwatch/daw/beijing/platform/plat1.htm. Accessed September 13, 2004.
van Donselaar, Gus. 1998. "The Freedom-Based Account of Solidarity and Basic Income." *Ethical Theory and Moral Practice* 1:313–33.
Walzer, Michael. 1970. *Obligations: Essays on Disobedience, War, and Citizenship.* Cambridge, Mass.: Harvard University Press.
———. 1987. *Interpretation and Social Criticism.* Cambridge, Mass.: Harvard University Press.
———. 1988. *The Company of Critics.* New York: Basic Books.
———. 1992. *Just and Unjust Wars.* 2nd ed. New York: Basic Books.
———. 1994. "Multiculturalism and Individualism." *Dissent* (Spring): 185–91.
———. 1998. "Pluralism and Social Democracy." *Dissent* (Winter): 47–53.
Ware, Robert. 1983. "Marx, the Theory of Class Consciousness, and Revolutionary Organization." *Praxis International* 3 (3): 262–73.
Washington, Johnny. 1986. *Alain Locke and Philosophy: A Quest for Cultural Pluralism.* New York: Greenwood Press.
———. 1994. *A Journey into the Philosophy of Alain Locke.* New York: Greenwood Press.
Weale, Albert. 1990. "Equality, Social Solidarity, and the Welfare State." *Ethics* 100 (3): 473–88.
Weber, Clare. 2006. *Visions of Solidarity: U.S. Peace Activists in Nicaragua from War to Women's Activism and Globalization.* Lanham, Md.: Lexington Books.
Wernick, Andrew. 2001. *Auguste Comte and the Religion of Humanity.* Cambridge: Cambridge University Press.

Wippman, David. 2000. "Can an International Criminal Court Prevent and Punish Genocide?" In *Protection Against Genocide: Mission Impossible?* edited by Neal Riemer, 85–104. Westport, Conn.: Praeger.

Wojtyła, Karol. 1981. *Toward a Philosophy of Praxis: An Anthology.* Edited by Alfred Block and George T. Czuczka. New York: Crossroads.

Yoder, John Howard. 1991. "The Conditions of Countercultural Credibility." In *The Making of an Economic Vision,* edited by Oliver F. Williams and John W. Houck, 261–74. Lanham, Md.: University Press of America.

Young, Iris. 1980. "Socialist Feminism and the Limits of Dual Systems Theory." *Socialist Review* 10 (2/3): 169–88.

———. 1983. "Justice and Hazardous Waste." In *The Applied Turn in Contemporary Philosophy,* edited by Michael Bradie, Thomas W. Attig, and Nicholas Rescher, 177–83. Bowling Green, Ohio: Applied Philosophy Program, Bowling Green State University.

———. 1990. *Justice and the Politics of Difference.* Princeton: Princeton University Press.

———. 1996. "Communication and the Other: Beyond Deliberative Democracy." In *Democracy and Difference: Contesting the Boundaries of the Political,* edited by Seyla Benhabib, 120–35. Princeton: Princeton University Press.

———. 2001. "Activist Challenges to Deliberative Democracy." *Political Theory* 29 (5): 670–90.

Zack, Naomi. 2005. *Inclusive Feminism: A Third Wave Theory of Women's Commonality.* Lanham, Md.: Rowman and Littlefield.

Index

ableism, 142, 171, 210
abolition, 139
Abramoff, Jack, 202–3
abuse, 74, 217
accountability, 37
action
    collective, 25, 33, 54, 71–114, 131, 134, 136–37, 222–23, 255, 247
    individual, 84, 145
    political, 74, 128, 263
    reflective, 54
activism, 56, 87, 92–96, 141–42, 182, 189, 202
    as duty of solidarity, 13, 101–7
    environmental, 147
    feminist, 53, 63, 83, 136, 208, 254, 261–63
    grassroots, 103–5
    nonviolent, 78, 110, 143–44
    political, 61, 63, 114, 149, 164, 175
    social, 7, 51, 58–70, 74–77, 114, 123–24, 132–33, 136, 156, 159–60, 167
    violent, 106–12, 102, 122, 194
advocacy, 62, 66–69, 72, 77, 104–5, 140, 199, 225
Africa, 257
African American, 75, 80, 97, 170, 201
ageism, 138, 171, 210
agency, 110
    individual, 137
aggregates, 120
AIDS, 39, 64, 257
Alcoff, Linda Martín, 182–83

alienation, 29, 73, 141
alliances, political, 37–38
altruism, 12–13
ambiguity, 162
America, 67, 131, 212, 255
American Association of Retired Persons (AARP), 118
Anderson, Ana Flora, 94, 247
anger, 51, 80, 83–84
apartheid, 64
Appiah, K. Anthony, 2
Aristide, Jean Bertrand, 193
Aristotelean virtue, 182
Arp, Kristana, 224
associations, 5, 19, 22, 35, 46, 57, 70, 113–23
    culture, 97
    political, 69
    ties of, 99, 142
    voluntary, 18, 73, 113, 125, 146–47, 255
autonomy, 19, 29, 31, 98, 138, 158, 247
    individual, 74–75
Axis Rule in Occupied Europe (Lemkin), 239

bad faith, 99
Bailey, Alison, 131, 182
Bangladesh, 231–32
Barstow, Anne Llewellyn, 257–62
Bartky, Sandra, 95, 128, 163–65, 166, 175, 226
basic needs, 29
basic rights, 96
Bastille, 39

Bates, Stanley, 84, 131, 254
Bayertz, Kurt, 10–11, 19–20, 23, 29, 35–38, 40, 91–92, 116, 240–41, 256, 264
Beauvoir, Simone de, 76–78, 144, 152, 162, 165, 191, 215, 223–26
  Ethics of Ambiguity, 76, 165
Beijing Platform for Action, 259
Bell, Linda, 176
beneficence, 31
Benhabib, Seyla, 179
Bernstein, Richard, 97
Blum, Lawrence, 38
Boff, Clodovis, 8
Boshammer, Susanne, 30
Bosnia, 232, 238
boycott, 62, 64, 74, 103, 110, 116, 136, 145, 149, 157, 228, 257
Brison, Susan, 199
Brownmiller, Susan, 232
Bush, George W., 47

camaraderie, 2, 5, 46–48, 79, 116–17
Cambodia, 231
Capaldi, Nicholas, 49
capitalism, 7, 40, 102, 132, 168–69, 211–12
Card, Claudia, 257, 260, 263
care ethics, 167, 173–77, 183, 235, 241
Catholic Social Teaching, 7–8, 31–33, 147, 242–48
Chaplin, Ralph, 9
charity, 37, 93
  universal, 32
Charter of Fundamental Rights of the European Union, 9, 28–29
children, 74, 217–19, 240
Chile, 37
Christian social ethics, 40
citizenship, 27, 33, 213
  rights of, 9, 50, 108, 264
  social bond of, 27
  See also civic solidarity
civic organization, 63
civic participation, 17, 104, 113–14, 122, 145, 148, 242
civic solidarity, 5, 11–12, 17–20, 27–33, 36, 39–46, 72, 199–201, 204, 223, 232
  as human solidarity, 65, 219, 242–52
  defined, 29
  international, 42, 246
civic virtue of solidarity, 31
civil disobedience, 112

civil inequality, 24
civil law, 23–24, 64, 155
civil rights, 9, 28, 50, 142, 157, 193, 208
  movement, 36, 63, 67–69, 72, 75, 103, 110, 137, 228
  transnational, 147
civil society, 5, 10, 27, 36, 41–43, 55, 50, 149, 154, 206, 264
Cladis, Mark, 13, 153
class, 130, 140
  consciousness, 132
  divisions, 169
  privilege, 132
  social, 218
  solidarity, 129
classism, 141–42, 171
coalitions, 56, 59, 68–69, 142, 147, 189, 198, 255, 260
  building, 65
  global, 255
  international, 257, 263
collective action. *See under* action
collective responsibility. *See under* responsibility
Collins, Patricia Hill. *See* Hill Collins, Patricia
colonialism, 132, 138, 210
commitment, 57–62, 160, 166, 175, 221–24, 254–63
  active, 72
  collective, 83, 134, 155
  existential, 75
  individual, 13–14, 35, 41, 64–66, 71–79, 83, 110, 113, 116, 124, 130, 167
  international, 66
  moral, 16, 38, 137, 156, 121
  multiple, 65
  mutual, 72, 81, 83, 119, 123, 135
  political, 56, 61, 121, 141
  of political solidarity, 32, 51–53, 101, 128, 152
  solidary, 75, 85
  to a goal, 86, 91, 94, 133–34, 191
common good, 27–29, 81
communalism, 18
communication, 53, 56, 58, 63, 85–90, 109, 130, 148, 150, 166, 178, 181, 185–86, 198, 236
  electronic, 104
  global, 113
communicative theory, 177–81, 207. *See also* discourse theory
The Communist Manifesto (Marx), 96
Communist Party, 8–9, 39

Index

communitarianism, 19
community, 35, 41–43, 46, 75–76, 92, 113–21
  civil, 242
  collective, 65
  global, 32, 247, 251
  human, 233–41
  impure, 139
  interdependent, 23–24
  international, 12, 33, 41, 65, 231–32, 242–62
  pure, 139
  solidarity and, 2, 5, 18–19, 31, 129, 223
comparative justice. *See under* justice
competition, 25
Comte, Auguste, 6
Congress, 64
Congressional Black Caucus, 123
consciousness, oppressive, 102
  shared, 21, 22
  social, 75
consciousness-raising, 13, 52, 58, 66, 73–74, 103–5, 126, 131, 179–80
consumer protection, 5, 9, 28–29, 55
consumerism, 10, 12, 66, 74, 87, 93, 145, 212
  conscious, 53, 57, 62, 74–75
  informed, 29, 74
  reflective, 74–75
Contingency, Irony, and Solidarity (Rorty), 238
cooperation, 7, 13, 38, 56, 58, 78, 73–94, 98, 109, 136, 166, 181, 205–7, 227, 256
  international, 251
coordination, 85–87, 149–50
Copelon, Rhonda, 261–62
cosmopolitanism, 113, 122
Crenshaw, Kimberlé, 140
crimes, 24, 55
  against humanity, 242, 249, 250, 258
  of war, 242, 250–51, 258, 261
  violent, 199
criminal justice system, 202
critical race theory, 2, 11
critical theory, 11, 146, 179
criticism, social. *See* social criticism
Critique of Dialectical Reason (Sartre), 120
Crocker, Lawrence, 91–92
crowds, 117–18, 122
cultural imperialism, 202–3, 212, 236
cultural pluralism, 236
cultural solidarity, 22
culture, 22, 45, 64, 74, 130, 135, 178, 212, 236–37, 245, 255, 261–62
  associations, 97

interdependence, 32
  military, 260
  rituals, 96
cyber protest, 104–5

Darfur, 231
Dean, Jodi, 37
decision-making, 33, 140, 173, 207–9, 217, 245
  democratic, 56, 146–47, 263
  and equality, 151–58
  political, 68–69, 75
  procedures, 84, 117
  rational, 72
  within political solidarity, 14, 66, 85, 114–23, 138, 144–50
democracy, 91, 179, 212, 240
  and decision-making, 56, 144–47, 263
  deliberative, 110, 146, 151–52, 155, 157
  discursive, 146
  in political solidarity, 14, 68, 114–15
  social, 145
  and society, 202, 215, 255
development, 7, 20, 244–46, 251
  sustainable, 28
dignity, 31, 144, 244, 247
  human, 9
disability, 67, 217
Discourse on the Origins and Foundation of Inequality Among Mankind (Rousseau), 23–24
discourse theory, 167, 177–81, 183. *See also* communicative theory
discrimination, 207–10, 217
distribution, economic, 87, 172
  of power, principle, 88
  of rights, 34
distributive justice. *See under* justice
diversity, 37, 74, 160, 163, 192, 237
  and political solidarity, 139–44
division of labor, 23, 41, 45, 106, 141, 204, 233–34, 240
  gender, 168
Doctors Without Borders, 198
domestic violence, 5, 54, 106, 124, 131, 140, 221–22
domination, 84, 89, 93, 110, 139
  logic of, 141
  systems of, 135, 136, 141, 144
  See also under groups
Doran, Kevin P., 22–26, 32–33, 60, 108, 235, 244–48

Index

Dorr, Donal, 246
double consciousness, 182–83
Dryzek, John S., 146–47
Du Bois, W.E.B., 2, 22, 182
Durkheim, Emile, 6, 10, 20–27, 39–49, 153, 233–37
Dussel, Enrique, 37
duties, 17, 71–112
    moral, mutuality as a, 81–83, 91–94
    negative, 19
    positive, 19–20, 33, 48, 58–60, 68–69, 78, 133, 153, 204, 254
    positive, of camaraderie, 117
    of solidarity, 32

Eastern Europe, 9
ecological interdependence, 32
education, 55, 218
    consumer, 29
egalitarianism, 31, 243
Egonsson, Dan, 31
empathetic understanding, 4, 129
empathy, 37, 79, 173–76, 199, 233–35, 240–41
employment, 30, 55
empowerment, 38, 52, 54, 58, 88–89, 148, 236, 251, 261, 263
Engels, Friedrich, 102
English Common Law, 53
environment, 28, 74, 113
    degradation of, 252
environmental activism, 78, 142–43, 147
environmental protection, 5, 9, 28–29, 55
epistemological privilege, 40, 155, 159–60, 164–76
epistemology, 15, 164
    feminist, 152–53, 165–86
    for political solidarity, 4, 181–86
    of provenance, 171
    standpoint, 168–72, 177
equality, 67, 75, 92, 115, 177, 179, 243
    civil, 154–55
    of resources, 243
    within political solidarity, 151–60
ethics, 35, 39–46, 98
    care, 173–77, 183, 235
    discourse, 177–81, 183
    existential, 76, 137, 191
    feminist, 49
    individualist, 76
    procedural, 47
    solidarity, 71–112

Ethics of Ambiguity (Beauvoir), 76, 165. *See also* Beauvoir, Simone de
ethnic cleansing, 232, 259
ethnicity, 68, 205
Europe, 27–28, 31
European Union, Charter of Fundamental Rights, 9, 20, 28–29
existentialism, 13, 75–78, 137, 191
exploitation, 32, 38, 53, 55, 135, 143, 183, 202, 211, 217, 253, 261

fair trade, 116, 119, 157, 227
family, 9, 17, 26, 48, 114, 140
Fanon, Frantz, 110–11
    The Wretched of the Earth, 111
Farmer, Paul, 193, 195, 261
Feinberg, Joel, 35, 43–46, 80, 195, 207–8
fellow-feeling, 166
female genital mutilation, 64
feminism, 38, 58, 69, 78, 142, 193, 216, 257–63
    and activism, 3, 63, 106, 136
    and epistemology, 165–87
    and ethics, 49, 173–77, 183, 235
    and feminist movement, 3, 35, 123, 131, 136, 140
    first wave, 208, 209
    and literature, 11, 138
    postcolonial, 152
    second wave, 209
    socialist, 141
    and solidarity, 3–4
    See also women's liberation
Ferguson, Ann, 89
Fraser, Nancy, 163, 177–80
fraternity, 10
free rider problem, 136, 255
freedom, 9, 29, 76–77. *See also* liberation
Freire, Paulo, 102, 107, 111, 126, 170–71, 213–15
French Revolution, 28, 39, 154
French, Peter, 35, 84–90
Friedman, Marilyn, 126
friendship, 9, 46, 51, 55, 79, 115, 117, 126, 176, 184, 199
Frye, Marilyn, 210–11

Gandhi, Mahatma, 102, 110
gay rights movement, 67
gender, 205, 210, 240, 248, 261
general will, 24
genocide, 15–16, 42, 211, 220, 247
    defined, 231
    rape as, 254, 257–63

Index

Gewirth, Alan, 196, 234
Gilligan, Carol, 173
   In a Different Voice, 173
global community, 32, 247, 251
global interdependence, 32–33
global justice, 49
global political solidarity. See *under* political solidarity
global warming, 252
globalization, 12, 74, 113, 212, 234–35, 263
goal, 81, 107, 122, 135
   collective, 108
   commitment to, 72, 86, 94
   formative, 54, 69, 81–82, 86, 108, 111, 190, 206
   of liberation, 15, 85
   of organization, 118
   of political solidarity, 34, 58, 68–70, 92–3, 130, 137, 139, 149, 158, 189–29
   political, 56, 133
   relation to, 78, 94–100, 225
   substantive, 69, 81–82, 86, 95, 108, 111, 190–91, 203, 206, 221–24
Goodin, Robert, 85, 89–90, 94, 98, 149–50, 219
Goodwyn, Lawrence, 8, 72, 104
Gould, Carol, 241, 257, 262–63
government, 29–30, 39, 41, 66
grassroots activism, 103–5, 263
groups, 41, 113, 116, 121, 123
   cohesian of, 17, 21
   dominant, 58, 80, 100–1, 152, 158, 166, 169–70, 177–80, 209, 212–14
   institutional, 120
   liability, 35
   participation in, 98
   pledge, 120
   social, 120–21, 125–27
   See *also* oppressed groups; solidary group
guilt, 79

Habermas, Jürgen, 177
Haiti, 57, 77
Halldenius, Lena, 29–31
Haraway, Donna, 172
Harlem Renaissance, 236
Hartsock, Nancy, 169–72, 174
Harvey, Jean, 129, 163, 204
Hawkesworth, Mary, 263
healthcare, 5, 28, 39, 42, 44, 55, 61, 63, 163, 195, 218–19, 242, 261
   universal, 20, 31, 46

Hechter, Michael, 24–25, 86, 118, 123, 120
Held, Virginia, 35, 74–75, 90, 119–20
heterosexism, 210. See *also* homophobia
Heyd, David, 49
Hill, Thomas, 73, 83, 105, 136, 193–95, 221
Hill Collins, Patricia, 189–90
Hirschmann, Nancy, 140
Hoagland, Sarah Lucia, 176–77
Hodge, John, 210
Hollinger, David A., 122, 133, 255
homelessness, 14, 145, 192
homophobia, 166. See *also* heterosexism
hooks, bell, 3, 58, 61, 131–32, 135, 138, 141
hope, 51, 60, 79–84, 92, 95
housework, 106
human nature, 40, 240–41
human rights, 9, 28, 45, 114
   crises, 113, 232–35, 241–44
   and need for solidarity, 65, 196, 207
   United Nations Universal Declaration of, 55, 248–50
   violation of, 12, 198
   women's, 258–63
human solidarity, 10, 12, 15, 20, 65, 150, 219, 231–64
   as civic solidarity, 42, 242–52
   as social solidarity, 27, 41, 233–41
   duty of, 32, 233–52
human trafficking, 53
humanism, 73
humanity, 232, 240, 252
Huntington, Patricia, 138
Hurricane Katrina, 198, 200–1
Hutus, 232, 241

Ibana, Rainer R.A., 26–27, 91
identity, 3, 38, 73, 125–26, 128, 133, 214–15
   common, 113, 134
   group, 133–35
   oppressed, 134
   shared, 121
   social constructed, 213–15, 240
identity politics, 141
immigrants, 97, 140
imperialism, 38, 138
   cultural, 202–3, 212, 235
In a Different Voice (Gilligan), 173
incremental solidarity, 233, 235–36, 241
individual, 22, 73, 85, 144–45, 148
   and community, 19, 26, 41
   and group, 33, 70, 120

rights of, 27, 29, 242
    See also action; autonomy; commitment; liberty; political solidarity
individualism, 7, 18, 19, 49, 75, 84, 240, 246
industrial revolution, 7
inequality, 23, 140
    civil, 24
    social, 207
The Inessential Woman (Spelman), 185
injustice, 55–70, 71–112, 191–97
    defined, 207–9
    experience of, 124–27, 135–36, 167, 171, 175
    global, 252–57
    and privilege, 142, 152, 159–64, 186
    social, 55, 64, 158, 197, 202–9, 212, 225
    systemic, 201, 251
integrity, 31, 45, 157, 261
interdependence, 74, 77, 94, 125
    cultural, 32
    ecological, 32
    economic, 32
    global, 32–33, 235, 244–45, 247, 252, 255
    human, 32
    intellectual, 32
    political, 29, 32
    and solidarity, 19, 84, 137–38, 155
    and social solidarity, 21, 23–24, 44–45
    technological, 32
intergovernmental organizations, 56
international aid agencies, 39
international coalitions, 257, 263
international community, 12, 33, 41–42, 65, 231–32, 242–63
International Covenant on Civil and Political Rights, 249
International Covenant on Economic, Social and Cultural Rights, 249
International Criminal Court (ICC), 251
international law, 248
international organizations, 56
international political solidarity. *See under* political solidarity
international relations, 246, 260
intersectionality, 140, 171
Isasi-Diaz, Ada Maria, 93

Jaggar, Alison, 141, 263
Jim Crow laws, 129, 159
just wage, 54, 116, 123–24, 136, 142, 149, 192, 227
just war, 108
    theory of, 247–48

justice, 9, 31, 207, 221
    as goal of solidarity, 54, 56, 96, 189–97
    comparative, 55, 206–7
    distributive, 29, 97, 156
    economic, 202
    global, 49
    See also social justice
Justice and the Politics of Difference (Young), 120

Kahane, David, 10, 27, 186
Kayb, Matthias, 30
King, Jr., Martin Luther, 110
Kolenda, Konstantin, 233, 235, 237
Kruks, Sonia, 106, 120, 137, 162, 171–72, 175–76, 180, 183–84, 224, 228, 239
Ku Klux Klan, 206
Kuipers, Ronald Alexander, 239

labor
    child, 74
    division of, 106, 141, 204, 233, 234, 240
    gender division of, 168
    sweatshop, 74
labor rights movement, 36
labor union, 9, 56, 61, 66, 87, 118, 120, 124, 149
Laborem Exercens (Pope John Paul II), 32
Ladd, John, 18, 26, 35, 73, 91–92
language, 53, 61, 128, 145, 212, 219, 236, 238, 255
    as oppressive, 53, 96, 152, 248
Latin America, 68
Latin American Liberation Theology, 193
law, 39, 42, 35, 96, 112, 233
    civil, 23–24, 155
    English Common, 53
    international, 248
    natural, 24
    rule of, 202
legal rights, 155, 208
legal system, 109
    civil, 64
Lemkin, Rapheal, 239
    Axis Rule in Occupied Europe, 239
Lenhardt, Christian, 10, 143, 193, 253
Leroux, Pierre, 29
Letter to D'Alembert on the Theatre (Rousseau), 154
liberalism, 30, 75, 138, 151, 157
liberation, 68, 85, 90, 141, 156, 163
    goal of, 13, 15, 36, 54, 58, 97–98, 139, 190–92

ideal, 34, 79
    struggle for, 17, 21, 40, 76–78, 92, 105–6, 142, 145–46, 160, 171
    and violence, 108–10
    women's, 69, 72
liberation theology, 8, 12
liberty, 29, 67, 75, 140, 209
    civil, 207
Libiszowska-Zótkowska, Maria, 8
Lindemann, Kate, 213, 215
Locke, Alain Leroy, 2, 10, 22, 233, 236–37
Locke, John, 209
Lugones, María, 93–94, 102–3, 115, 132, 139, 184–85
Luther, Martin, 96

MacKinnon, Katherine, 248
Macpherson, C. B., 209
Manning, Rita, 173–75, 235–36
marginalization, 55, 203, 211
Marx, Karl, 10, 102, 132–33, 143, 168, 171, 253
    The Communist Manifesto, 96
Marxism, 99, 126, 137, 168, 211
Mason, Andrew, 29, 39, 81, 91, 93, 238, 251
Mater et Magistra (Pope John XXIII), 7
Maternal Thinking (Ruddick), 174
May, Larry, 35, 43–46, 80–82, 108, 126, 129, 133, 240–41, 263
McGary, Howard, 35, 131, 134–35, 208
Merleau-Ponty, Maurice, 106
Metz, Karl, 6
migrant workers, 63–64
military intervention, 108–9
Mills, Charles, 2, 181–82, 209, 240
Min, Anselm Kyongsuk, 8
mob action, 122
Mohanty, Chandra Talpade, 37–38, 148–49, 208
Moody-Adams, Michele M., 214–15
moral obligations, 30, 36, 40, 42, 65, 66
    of political solidarity, 71–112
moral privilege, 155, 165
moral sentiments, 13, 79, 226
    hope, 82–83
Mueller, Franz H., 7
multiculturalism, 145, 179
multinational corporations, 64
Mussett, Shanon M., 226
mutuality, 187, 247, 252
    as moral duty, 13, 58, 81–83, 90–94, 109, 155–56, 206
    of interest, 123
    solidarity as, 37, 158, 237

Narayan, Uma, 140
National Association for Advancement of Colored People (NAACP), 118
National Organization for Women (NOW), 69, 123
Native American, 202–3
natural disasters, 54, 198–201, 221
natural law, 24
Nazism, 26, 73, 206
neocolonialism, 74
New Orleans, 200–1
New York Times, 218
Nicaragua, 37, 223, 263
Nino, Carlos Santiago, 234
Noddings, Nel, 173
nonmaleficence, 31
nonviolence, 13, 144
    activism, 78, 110, 143
    militant, 110
    resistance, 107
    See also violence
Nuremberg Tribunal, 250–51

Okin, Susan Moller, 262–63
oppressed groups, 152, 215
    identity of, 130, 134, 138
    and solidary group, 114, 124–38, 167
oppression,
    defined, 128, 200, 205, 209–16
    experiences of, 72, 223, 262
    forms of, 139–43
    internalized, 102, 110, 126
    logic of, 101, 108, 184
    and moral sentiments, 79–82
    and political solidarity, 14–15, 34–38, 51–70, 189–197, 264
    and privilege, 152, 158–64, 167–87
    responsibility for, 75, 83–94, 97, 100–2, 194
    systemic, 64, 101, 103, 134–35, 152, 163, 209–10
    violent, 103, 106–12
organizations, 35, 53, 70, 113–18, 123
    civic, 63
    formal, 84, 122
    goals of, 118
    intergovernmental, 56
    international, 56

National Organization for Women (NOW), 69
political, 68, 69, 72
social justice, 127

Pakistan, 232
parasitical solidarity, 5, 18, 20, 36, 46–48, 50, 79, 203
Parks, Rosa, 103
Pateman, Carole, 209
patriarchy, 40
Paulhus, Normand, 246
peace politics, 174
Pedagogy of the Oppressed (Freire), 111, 213. See also Freire, Paulo
personal transformation. See under transformation
Pesch, Heinrich, 7
philosophy, 7
    moral, 18
    political, 18, 19
    social, 11, 43, 46, 114, 138
pity, 51
pledge group, 120
pluralism, 122
Polish Solidarity, 8–9, 39, 72, 104, 193, 244
political solidarity,
    as a movement for social change, 67, 81, 124
    commitment of, 125, 128, 152, 166
    and decision-making, 144–49
    defined, 10–13, 21, 33–38, 58
    democracy in, 115
    distinguished from other forms of solidarity, 5, 17–20, 39–46, 124–38, 200, 204
    and diversity, 138–44
    epistemology for, 165–83
    and genocide, 232
    global, 12, 15, 20, 42, 59, 65, 77, 86–87, 231–32, 252–64 (see also global solidarity)
    goal of, 3, 37, 54, 138–44, 189–29
    international, 58–65, 115, 122, 145, 190, 195, 232, 256, 263
    local, 63–87, 59, 115, 159, 221–22, 263
    logic of, 194
    moral relations of, 36, 47, 56, 71–112, 122
    strong, 60, 62, 66, 115, 121
    struggles of, 121, 139–40, 153–56
    theory of, 6, 32, 51–70, 121–25, 158, 161, 165, 169, 193, 196
    weak, 60, 66, 115, 121, 136, 153, 156–57

pollution, 28, 42, 252, 253
Pope John XXIII, 7
    Mater et Magistra, 7
Pope John Paul II, 7–8, 32–33, 244–47
    Sollicitudo Rei Socialis, 7, 32–33, 244–47
Pope Leo XIII, 7, 244
Pope Pius XI, 7
    Quadragesimo Anno, 2
Pope Paul VI, 7, 32, 244
    Populorum Progressio, 7, 32–33, 244
Populorum Progressio (Pope Paul VI), 7, 32–33, 244
positive duties, 19–20, 33, 48, 58, 60, 68–69, 78, 133, 153, 204, 254
    of camaraderie, 117
postcolonialism, 212
postmodern, 137
poverty, 32–33, 65–66, 68, 74, 159, 193–96, 242–43, 251, 257
power, 80, 88–89
powerlessness, 211
pragmatic solidarity, 193, 195, 261
pragmatism, 237–38
praxis, 8, 15, 20, 35, 93, 103, 105, 111, 170–71, 183–84, 191, 221–25
prisoners, 218–19
    of war, 218–19, 250
privilege, 77, 80, 82, 100–1, 104, 109, 125, 128, 139, 142, 151–87, 213
    class, 132, 252
    epistemological, 14–15, 155, 159–60, 164–86
    moral, 155, 159–60, 165
    racial, 131, 181–82
    social, 135, 158–59, 161–62, 165, 264
proletariat, 99, 132, 143, 253
property, 75, 107, 154, 209, 213, 240, 250
protest, 36, 53–54, 63–65, 87, 99, 103–7, 110, 136, 145, 257, 260
    culture of, 225–27
    cyber, 104–5
    symbolic, 83, 105, 193–4, 221

Quadragesimo Anno (Pope Pius XI), 7

race, 130–31, 205
    solidarity, 2
    theory, 11
    traitors, 131, 181–83
racial justice movement, 35
racial solidarity, 2–4, 22, 129, 197
racism, 38, 63–64, 107, 131, 167, 181–83, 210

and sexism, 132, 135, 139, 171
  struggles against, 123, 138, 140–42, 201–203
  See also civil rights
rape, 15–16, 120, 131
  mass, 231–64
rational choice, 75, 130
rationality, 49, 209
reciprocity, 23, 33, 41, 81, 115, 134, 147, 191, 224
  as obligation, 58
  cultural, 237, 240
  in relationships, 56, 93
Red Cross/Crescent Society, 244
reflective action, 64, 74
Rehg, William, 177
Rerum Novarum (Pope Leo XIII), 7, 244
resistance,
  communities of, 96
  in political solidarity, 52–54, 61–62, 74, 101, 149
  logic of, 102–3
  nonviolent, 107
  struggles, 3, 111–12, 120
  violent, 106, 110, 112
respect, 101
responsibility, 33, 81, 85, 89, 134, 137, 157
  collective, 7, 13, 35, 39, 69–70, 80, 84–91, 119–21, 131, 156–57, 219
  equality of, 156
  moral, 88–90
revolution, 34, 55, 99, 120, 132–33, 143, 154, 191, 193, 253–54
  and solidarity, 67–68
Rich, Adrienne, 102
rights, 19, 29, 55
  basic, 196
  disability, 67
  distribution of, 34
  economic, 28, 208
  individual, 27, 29, 242
  intellectual, 208
  legal, 155, 208
  of citizenship, 108
  political, 28, 36
  social, 28
  See also civil rights; human rights; women's rights; workers' rights
Rippe, Klaus Peter, 11, 37–38, 56
Rorty, Richard, 75, 234, 237–39
  Contingency, Irony, and Solidarity, 238
Rousseau, Jean-Jacques, 20, 23–27, 29, 33, 153–54, 217

Discourse on the Origins and Foundations of Inequality Among Mankind, 23–24
  Letter to D'Alembert on the Theatre, 154
Ruddick, Sara, 3–4, 174, 177, 184
Rwanda, 231, 232, 241

Salzman, Todd, 261
Sandel, Michael, 31
Sandinistas, 37
Sartre, Jean-Paul, 183–84, 215
  Critique of Dialectical Reason, 120
Sass, Hans-Martin, 31
satyagraha, 102, 110
Scheler, Max, 6, 26–27, 166, 185
Scholz, Sally J., 2, 74, 76, 96, 101, 107, 112, 134, 137, 141, 209, 223, 236, 247, 249, 255, 257
Schott, Robin May, 261
Schuyt, Kees, 30, 40
Scott, Janny, 218
segregation, 210
self-defense, 111–12, 159
  collective, 111
self-determination, 58, 147–48, 210, 215, 247
self-identity, 120, 128, 130, 148
self-interest, 51, 75, 137, 145, 222
self-respect, 135, 148, 214
sentiment, 22, 30, 44, 49, 54, 67, 241
  bonds of, 81
  moral, 79–82, 226
Serbia, 232, 261
seriality, 120
sexism, 135, 138, 166, 170
  activism against, 53, 61, 151
  and racism, 38, 61, 107, 131–32, 140–43, 171–72, 210
  and violence, 194, 217, 257, 258 (*see also* rape)
sexuality, 205
shame, 79–81
shared consciousness, 3, 21–22, 49, 52, 125–27, 131–34, 187, 233
shared experience, 3–4, 21, 40, 41, 46, 125, 127, 129
Shelby, Tommie, 2, 38
Shue, Henry, 196, 227–28, 234, 254
sisterhood, 3, 38, 131, 175, 185
slavery, 80
social activism. *See under* activism
social consciousness, 75, 134–35

Social Contract (Rousseau), 24, 154
social contract theory, 114, 154, 209
social criticism, 67, 70, 78, 82, 103, 160, 171, 226, 260, 263
    as duty, 13, 94–100, 108, 135, 253
    within solidarity, 69, 106, 138–39, 142–44, 163–64, 174, 196
social groups, 120–21, 125–27. *See also* dominant groups; oppressed groups
social injustice, 55, 64, 158, 197, 202–6, 212, 225
social justice, 42, 78, 122
    as goal of solidarity, 52–55, 58–66, 189–197, 202–3, 205–29, 257
    and Catholic Social Teaching, 7, 32, 246
    in civic solidarity, 30, 32
    organizations and associations, 115–16
social ontology, 4
social security, 9, 28
social solidarity, 5, 10–11, 20–27, 198–201, 221–23
    as human solidarity, 65, 196–97, 232–41, 252, 256
    compared, 30, 33, 36–46, 79–82, 93, 124, 159–61, 175, 186, 204–7
    and identity politics, 128–38, 178
socialism, 4, 7, 36, 48, 140, 142, 193, 212
The Socially Responsive Self (May), 45
society, 39, 55, 113–14, 131, 217
    civil, 10, 50, 154, 206, 264
    cohesion of, 10, 19, 22–24
    democratic, 202, 215, 255
    good of, 27–31
    relation to, 58, 78, 101, 225
    transnational civil, 147
    See also social solidarity
sociology, 6, 22
solidarism, 7
solidarity,
    as mediating between individual and community, 18, 50, 66, 69, 144, 153, 160, 204, 227
    as a moral concept, 19, 113
    as an ontological concept construction, 2
    as a political movement, 3
    as similarity, 47
    as a social construction, 2
    as unity, 19
    administrative, 30
    anamnestic, 143, 253
    bonds of sentiment, 79–82
    and charity, 37
    civic virtue of, 31
    class, 129
    and commitment, 35
    continuum model of, 40–41
    cultural, 22
    duty of, 32
    epistemological, 4
    and familial analogy, 2
    familial models, 129
    feminist, 4
    forms of, 4–5, 18, 39, 79, 113
    functionalist, 25
    incremental, 233, 235–36, 241
    index of, 80
    individuals within, 142
    international, 59, 115, 145, 195, 232
    logic of, 108
    means of, 95
    mechanical, 10, 22, 44, 49
    moral, 4, 129
    national, 59, 115
    normative, 25
    of the oppressed, 129
    organic, 10, 22–23, 44, 235–36
    parasitical, 5, 18, 20, 36, 46–48, 50, 79, 203
    principle of, 29
    project-related, 11, 37
    rational choice theory of, 130
    representable, 26
    and revolution, 67
    and shared strengths, 3
    socialist, 4
    structuralist, 25
    three characteristics of every form, 17, 18–20
    transnational, 262
    unrepresentable, 26–27
    values, 13
    workers', 93
    world, 236, 237
    See also civic solidarity, human solidarity, global solidarity, political solidarity, pragmatic solidarity, race solidarity, racial solidarity, social solidarity
Solidarity Forever, 9
solidary group, 35, 82, 101, 109–10, 113–50, 180, 208, 223–24
    and equality, 85–86, 151–60
    and oppressed group, 14–15, 124–38, 164, 167, 186, 194, 202, 215
    and social criticism, 58, 96–100

Index

Sollicitudo Rei Socialis (Pope John Paul II), 7, 32–33, 244–47
Southern Christian Leadership Conference (SCLS), 110
sovereignty, 247, 251
Spain, 47
Spelman, Elizabeth, 184–85
   The Inessential Woman, 185
standpoint epistemology, 167–72, 174, 177, 183–84
state, 18–19, 27–33, 55, 101, 147, 242, 247, 255, 258
state of nature, 23
Steinvorth, Ulrich, 47
Stern, –ernhard, 236–37
Stout, Jeffrey, 27
Stubblefield, Anna, 2
subaltern counter publics, 179
subjectivity, 132, 137–38, 144
subsidiarity, 7, 31, 147
Sudan, 231
Sunstein, Cass R., 10
suffrage, 68, 75
sustainability, 12, 28
sweatshop labor, 53, 74
sympathy, 2, 6, 9, 17, 47–51, 60, 79, 176, 198–200, 205, 235, 241

Taylor, Charles, 128, 213–14
terrorism, 47, 259
Third World, 65, 148, 219, 263
   women, 37–38
Thome, Helmut, 25, 91
trade, 116
   fair, 116, 119, 157, 227
trade unions, 39
transformation, 70, 78, 111
   personal, 53, 74, 92, 102–4, 117, 156, 160, 166, 176, 190–92, 221–23
   social, 53
transnational civil society, 147
transnational solidarity, 262. *See also* political solidarity
Tribunal for Women's Human Rights, 258
Tutsis, 232, 241
tyranny, 51, 54–55, 69, 77–79, 85, 91, 97, 108, 264
Tyson, Timothy, 110, 228
Ullman-Margalit, Edna, 10
unions, labor, 9, 56, 61, 66, 87, 118, 120, 124, 149
United Nations, 239, 248, 251, 258, 259

United Nations Convention on the Prevention and Punishment of the Crime of Genocide, 231–64
United Nations Declaration on the Elimination of Violence Against Women, 249
United Nations Universal Declaration of Human Rights, 55, 248–50
United States, 41, 53, 74, 104, 149, 198, 217, 227, 245, 251, 257, 263–64
   government of, 118
   policy, 47, 57–58
   and racism, 63, 129, 159, 167, 201
   and value of solidarity, 27–28, 31, 65
   women's movement, 106, 139, 208
unity, 115–18, 128, 227, 241
   camaraderie as, 117
   in diversity, 233, 236–37
   international, 64
   of cause, 108
   of interests, 127
   of political solidarity, 36, 38, 57–59, 68–71, 108–9, 122 (*see also* solidary group)
   of purpose, 122
   solidarity as, 10, 19, 26, 227
Urban Plunge, 1–2

van Donselaar, Gus, 31
vegetarianism, 48, 143
violence, 55, 67–68, 144, 159, 195, 197, 202, 247, 262
   activism, 102, 106–12, 122, 163, 194
   against women, 56, 256–63
   as a response to political solidarity, 136
   definition of, 107, 212
   domestic, 54, 106, 124, 131, 140, 221–22
   justifying, 111
   logic of, 108, 206–7
   racial, 54 (*see also* racism)
   sexist, 194, 221–22, 257–58 (*see also* sexism)
   systemic, 103
Visions of Solidarity (Weber), 263–64
voluntary associations, 18, 73, 113–14, 122, 125, 137, 145–47, 255
vulnerability, 27, 31, 36, 42, 98, 136, 150, 200, 229, 242–43, 254, 257, 264
   political, 219
   social, 13, 15, 29, 51, 54–59, 69, 79, 189–194, 197, 207, 217–20, 226, 251–52

wage, 61, 131
   just, 116, 123–24, 136, 142, 149, 192, 227

Walzer, Michael, 9, 67, 82, 84, 95–100, 108–14, 133, 142, 145, 191, 196, 227, 228
war, 108, 247–48, 250, 257, 259. *See also* just war
war crimes, 242, 250–51, 257, 260–61
Ware, Robert, 127
Washington, Johnny, 236–37
Weale, Albert, 242–43
Weber, Clare, 263–64
welfare, 5, 29–31, 44, 46, 242
Wernick, Andrew, 6
white supremacy, 22, 197
Wippman, David, 251
Witness for Peace, 263
Wojtyła, Karol, 246
women, 68, 74–75, 179, 203, 208–11, 215–16, 239–41, 248, 254
   and resistance, 102–3, 106, 148–49
   and sexist oppression, 61, 97, 138–40, 143
   solidarity among, 3–4, 128, 131–32, 135–36, 166, 175, 197
   violence against, 56, 221–22, 232, 256–63
   See also feminism

women's liberation, 36, 67, 69, 72, 83, 106, 139, 151, 257
   United States, 139
   See also feminism
women's organizations, 53
women's suffrage, 68, 74
workers, 32, 37–38, 53, 62–66, 116, 124, 136, 192, 224, 227
   Marxism and, 102, 132, 143, 168–70, 253
   rights of, 7–9, 28, 54, 74, 93, 140, 142
World Bank, 243
world traveling, 93–94
World War II, 72, 231
The Wretched of the Earth (Fanon), 111

Yoder, John Howard, 246
Young, Iris, 106–7, 110, 120–21, 126–28, 141, 146, 148, 179, 203, 207, 211–12
   Justice and the Politics of Difference, 120
Yugoslavia, 231–32, 261

Zack, Naomi, 141

Made in the USA
Lexington, KY
19 January 2017